The Filmmakers' Legal Guide
Second Edition

Tony Morris

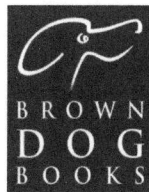

BROWN
DOG
BOOKS

The Filmmakers' Legal Guide
© Tony Morris 2015 & 2019

First edition published 2015
Reprinted 2017, 2018
Second Edition published 2019

Published under licence by Brown Dog Books and
The Self-Publishing Partnership, 7 Green Park Station, Bath BA1 1JB

www.selfpublishingpartnership.co.uk

ISBN printed book: 978-1-83952-019-8
ISBN e-book: 978-1-83952-020-4

Cover design by Kevin Rylands
Internal design by Andrew Easton

Cover photo: Cecil B. DeMille and crew on set during the silent era, reproduced
by kind permission of The Cecil B. DeMille Archives, Brigham Young University,
Provo, Utah

This book is printed on FSC certified paper

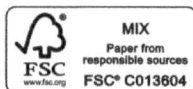

MIX
Paper from
responsible sources
FSC
www.fsc.org   FSC® C013604

Printed and bound by CPI Group (UK) Ltd, Croydon, CR0 4YY

FOREWORD

When the first edition of The Filmmakers' Legal Guide arrived in 2015 I knew it would immediately become a well-thumbed resource and, in fact, it has rarely left the side of my desk.

In the few short years following publication, the number and complexity of the legal questions facing filmmakers has increased. In the second edition of his book, Tony Morris has taken on board some of the interesting new challenges faced by filmmakers and content creators in the ever-changing digital landscape, including virtual reality productions, the use of IP in social media and the increasing popularity of shopping agreements. Of great interest and of exceptional use are his new and revamped Appendices. Here you will find a whopping great eighteen contracts covering an extensive range of a filmmaker's needs.

As a filmmaker myself I have found the Brexit uncertainty unsettling and, in particular, its effect on the legal regime. As with any new trend or unusual situation I have turned to Tony, who is not one to best-guess or make predictions, and who, instead, has examined a few key areas of concern. His thoughts on trade marks and copyright are of particular interest. He has also provided a succinct analysis of the perils of the new data protection rules, introduced by the UK government with Brexit in mind, and considered their potential effect on filmmakers.

Finally, this new edition of a filmmaking classic proves once again that filmmakers' legal challenges need not be overwhelming if you have this trusty, easy-to-understand guide at your fingertips.

Elliot Grove
Founder
Raindance Film Festival
British Independent Film Awards
January 2019

FOREWORD TO FIRST EDITION

In my two and a half decades working with films and filmmakers at Raindance I have found there are two sides to making a film. The first is the side that hundreds of 'how-to' books show you - how to write, direct, shoot and edit a film. The second side is the side where we, as filmmakers, create content or intellectual property. It's on this second side that knowledge and 'how-to' is terribly represented. Until now.

Tony Morris has created The Filmmakers' Legal Guide. In all my years I have never read a book so blindingly clear and easy-to-understand as this one. I got an advance copy and refer to it constantly. The thing that Tony does so brilliantly is to make the complicated simple; simply put, too, as most screenwriters and filmmakers are stunningly naive about the works they create and are even more clueless about how to protect and enshrine their work so it can be monetised.

The Filmmakers' Legal Guide is the most essential resource a filmmaker can have. Where anyone can do a tutorial on how to run a camera or a new piece of software, nowhere else can you find so much relevant and useful information about the legal side of things. Get the practical legal issues wrong and the film you create is nearly useless.

Tony Morris is engaging and entertaining. He's a fount of great knowledge and information. I believe all filmmakers should send messages of gratitude to him for sharing this hugely detailed and plain, straight, useful, essential book.

Elliot Grove
Founder
Raindance Film Festival
British Independent Film Awards
September 2015

CONTENTS

INTRODUCTORY

RIGHTS

CONTRACTS: OVERVIEW

MISCELLANEOUS

Introduction

INTRODUCTORY

1   Author's introduction and acknowledgments

1.1   For many years I have worked with an eclectic range of filmmakers and, since 1997, I have lectured at various film schools and presented numerous masterclasses on legal issues for filmmakers. Invariably, the time allotted is never enough to answer students' specific – and, usually, multi-layered – burning questions. In the course of doing my best in truncated Q & As, I was frequently asked if there was a book I could recommend for producers in which the topics I address were all to be found. I was unable to find one and thus the first edition of The Filmmakers' Legal Guide (**Guide**) was born. It was written in response to the needs of film production students but with the intention of becoming a 'go to' resource for filmmakers at all levels. Published in October 2015, the success of the book exceeded my expectations. Originally intended for Kindle only, I was persuaded to publish a hard copy. Having sold out the first two print runs and with stocks of the third beginning to run low it was time to start on a new edition.

1.2   The second edition of the Guide supplements the material from the first in a number of ways. Additional topics covered include some thoughts on legal issues arising in virtual reality productions, the effect of the General Data Protection Regulation and the increasing popularity of shopping agreements. I have revamped the Appendices extensively. The seven forms of contract from the first edition have been replaced with eighteen covering an extensive range of a filmmaker's needs. I have taken into account the subjects about which students most frequently ask questions; so, for example, I have supplemented the original text with additional information on topics such as filming in public. I have added more examples to a number of sections of the Guide.

1.3   A number of people have contributed to the success of the book and I would like to thank them for their help and inspiration. The extraordinary response to the Guide has been led by Elliot Grove, the founder of the Raindance Organisation and the British Independent Film Awards. Elliot is one of those people whose energy and insights on all things film enthuse everyone and anyone who come within his orbit. Lubna Salad, then a Raindance student, encouraged me to finish the first edition within a reasonable time frame and ensured that I arranged publication of the hard copy version for which she organised the launch. Chris Auty and his team at the National Film and Television School were early adopters of the Guide and have made it a recommended text for their production students to whom I have been invited to present seminars on several occasions. Charlie Watts at the University of Portsmouth has also been an important cheerleader and I have enjoyed delivering a number of very well attended lectures to production and other students in my hometown. Stuart Wright interviewed me twice for his Britflix podcast and has been a steadfast promoter of the Guide.

1.4 In preparing this second edition I would also like to mention the following: Joel Breton, founder of Vive Studios, was generous with his time in talking through some of the legal issues that most concern him as a creator of virtual reality content. Several of my colleagues at Swan Turton LLP are consistently helpful in brainstorming sessions: Anne Mannion on contentious matters and defamation, Charlie Swan on IP and Antony Gostyn on all things film; Nicky Androsov provided insight on GDPR. Finally, I would like to thank all those clients on whose films and other projects I have worked over the years that have enabled me to develop my skills and knowledge, particularly those whose anonymised legal problems have found their way into the Guide as examples.

2   Objectives

2.1   In writing this Guide, I have endeavoured to address the practical needs of filmmakers. The pitch is not to lawyers and the Guide is not intended to be a legal text book. No apologies are made for the paucity of references to decided cases, sections of statutes and quotes from learned legal tomes.

2.2   Although written from the standpoint of an English lawyer applying English law principles, much of the practice described will be of more general application. Intellectual Property Law has been largely harmonised throughout the EU, of which the UK was still a member at the time of finishing the manuscript for the Guide. Nevertheless, there are some differences of application – one example being that of moral rights. In relation to certain subject matter, the US First Amendment may enable a documentary maker to use a broader palate from which to analyse and comment than the equivalent English law. There are some references to these similarities and differences in the text.

2.3   Inevitably Brexit looms as large over the film industry as it does over every other area of the UK's commercial, creative and social activity. At the time of going to press no one was able to accurately anticipate how extensively our industry will be affected by Brexit. I have not attempted to best-guess or make predictions. A few areas of concern are mentioned at section 54. Other comments are included within the text where relevant; see for example observations on copyright at paragraph 5.28, on trade marks at paragraph 14.6 and licensing at 49.8.

2.4   There are numerous areas of the law that are relevant to filmmakers: contract, intellectual property, employment, finance, tax and so on. Each of these legal topics is governed by numerous statutes and extensive common law and addressed in lengthy text books. In applying the law to the practical needs of the filmmaker within the parameters of this Guide it is only possible to review key relevant principles.

2.5   The Guide is not intended to be a substitute for tailored advice on the idiosyncracies and intricacies of individual projects. Filmmakers are recommended to take informed advice at a level that will equip them to deal effectively with the specific legal requirements of any particular project in which they are involved – and in some cases that may involve lawyers practising in more than one jurisdiction. One size does not – and never does – fit the legal requirements of every production.

2.6   The information in the Guide is based on the laws of England and Wales as they stood as at 1st January 2019.

3 A guide to the Guide

3.1   The term 'film' is used throughout this Guide. It is used to include every type of audio-visual production: theatrical films, television programmes, animation, documentaries, shorts, 'videos', commercials and promos or works produced with online distribution as their primary medium of exploitation.

3.2   The term 'filmmaker' has been adopted to distinguish between the role of those engaged in the overall process of production – both the management of the commercial aspects and the creative process of a film – and that of an 'executive producer'. Executive producer credits may be given to those who perform a wide variety of different roles. Frequently the title of executive producer is accorded for raising finance for or investing in a film. In other circumstances, the credit may be given for providing input or services to a film where the provider may not otherwise have been paid. Depending on the context, the term 'filmmaker' may refer either to (a) one or more individual producers or (b) a production company.

3.3   Reviewing the legal aspects of film development and production is not easily dealt with as a linear exercise. The eclectic nature and intricate interdependencies of the filmmaking process make it a challenging task to determine the ideal sequence in which to address each of the component parts of the subject or to isolate certain comments under standalone headings. Accordingly, cross-references to relevant sections and paragraphs are included where helpful.

3.4   A finished film is generally a collaborative work that relies on numerous contributions and a variety of content, and which also comprises a collection of 'rights'. The term 'rights' is used to denote a mix of legal entitlements. There are various species of intellectual property rights recognised and codified by statute such as copyright and trade marks, as well as permissions or licences that are bolted together with a series of contracts. There are rights that are created by filmmakers, rights that are acquired by filmmakers from third parties and rights that are granted by filmmakers – perhaps via distributors – to those who exhibit or otherwise make films available to the public. In order to see the whole, each of these component parts is examined separately. The substance of the contracts that are employed to bolt these rights together is critical. Nevertheless, filmmakers' contracts mean nothing without content. A film's content is dependent on a host of rights and, therefore, rights and content are examined first.

RIGHTS

4   Intellectual property

4.1   Intellectual Property (**IP**) is a legal concept which refers to the creations of the mind and in which certain exclusive rights are recognized by law. IP is at the heart of all creative output – books and magazine articles, musical compositions and sound recordings, drawings, designs, paintings, sculptures and photographs, films and digital works.

4.2   IP laws establish, grant and provide for the protection of various species of intellectual property rights that include copyright, moral rights, performers' rights, trade marks, designs, trade dress or get-up, confidential information and, in certain jurisdictions, trade secrets. There are also sub-sets of rights that arise out of the use and exploitation of IP and which include reproduction rights, neighbouring rights and mechanical rights. Patents – rights in inventions – have been intentionally excluded from this Guide. Design rights, which are rights that arise in the shape or configuration of a physical object, have also not been addressed. Nevertheless, there are circumstances in which design rights may attach to a prop or other physical item created for a film.

5   Copyright

5.1   The nature of copyright

Copyright arises as a matter of law in original literary, musical, dramatic or artistic works. Copyright protection does not extend to protecting an idea, but the expression of an idea. In other words, in order for an idea to be protected by copyright it necessarily needs to be reduced to a permanent form, which can be either tangible – the written word, an illustration or photograph in a physical format, a film, a sound recording or audio-visual programme on disc – or intangible – an MP3 or other digital file. In order to establish copyright, the author must have expended sufficient skill and labour in creating the work so as to make it original. The threshold for originality is not an onerous one to achieve. The protection of ideas is dealt with in more detail at section 7 below.

5.2   A film contains an array of copyrights in its component parts – i.e. script, music, still photographs, existing footage. Copyright also arises in a finished film itself, the ownership of which is addressed at paragraph 5.12. Owning or having sufficient right to use copyright material included in a film is a necessary prerequisite for anyone who intends to exhibit, broadcast, distribute or otherwise exploit that film. The owner of a copyright has the legal right to exploit the subject matter of that copyright, to protect it from infringement and to enjoy the income streams to be derived from its exploitation.

5.3   First owner of copyright

The first owner of a copyright is its author. The writer of a screenplay will be the first owner of its copyright. The composer of a song or piece of instrumental music will be the first owner of its copyright. The photographer is the first owner of copyright in a photograph. The artist who draws a picture or who paints a portrait is the first owner of copyright in such works. For the purposes of copyright law, a computer programme is a literary work. The programmer who writes code is the first owner of copyright in a computer programme. Digital effects included within a film will include elements of code in which copyright will subsist as a literary work. Exceptions to the rule are examined at paragraphs 5.5-5.8.

5.4   In order for a work to qualify for protection under English law, its author must be a 'qualifying person' for the purposes of the Copyright, Designs and Patents Act 1988 (**Copyright Act**). What constitutes a 'qualifying person' is subject to

a host of detailed provisions. A qualifying person principally includes: British citizens, British Dependent Territories citizens, British Nationals and British subjects, individuals domiciled or resident in the UK, or companies incorporated under the law of any part of the United Kingdom. Reciprocal protection to copyrights created by nationals and citizens of other jurisdictions is also provided by two international treaties. A majority of countries are signatories to the Berne Convention, originally signed in 1886, and now administered by the World Intellectual Property Organisation (**WIPO**). There is also the Universal Copyright Convention (**UCC**), to which the UK and more than eighty other countries are signatories.

5.5   Copyright created by an employee

The principal exception to the rule that the author is the first owner of copyright arises when a copyright created by an employee 'in the course of employment will belong to the employer'. The expression 'in the course of his employment' is not defined by the Copyright Act but in settling disputes the distinction applied by the courts is whether the individual whose work is the subject of competing claims of ownership was working under a 'contract of service' (e.g. as an employee) and not providing services as a freelancer or independent contractor under what is termed a 'contract for services'.

Freelancers or independent contractors will be the first owners of copyright works they create; see the discussions at paragraphs 5.9 and 6.2-6.6.

5.6   If an app development studio employs a programmer to write code for its customers, copyright in that code will be owned by the app development studio and not the programmer. If a production company employs an in-house composer to write the music for the soundtracks to its films, the copyright in that music will be owned by the production company and not the composer. Problems may arise when the composer writes music for someone other than her/his employer or the programmer writes an app with a view to selling it online for her/his own account and the work in either case is undertaken at home and/or outside normal working hours.

5.7   In order to determine ownership of copyright in circumstances such as these, the terms of the relationship between employer and employee will require examination. The specific terms of the employee's contract of employment may contain the answer. Many, if not most, programmers' employment contracts provide for an employer to own all and any code the programmer writes, irrespective of when and in what circumstances. However, what if the music the composer writes at home includes certain themes previously rejected by the production company? Suppose the programmer for a banking software house uses his employer's laptop while on holiday to create a fantasy games app? There are no hard and fast answers. Each case requires to be examined on its own facts. These examples should nevertheless serve as a warning to unwary filmmakers engaging friends and acquaintances to work on their productions in their own time, where those friends are employed in jobs that involve the provision of services similar to those required by the filmmaker. Additionally, for those with aspirations to create or work on their own productions, when accepting a full-time job or other employment, the terms of the IP provisions and any restrictions in the employment contract should be carefully considered and, where possible, negotiated so as to ring-fence and protect personal projects from any claims that an employer may be entitled to ownership of or a first look at them.

Example

*Ivan, a recent film school graduate, develops a sitcom format with his friend, Yolanda, who is employed as a script-editor by a production company, Upcoming Films Limited. Ivan and Yolanda co-write a pilot script and also collaborate in creating a format bible that includes detailed descriptions of characters and situations, extensive treatments for a dozen episodes and other original material. Yolanda's employment agreement provides that she must disclose to Upcoming Films all and any 'programme and other ideas, treatments, outlines and all and any other proposals that she originates, creates or on which she collaborates at any time during the term of her employment (**Works**) irrespective of whether the Works have been originated, commissioned or created by or at the request of Upcoming Films which shall have a first option to further develop, produce and exploit said Works in its absolute discretion and on such terms as Upcoming Films may determine'.*

In these circumstances, Yolanda is obliged to disclose the project to her employers who are nevertheless unable to do anything with it without first entering into an appropriate contract with Ivan. Equally, Ivan is unable to deal with the Works without negotiating a release or other arrangement with Upcoming Films.

The Works in the above example are works of joint authorship; see paragraph 5.11.

5.8   As a general principle, a company should endeavour to keep ordered and careful records of which of its employees or contractors creates original copyright works, referencing those contracts pursuant to which the works were created. Even if created by an employee in the course of employment, the term of copyright protection of a work will be determined by the date of the death of the creator(s), being the individual employee(s) in question; see paragraphs 5.14-5.16.

5.9   Copyright created by freelancers

More often than not many, if not most, of those engaged by a filmmaker to work on and contribute to the production of a film will be self-employed freelancers. The mere act of hiring a freelancer to work on a film will not automatically vest ownership of copyright works created by the freelancer in the filmmaker. In the absence of a clear written agreement that provides for the outright transfer – technically, an assignment – of such copyright works to the filmmaker, the filmmaker's rights will be limited to a licence. The extent to which a filmmaker is granted rights to use a commissioned work is discussed in more detail at paragraphs 6.2-6.5.

5.10   Works made for hire

US copyright law vests ownership of copyright in 'works made for hire' in those who commission an author to create a work. This language is used in US employment contracts as well as in agreements by which freelancers or outside contractors are engaged to create an original copyright work. This concept extends beyond the English concept of a work created by an employee in the course of her/his employment. With increasing frequency, similar language is being imported into English law contracts as an addition to the traditional language used to vest copyright in a filmmaker (or other commissioner) of copyright work. This language is particularly prevalent where there is an intention to distribute a production in the US. The objective in doing this is to assuage the concerns of US distributors that they might otherwise express as to the ownership and control of works in which they are granted rights.

Example

Screenwriter hereby assigns to Producer absolutely the entire copyright and all other rights in the nature of copyright subsisting in the Screenplay with the benefit of full title guarantee for the life of copyright together with all and any renewals, revivals and extensions and, for the purposes of US Federal Copyright

Law, the Screenplay shall be deemed to be a 'work made for hire'.

For an explanation of 'full title guarantee', see paragraph 6.4.

5.11   Joint authorship

Where a copyright work is created by two or more persons it is considered to be a work of joint authorship. No single author of a work of joint authorship may deal with that work without the consent of the other author or authors. In other words, if there are two writers of a screenplay, neither may sell the work to a producer without the consent of the other. Neither one of two composers of a musical score can grant a synchronisation licence to a filmmaker to use that score on a film's soundtrack without the consent of the other. A work is one of joint authorship where the contribution of each author is not distinct from that of the others. This means that the finished work does not exhibit distinct works from separate authors but is seen or experienced as a whole piece. Where a finished work comprises clearly distinct and separate components then it will be a 'collective' work.

Examples

The paintings of Gilbert and George and the operas of Gilbert and Sullivan are experienced as complete works and are works of joint authorship. The pilot script and format bible described in the example at paragraph 5.7 on which Ivan and Yolanda collaborated are works of joint authorship.

By contrast, the classic jazz composition 'Around Midnight' was written by Thelonius Monk and originally published in 1944 as an instrumental. The lyrics were written some time later by Bernie Hanighen. In this particular case, as the lyrics may be separately identified, the song as an overall work is not one of joint authorship. Separate copyrights subsist in each of the music and the lyrics.

5.12   First owner of copyright in a film

The first owners of copyright in a film are its principal director and producer. For the purposes of establishing the author of copyright, the identity of a film's producer may not always be easily determined. It may be that there will be two – or even more – producers who will properly demonstrate that they are to be regarded as owners of copyright. It is important, therefore, that clear agreements are put in place at the inception of a project to determine ownership of copyright and control of the rights of exploitation. The production company responsible for making the film will often be the owner of copyright, though in more complex arrangements there may be another entity designated to acquire and own the copyright in the finished film and all of its underlying rights; consider, for example, the various arrangements described at sections 38, 41, 42 and 43.

5.13   The filmmaker or other party intending to own and control copyright in a finished film should always enter into written agreements that provide for the outright assignment of copyright and all other rights to the filmmaker (or, if applicable, the filmmaker's production company) from each and every individual or organisation responsible for creating any original work that is or may be included in the film – screenplay, original music, digital visual effects, etc.

5.14   Term of copyright

The term of copyright protection in a literary, artistic, musical or dramatic work will expire seventy years after the end of the year in which the author of that copyright dies.

Examples

The composer, Edward Elgar, died on 23 February 1934. His compositions went out of copyright on 31 December 2004.

The playwright and two-time Oscar-winning screenwriter Robert Bolt died on 21 February 1995. The copyright in his works will expire on 31 December 2065.

Following the death of the author of a copyright, unless transferred during the author's lifetime, ownership of the copyright will devolve in accordance with an author's will or, if the author dies without leaving a will, then in accordance with the rules on intestacy. Thus, any dealing with a copyright formerly belonging to a deceased author will be managed by the executors of the author's will or by her/his personal representatives in the case of intestacy. An initial resource for locating wills and executors may be obtained from https://www.gov.uk/search-will-probate

5.15   The copyright in a work of joint authorship will expire at the end of the year that is seventy years after the death of the last of the authors.

Example

Michael Flanders and Donald Swann, who were active in the 1950s and 1960s, were prolific co-writers of comic songs. Flanders died in 1975, Swann in 1994. Copyright in their jointly written compositions will expire on 31 December 2064, which will be seventy years after the end of the year in which Swann died.

5.16   Term of film copyright

Copyright in a film will expire seventy years after the end of the year in which the death occurs of the last to survive of the following: the principal director, the author of the screenplay, the authors of any dialogue in the film (if other than the principal screenplay writer(s)), or the composer of any music specially written for the film.

Example

Henry, the screenwriter and the writer of the dialogue of a British film made in 1940, died shortly after principal photography began. Herman, the director, was killed in a plane crash in 1964. Hector, the composer of the original musical soundtrack, lived until 1971. All of the creative team and the producers of the film were British. The copyright in the film will expire at the end of the year that is seventy years after the last of the deaths of the authors of the film, being that of Hector. Copyright will therefore expire on 31 December 2041.

Once a work ceases to be protected by copyright it will pass into the public domain and may then be used without permission of either the authors or the authors' estates; of more significance, once a film is out of copyright the production company or other entity in which the copyright was vested, will no longer be able to control the film's exploitation.

5.17   Dramatic work

A 'dramatic work' is a work of action, with or without words or music, which is capable of being performed before an audience. For the purpose of copyright, dramatic works include plays, mimes and dances. Other elements of a dance production may be protected by other areas of copyright; for example any accompanying music may be protected as a musical work; written or diagrammatic choreography may respectively be protected as literary or artistic works. For a dramatic work to benefit from copyright protection it must be recorded in a permanent form, whether in writing or in some other medium. As with other species of work, in order to establish copyright the author must have expended sufficient skill and labour in creating the work so as to make it original.

5.18   Term of sound recording copyright

Copyright in a sound recording will expire seventy years after the end of the year in which that sound recording was produced, or, if later, the year in which it was first 'communicated to the public'. Until late 2013, the copyright term for a sound recording was only fifty years. Thus there were sound recordings first released between 1944 and 1962 in which the copyright had expired, but in which copyright revived as a consequence of the 2013 legislative change. Specific rules apply to these recordings. Should a filmmaker wish to use such a recording as part of a film soundtrack, the position will require consideration on a case-by-case basis in order to ensure that the requisite rights are cleared from the correct source.

5.19   Comparative position

There are important differences between the UK/EU and the US (and, indeed, as between certain other territories) with regard to the length of protection of certain copyrights. It is dangerous to assume that because a copyright may be protected in the UK/EU it will automatically be protected for the same length of time in the US and vice versa. Equally, a work that is in the public domain in the US may well not be in the public domain in the UK/EU. It is beyond the scope of this work to analyse the US copyright registration provisions and the effect of not registering or renewing such registrations. Although international treaties provide for the reciprocal recognition and enforceability of intellectual property rights as between the signatories to those treaties, the position is not uniform globally; see paragraph 5.4. When considering the use in one country of a copyright work that originates in another, situations can arise whereby it may become necessary to ascertain the law by which copyright in that work is primarily protected before examining how the work is to be treated in the country in which rights are sought to be used.

5.20   Copyright registration

There is no collective system for registration of copyright in the UK or, indeed, in other major European jurisdictions. Thus, proving authorship and ownership of copyright may not always be straightforward. Assistance will be provided by keeping records of when a copyright work is created and details of when and to whom it may be sent for evaluation, review or otherwise. A system of registration exists in the US via the Library of Congress in Washington http://www.copyright.gov/ The Writers' Guild of America offers a service for registration of scripts https://www.wgawregistry.org/ In the UK, Raindance will also register scripts for the purposes of protecting copyright https://www.raindance.org/london/script-registration-service/ US Library of Congress registration creates a rebuttable presumption in favour of the registrant that s/he is the owner of copyright. Registration in the US, however, does not automatically mean that the registrant will own the copyright in the UK or elsewhere. There is a school of thought that registering in Washington ahead of first publication gives notice of the detail of a work that leaves it more easily open to being copied. In the event that a copyright is infringed in the US, registration at the Library of Congress may become significant in determining the amount of damages and the recoverability of attorneys' fees arising from pursuing the claim through the courts.

5.21   Copyright notice

One way in which authors may at the very least provide notice of their ownership of copyright in a work is by using a copyright notice in the form © followed by the name of the copyright owner and the year of first publication.

Example

The Filmmakers' Legal Guide © Tony Morris 2019

This form of copyright notice is prescribed by the UCC. Its inclusion is one of the prerequisites for ensuring the work is protected by copyright in UCC countries. The Berne Convention does not have the requirement. Nevertheless, use of the © mark is good practice.

5.22   Copyright infringement

The owner of a copyright work is entitled to protect that work from infringement. In addition to the copyright that subsists in a finished film, the copyrights in the separate component parts – whether, artistic, literary, dramatic or musical – may be protected. The term 'plagiarism' is sometimes used in common parlance. Irrespective, the legal cause of action that arises when an original work is copied or 'plagiarised' is copyright infringement.

5.23   In order to constitute infringement, either the whole or a recognisable part of a work may be copied. A copyright in a literary, dramatic, musical or artistic work is infringed if a work is copied in any material form which may include storing the work in any medium by electronic means. Copying in relation to a film or broadcast includes making a photograph of the whole or any substantial part of any image forming part of the film or broadcast. Infringing a copyright will include the making of copies which are transient or which are incidental to some other use of the work.

Example

Failing to clear a thirty second clip from a US produced television programme that had been first broadcast in 1965 and which was therefore in copyright at the time of its unlicensed inclusion in a 1998 UK theatrical film was an infringement of the copyright in the television programme. The owners of the copyright in the US television programme brought proceedings against the British filmmaker in the Los Angeles Court. The programme owner was able to establish jurisdiction of the California courts as the film had been shown in California and an infringement of the programme copyright had therefore occurred within that jurisdiction. The filmmaker submitted to judgment for damages. The method for calculating damages in the California courts resulted in the filmmaker making a materially larger payment to the programme owner than might otherwise have been the case in England. In California, a compensatory element inflated the total amount to be paid beyond what would have been paid for a licence.

5.24   Under English law, remedies for infringement of a copyright will include damages and, in some circumstances, an injunction to prevent further infringement. An injunction may be granted if a party whose copyright has been infringed can show that greater damage will be suffered by permitting an infringing work to remain on the market than may adequately be compensated by way of money damages. Copyright damages are assessed by English courts in one of two ways; it is for the party making the claim to decide which:

(a)   an account of profits; i.e. the amount by which the infringer has profited from its unauthorised use of a copyright; or

(b)   the amount that a willing licensee would have paid to a willing licensor for the use of a copyright had it been made subject to a valid licence for the purposes for which it has been used; this is known as the 'user principle'. In assessing the quantum of damage, it is not open to the owner of an infringed copyright to argue that a licence would not have been granted to the infringer under any circumstances and thereby require a greater sum than will be determined by applying the test used by the Courts.

In the example at 5.23, had the case been brought in England, the court would have assessed the damages as a sum equivalent to an arm's length licence fee. It is often problematic for loss of profits to be assessed and, in the case in question, the film had, ostensibly, not made a profit.

In some cases the Courts may award additional compensatory damages if the infringement of copyright is 'flagrant'; i.e. where the infringement is intentional.

5.25   In England and Wales, the Intellectual Property Enterprise Court (**IPEC**) provides a dedicated forum for the resolution of disputes concerning all species of IP. IPEC's cap on the amount of legal fees recoverable by a successful party is designed to encourage disputing parties to concentrate on key issues with a view to streamlining the resolution of disputes.

5.26   Copyright searches

As part of the process of preparing delivery materials for distributors – particularly where a film is to be theatrically released and especially in the US – copyright searches may be undertaken. The object of such a search is to ascertain whether or not a film may or could infringe the copyright in a pre-existing film or copyright in another work. Leading providers of these searches include Thomson CompuMark http://trademarks.thomsonreuters.com/ and The Law Offices of Dennis Angel www.dangelesq.com Both the electronic records of and those on site at the US Copyright Office will be searched. Industry sources are reviewed, including databases from journals such as Variety and The Hollywood Reporter, in order to report on specific works and other properties and rights related to those works.

5.27   Copyright searches may also be undertaken in connection with chain-of-title investigations; see section 37 for a discussion of chain-of-title. A copyright search may be useful when picking up a project that has been part-developed or where a book has been subject to a previous option that has lapsed. Filmmakers may also want to establish the history of the origination and publication of a work as well as any history of its registration in the US and any renewals. Searches may reveal the history of assignments. Inevitably the extent of such a search may be restricted by what is available from public records.

5.28   Copyright law has been harmonised in the EU. It is not generally believed by IP lawyers that, consequent upon Brexit, there will be any change in English law of copyright and so, following Brexit, the principles and application described in this section 5 should continue to apply in both the UK and in the remaining 27 member states of the EU.

6   **Acquiring copyright: assignments and licences**

6.1   Acquiring an interest in copyright

In order to transfer ownership of a copyright work there must be an assignment (transfer) in writing signed by the person making the transfer. If a copyright is being acquired from the author, then it is the author who must sign the assignment. Where the author has transferred ownership of a copyright to another party, the assignee or, if the assignee is a limited company, then the duly authorised signatory of the company, will need to sign any subsequent assignment of the copyright.

6.2   Commissioning a copyright work

As mentioned previously, and no apologies are made for repeating this critically important point, it is a common misunderstanding that a party who commissions another to create a copyright work will automatically own the work that is commissioned. By contrast, a copyright will vest in the party commissioning its creation where the specific terms of a written agreement provide for that to be the case. In other words, for filmmakers who hire any other party to contribute original copyright work to be used in a film (or in any other commissioning arrangement) best practice is to ensure that:

(a)   the terms of the commission are in writing;

(b)   there is a clear and unconditional assignment to the filmmaker by the commissioned party of all copyright and any other rights in and to the subject matter of the work commissioned;

(c)   there is an obligation on the author to deliver up to the commissioner the requisite physical and/or digital media and materials reproducing the copyright work.

6.3   By way of example, if a filmmaker commissions a screenwriter to write a script for a film, unless there is a written assignment of the screenplay from the screenwriter to the filmmaker, ownership of the copyright will remain with the screenwriter. An assignment may be made of a future copyright. In other words, even if the screenwriter's agreement is put in place before the screenplay is written (as opposed to an agreement for the acquisition of a finished screenplay) the screenwriter's agreement may provide for the copyright in the screenplay to be assigned.

Example

Screenwriter hereby assigns to Producer absolutely the entire copyright and all other rights in the nature of copyright subsisting in the Screenplay with the benefit of full title guarantee for the life of copyright together with all and any renewals, revivals and extensions.

Renewals, revivals and extensions of copyright may arise if there is a change of legislation; see paragraph 5.18.

6.4   Full title guarantee

An assignment providing for copyright to be transferred 'with full title guarantee', is one by which the assignor – the party transferring the copyright – guarantees that s/he owns all the relevant rights, that the assignor is fully entitled to dispose of them as contemplated, that the assignor will do all she/ he can to complete the transfer, and the rights transferred are not subject to any claims or interests of any other party.

Omitting the language 'subject to full title guarantee' will not affect the validity of a transfer of ownership. Where a transferor cannot be certain that s/he owns a copyright outright, the owner will only be able to 'assign and transfer such right title and interest as assignor may own in and to the copyright work' (as defined in the assignment or other agreement in question). This is known as a 'quitclaim'. In circumstances where rights are qualified in this way the transferring party will only be able to give limited warranties as to the provenance of the copyright; (see para 25.8). Those acquiring such a copyright will necessarily need to proceed with caution.

6.5   In the absence of a written assignment of copyright, a transaction involving the use by one party of the copyright work of another will take effect in English law as a licence. If there is no written licence then the use that may be made by the licensee (or commissioning party) will be limited to those uses that were in the contemplation of the parties at the time the work was commissioned. In order to assess the extent of limitations on a commissioner's use of a copyright work – in circumstances where a work is not made the subject of a written assignment – the entire fabric of the dealings between the parties will need to be considered.

6.6   The following are examples based on real situations where no written terms had been agreed between the parties.

Examples

An image was licensed by a filmmaker from a photographic library for use as a still on the sleeve of the DVD release of a film and in posters advertising the DVD. The invoice from the library specified those uses and the printed terms limited uses to those specified on the invoice. The filmmaker was not able to imply the right to sell t-shirts and other merchandise promoting the film that included the image.

An aspiring musician persuaded a flatmate to make a short, no-budget film to accompany the musician's home studio recording of one of his songs. The filmmaker was told that the resulting video would be used for the sole purpose of helping the musician to secure a record deal. The benefit to the filmmaker was in the production of a short film that he could then use to showcase his skill and talent. In the absence of any written terms between the filmmaker and the musician, the record company subsequently signing the musician could not then use the film for promoting the resulting record release through commercial channels – such as MTV – without securing the relevant permission from the filmmaker.

A production company was hired by a major brand to make a short animation that was specified as being part of an upcoming summer, online advertising campaign. Permission was not deemed to have been given for the brand to use the characters in the animation in other media nor to use the promo on television nor at the cinema. There was nothing in writing that specifically permitted these additional uses nor was it to be clearly inferred from the circumstances of the parties' dealings.

6.7   Acquiring a licence of copyright work

There are many circumstances where a copyright owner may be happy to permit a filmmaker to use a copyright for a film but where there will be no intention to transfer outright ownership of that copyright. For example, a documentary maker may require the use of original photographs, existing footage or pieces of music. The required rights will generally be granted by way of licence. At the very least, the licence should specify the following:

•   the precise rights granted to the filmmaker;

•   limitations, if any, on the way in which the copyright may be used;

- the period of time – or term – during which the copyright may be used by the licensee;

- the media in which the film reproducing the copyright may be exploited;

- those territories in which the rights may be exploited; if the intention is that the rights may be exploited globally, then the licence should say so;

- the amount of any licence fee.

6.8   In acquiring a licence of an existing copyright, whether of footage, music, an image, a literary work or otherwise, the filmmaker should take care to ensure that the licence granted by the copyright owner will be sufficient to enable the licensed material to be included in the finished film, used in all required media and territories and, preferably, for the life of copyright of the film. In other words, where a filmmaker does not acquire an outright assignment of copyright, the licence or commissioning agreement should ideally provide for use of the licensed material:

'for all of the purposes of the film by all means and in all media now known or hereafter invented for the life of copyright of the film to include all extensions, renewals, reversions and revivals and in all territories of the world'.

Example

A documentary maker produced a film that told the story of the French Foreign Legion. The documentary maker endeavoured to acquire licences from third party copyright owners that extended for the life of copyright of the documentary. Amongst numerous clips and photos was footage licensed from French Military Authorities for which the written licence was limited to a ten-year term. The documentary was shown on numerous television channels around the world and released on DVD. Subsequently, ownership of the copyright in the documentary was acquired outright by a distributor. At the end of the tenth year the distributor was contacted by the French Military Authorities and asked if it wanted to renew the licence. Had it declined the opportunity to renew, the distributor would have had to remove the documentary from its catalogue or, at the very least, edit the documentary to remove the footage in question.

6.9   Licensing a musical composition or a sound recording comes with its own challenges. Licensing arrangements for exploitation of musical compositions and sound recordings may vest in a UK licensee certain rights of use in, say, a

US originated recording. However, the record company who had a UK chart hit may not necessarily be entitled under its licence from the US copyright owner of the sound recording to grant a synch licence to a filmmaker. Determining who is lawfully entitled to grant licences to use copyright works is critical. The subject of music is considered at section 13.

6.10   In some agreements the territory is expressed to extend to *'the world and its solar system'* or even to *'the Universe'*. There is nothing objectionable to these formulations that are rooted in a case that was brought against a record company many years ago. An artist claimed that by limiting the territory of his agreement to 'the world' the record company was not permitted to make the recording available for satellite broadcast via MTV and other similar networks which involved transmitting signals beyond the atmosphere of the Earth. The case was apparently settled with no finding.

6.11   There will be circumstances in which the author of a copyright will no longer be its owner and the assignee and/or subsequent owners may not easily be traced, thereby making clearance a less than easy task to accomplish. Copyrights may have been acquired by companies that have since been dissolved. Executors of a deceased writer or photographer or other artist may have assigned ownership of copyrights to raise money to look after dependent family members. In such cases the filmmaker will necessarily need to take all reasonable steps to ascertain the identity of the current copyright owner in order to clear rights required.

6.12   If a copyright owner cannot be traced, a prudent filmmaker should keep careful records of the steps taken to identify and/or locate the owner and should also accrue a sum of money to cover what would be considered a reasonable licence fee. If subsequently challenged, the filmmaker will be able to show that s/he acted in good faith. As far as English law is concerned, the filmmaker acting in good faith will likely be covered if a claim is made – certainly to the extent that the amount accrued is shown to be what a willing licensor would have required a willing licensee to pay for the use of the copyright work in question.

6.13   Bona vacantia

Assets that were not transferred out of companies prior to their dissolution will vest in the Crown as bona vacantia (literally *'vacant goods'*). Rights in such copyrights may be acquired from the Treasury Solicitor, though the procedure may be complex and not necessarily speedy. More details may be found at https://www.gov.uk/government/collections/bona-vacantia-companies-guidelines

7   Protecting an idea

7.1   No copyright in an idea

There is no copyright in an idea. Copyright arises in the expression of an idea. In order to benefit from the protection of copyright, the creator of an idea needs to record that idea in a permanent form. As mentioned at paragraph 5.1, what constitutes 'permanent form' extends to include both physical and digital media: written documents, drawings, photographs, illustrations, sculptures and models, sound and audio-visual recordings, digital files and computer code.

Example

A documentary filmmaker meets a commissioning editor from a network. During the course of the meeting, the filmmaker explains an idea that she has for a programme series dealing with testing drugs on human guinea pigs. She mentions the names of pharmaceutical companies she believes to be involved in the practice and those of individuals who have acquired evidence to support her claims. The network then commissions an in-house team to investigate the issue and to produce programmes addressing the matter. The filmmaker had no claim for infringement of copyright as she had not written a treatment or outline and had failed to put any of her research in writing or otherwise record it in permanent form. There is a possibility that disclosure of the information may have been protected by the common law of confidentiality. However, in the absence of making any attempt to preserve confidentiality, the filmmaker faced an uphill struggle to prove her case in court.

The general principles of protecting confidential information are considered at paragraphs 7.5–7.8 and at section 15.

7.2   For a filmmaker, protecting ideas can be more challenging than for creatives operating in other media. This is particularly the case where the project is documentary in nature, where there is no script as such and where the finished form of the work may only emerge during the course of post-production.

7.3   Once an author has created an original work it will be protected by copyright. An outline or a treatment will be protected by copyright – provided it is original. The principles of copyright infringement discussed at paragraphs 5.22-5.25 apply to treatments and outlines as well as to complete scripts. A film that is produced from an outline or treatment for which the filmmaker has not obtained a clearance may infringe the copyright in that outline or treatment.

7.4   Protecting a format

Successful formats (whether created for television or otherwise) may have considerable commercial value, though there is no copyright in a format as such. To protect a format, its creators need to record the elements of the format in permanent form; the more detail that is recorded, the more robust the format will be. Such detail may include descriptions of the scenarios, characters, catch-phrases, slogans, artwork, photographs, logos, trade marks, set designs and general get-up, costume design, musical selections and so on. By building up a dossier that contains all of this detail in permanent form – be it written, graphical, digital or otherwise – the format creator will be able to demonstrate the existence of a substantial copyright work that may then be protected against infringement. One very effective way of protecting a format is to produce a pilot programme, or even a trailer or a 'sizzle', and thus to create a complete copyright audio-visual example of how a programme developed from the format and filmed will look; in such a case the filmmaker will have a definitive copyright that can be protected. There is a contrary school of thought suggesting that by filming a pilot, or even a trailer or a 'sizzle', a format creator may give too much away; those viewing a pilot, trailer or 'sizzle' are afforded the opportunity of reviewing the format and changing it sufficiently to avoid a claim of infringement. Given that experienced producers may express such wildly differing opinions, those developing a format must necessarily take a commercial view about how they may most effectively proceed when disclosing the details of a format to a third party.

7.5   Non-disclosure/confidentiality agreements

Although there is no copyright in an idea as such, ideas and information may be protected. The device by which protection may be afforded is a Confidentiality Agreement or Non-Disclosure Agreement (**NDA**). In its simplest form an NDA is a written agreement providing that in consideration for the disclosure of information the recipient undertakes to keep that information confidential and not use it for any purpose other than to evaluate it. An NDA may be used to protect not just material for a documentary or a format but information of any kind. Such information may include storylines, scripts, the amount to be paid for the film rights, cast lists, location availability and any other particular elements of a project that may be considered to be confidential. The requirements to make such an arrangement in the form of a contract binding are considered at paragraphs 24.1-24.7.

7.6 Commissioning broadcasters and others requested to sign NDAs may and, from experience, often will refuse to do so; they will be wary of assuming a contractual obligation that shuts them out from making programmes about subjects or using information of which they may already have knowledge; this notwithstanding that standard forms of NDA will generally exclude from protection information of which the recipient may demonstrate it is already in possession. If refused an NDA, a film or programme maker will necessarily need to take a view as to whether information may safely be disclosed. English law recognises that an implied duty of confidence may arise in certain circumstances. Arguably such a duty will protect a filmmaker who discloses details of a project to a potentially interested party; see section 15.2.

7.7 Having shared information without an NDA, a filmmaker is advised to follow up immediately by confirming, in writing, brief details of the information made available and the basis upon which it was shared; viz. to enable the network (or other recipient) to evaluate the information for the sole purpose of producing films or programmes in conjunction with the party disclosing the information. The filmmaker should also assert that:

(a)   the circumstances in which the information was shared create an obligation of confidentiality, and

(b)   the material has been recorded in a permanent form that is subject to copyright protection, ownership of which is vested in the film or programme maker.

Example

A filmmaker, Douglas, develops a sitcom set in a car repair workshop entitled, 'The Panel Beaters'. Douglas pitches the proposal to Matthew, a network commissioner, at an impromptu meeting arranged at the end of a panel session during a festival. Matthew declines to sign the NDA that Douglas proffers. Douglas, nevertheless, proceeds to explain the main elements of the situation, to describe each of the four main characters and some of the minor roles and also outlines a number of storylines that are contained in written treatments that he has developed into six scripts. Douglas shows the treatments to Matthew and leaves copies with him. Matthew informs Douglas that he will review the proposal with his colleagues at the network. Very shortly after the meeting, Douglas sends an email to Matthew that reads:

Dear Matthew,

I refer to our meeting of earlier today when I explained to you the key elements of my sitcom presently entitled 'The Panel Beaters' and left with you written treatments for the six episodes that I have written. I also described the four main characters and some of the minor roles. The treatments, scripts, characters, situations, scenarios and all other component parts of 'The Panel Beaters' are original literary works in which ownership of the copyright is vested in me.

At the end of the meeting you said that you would give some thought as to whether 'The Panel Beaters' would be of interest to the network. I look forward to hearing from you and, in the interim, take this opportunity of confirming that all of the information that I gave to you about 'The Panel Beaters' is confidential so that it may only be used for the purposes of discussing my project with your colleagues at the network and for no other purpose; in particular the information that I shared with you may not be adapted or used in or for any other programme or as part of any other programme format without my prior written consent.

Yours sincerely

Douglas

7.8   Experience shows that even with a signed NDA, the integrity of information may not always be respected, even by major players. Nevertheless, by acting sensibly and taking a professional approach, a filmmaker can maximise her/his position in the event that what s/he regards as confidential information about an original copyright work – or a copyright work itself – is misused. A short form of NDA is to be found at Appendix 1.

8   Moral rights

8.1   Nature of moral rights

Moral rights exist outside of and in addition to copyright. In contrast to copyright which protects ownership – and hence the economic rights to a work – moral rights are concerned with protecting the personality and reputation of authors.

8.2   Authors of literary, dramatic, musical and artistic works and film directors are granted a number of moral rights by virtue of the Copyright Act of which the most relevant to filmmakers are:

- the right to be identified as the author of the work or, in the case of a director, to be identified as the director of a film; this is known as the right of paternity;

- the right to object to a derogatory treatment of a work or, in the director's case, of a film which amounts to a distortion or mutilation, or which is otherwise prejudicial to the honour or reputation of the author or director; this is known as the right of integrity;

- the right not to have a work falsely attributed.

Under English law, the rights of paternity and integrity last as long as the copyright in the work. The right not to have work falsely attributed expires twenty years after the death of an author.

8.3   Right of paternity

Under English law the right of paternity, i.e. the right to be identified as an author, may not be exercised unless it has been asserted. In other words, the author or director is required to indicate his or her wish to exercise the right by giving notice to this effect (which is recommended as being in writing and signed) to those seeking to use or exploit the work or film. Such an assertion will usually be addressed in the contract by which the author is engaged. In the case of a film, the director's assertion will usually be provided for in the agreement by which s/he is engaged by the production company.

8.4   Waiver of moral rights

Moral rights may be waived under English law. The right of paternity may only be waived once it has been asserted. An author or director may waive both the right to be identified as an author and the right to object to derogatory treatment. Such a waiver may be effected by contract. Many standard form agreements written under English law provide for a waiver. Where the author of a work is required to waive the moral right of paternity, it is recommended that part of the consideration for doing so is to require the filmmaker by whom the waiver is sought to provide an appropriate credit. Additionally, where the right of integrity is required to be waived, an author may consider that safeguards will be required to protect the integrity of a work so that it does not become subject to a derogatory treatment.

8.5   Derogatory treatment

Instances of whether there is an infringement of the right to prevent a derogatory treatment may be difficult to determine. Examples of derogatory treatment include the use of an anti-war protest song in a film that extols the virtues of war or replacing the words of a love song and using it as the soundtrack to a commercial that advertises a brand of toilet cleaner. A recent instance demonstrates the requirements of a novelist contemplating the grant of an option to a filmmaker.

Example

A novelist tells the story of a devoutly religious Amish couple whose love is only ever platonic. The male is murdered before they can be married. The filmmaker acquiring screen rights may envisage the inclusion of a full-on bedroom scene before the murder. The novelist may consider that such a scene would erode the integrity of the original work and, in the grant of rights, endeavour to preserve his characters' on-screen chastity.

8.6   The position in English law should be contrasted with the way that moral rights are viewed in other jurisdictions. Moral rights are not recognised in the US. Invariably, US contracts will require all those contributing to a production or otherwise commissioned to create copyright works to waive their moral rights. A waiver under English law or under the law of a US state may be enforceable in the US and/or in the UK; however, that position will not necessarily be the same elsewhere.

8.7   The laws on moral rights and the extent to which they may be waived vary significantly. In parts of continental Europe, notably France, moral rights are 'inalienable, irrevocable and perpetual'. Further, France will recognise the moral rights of authors from any part of the globe, even from those jurisdictions whose laws do not provide for moral rights, i.e. US. The French courts may also uphold the moral rights of deceased authors whose works are out of copyright.

Example

A colourised version of a black and white movie, 'The Concrete Jungle', financed and produced in the US and of which the author was a US national, was distributed and exhibited in France. John Huston, who both wrote the screenplay and directed the film, successfully demonstrated that the colourised version constituted a derogatory treatment of the original and a French court granted an order to prevent further exploitation of the colourised version.

8.8   The position in other jurisdictions varies and may require specific advice on the treatment of moral rights if there is concern about exploitation of any work in which authorship is not credited or of which a treatment may be derogatory.

8.9   False attribution

Authors of copyright works and film directors are also granted the moral right not to have a work or film falsely attributed to them.

Example

A production company was engaged to deliver an online promo for a leading brand of liqueur. The production company was owned by a well-known, award winning features director. The director was not involved in any aspect of the promo, but the brand owners implicitly suggested the director had been responsible for creating the promo. The production company successfully stopped the brand owner from attributing its owner as director of the promo.

8.10   Works to which moral rights do not apply

Moral rights do not apply:

•   to computer programmes;

- where ownership of a work was originally vested in an author's employer;

- where a copyright work is being used in newspapers or magazines or in reference works such as encyclopaedias or dictionaries.

8.11   Moral rights in performances

Performers also have moral rights which include the right to be identified, or credited, as the performer and to object to derogatory treatments of their performances. The principles applicable to the protection of these moral rights are the same as those applicable to authors. Performers' rights are examined in more detail in section 9; moral rights in performances at paragraph 9.6.

9   Performers' rights

9.1   Nature of performers' rights

A performer has a right in his or her performance. In addition, a performer has a number of economic rights that arise from a performance being the rights of reproduction, distribution and the so-called rental and lending right. A performance may include acting, singing, playing a musical instrument, conducting an orchestra or other musical ensemble, dancing, mime, performing magic tricks and illusions, reciting poetry, stand-up comedy, stunt performances, ventriloquism, circus acts, escapology, contortionism, acrobatics, knife-throwing, fire-breathing, snake-charming, sword-swallowing, juggling, plate-spinning, puppetry, balloon-folding or any other activity comprising a performance.

9.2   Performers also have rights in recordings, films or broadcasts of their performances. A performer has the right to determine how, when and by whom that performance may be exploited. In order to exploit a finished film, it is necessary for filmmakers to ensure that adequate consents have been obtained from each of the performers participating in the film.

9.3   Performers' consents

English law does not require consent to be in writing. A performer's consent may be implied from the circumstances in which the performance is given. The actor cast in a walk-on part in an episode of a television soap for which he has had a script and learned his lines, who turns up at a studio, puts on a costume and make-up and is then directed on set clearly consents to having his performance filmed. However, in the absence of written consent, there may be limits on the extent to which a filmmaker may exploit a performance. Those limits will be determined by what was in the reasonable contemplation of the parties at the time the performance was given. Limits may apply to:

•   the medium within or the purpose for which use may be made of the performance; i.e. television only;

•   the period during which the performances may be used or the number of permitted transmissions;

•   the territory within which the performance may be exploited.

Examples

A group of undergraduates collaborated on a short, dramatic film that was made specifically for an international student film festival. There were no written agreements between the students. Having won first prize, subsequently, one of the students granted a licence of the film to an international television distributor without reference to the rest of the team. The actors successfully objected to the distributor's activities. Their consent could only implicitly extend to the showing of the film at the student festival.

A back-up singer at a charity concert signed a short form consent for her performance to be filmed for a live broadcast. She successfully prevented compact discs and MP3s being distributed without her further consent being secured.

A well-known Shakespearian actor was standing with other members of the audience on the concourse outside the National Theatre. Whilst waiting for the doors to open for the premiere of a new production of 'Hamlet', the actor gave an impromptu performance of the 'To be or not to be' soliloquy. Unseen, a filmmaker who was nearby, recorded the performance on his iPhone and uploaded it to YouTube. The actor successfully had the film taken down. No consent was given, either expressly or implicitly, for his performance to be recorded or used in this way by the filmmaker.

9.4   As a matter of course, filmmakers should ensure that all performers sign a written consent irrespective of how insignificant their respective roles may be. Ideally, consent should extend to permit filming and recording of the performance in question and to enable filmmakers and those deriving rights from them to make copies and to exploit films reproducing the performances by all means and in all media throughout the territory of the world for the life of copyright of the film.

9.5   The written consent of a performer should ideally be sought and obtained before filming or making any other permanent record of a performance. The more established a performer, the stronger his/her position will be in relation to the negotiation of the consideration for such consent. Extras, walk-ons and even supporting cast may be paid a complete buyout on a minimum scale. Leads in larger productions may command big fees, perquisites and a net profit participation. If not included in a contract that covers the entirety of the agreed terms between filmmaker and performer, at the very least the key elements of a consent should be incorporated in a form of release. Performers' contracts are addressed at sections 30-32; examples of a performer's contract and a short form consent are included at Appendices 11 and 12.

9.6   Moral rights in performances

A performer also has moral rights in her/his performance. The right to be identified as a performer will generally be satisfied by the provision of a credit. A performer also has the right not to have a derogatory treatment made of a performance.

Example

A young filmmaker persuaded her friend to permit the friend's six-year-old daughter to be filmed in her pyjamas for what was described by the filmmaker as a short film about telling bed-time stories. The parent or legal guardian of a minor is regarded by law as having the right to provide consent for that minor. The footage was edited in such a way that the child was implicitly connected with the activities of a paedophile. The child's mother successfully prevented the film from being shown and secured an undertaking from the filmmaker to destroy it. The use proposed by the filmmaker constituted a derogatory treatment of the performance that had been given by the six-year-old.

The engagement of children in filmmaking is discussed at section 34.

9.7   Term of performers' rights

A performer's rights continue to exist until seventy years after the date upon which a performance is given or, if recorded (and for these purposes 'recorded' or 'recording' includes 'filmed' or 'filming'), seventy years after the end of the year in which the recording or film is first released.

9.8   Fair use of performances

Fair use of performances may be made in circumstances that are substantially the same as the fair uses that may be made of copyright works. Amongst these are incidental inclusion, criticism or review, use for instruction and examination and in educational establishments. A discussion of these principles is to be found at section 11. Thus the rights in a performance or in the recording (or filming) of a performance are not infringed by the use of a short extract from the performance or from the recording of a performance provided that:

(a)   the performance or recording has been made available to the public, and

(b)   the use of the quotation (or extract) is fair dealing with the performance or recording, and

(c)   the length of the extract is no more than is required for the specific purpose for which it is used, and

(d)   the extract is appropriately acknowledged or credited on screen.

When taking advantage of these provisions a filmmaker may not use so much of a filmed/recorded performance as will constitute an infringement of the original performance. In particular fair use does not give free rein to those who may wish to sample a sound recording without consent of the copyright owners of the recording and of the underlying musical material. See the discussion at paragraph 11.5; music is discussed in detail at section 13.

9.9   Consents of minors

Under English law minors and persons acting under a disability, such as mental incapacity, are not able to give a consent for their performances to be used. Consents for minors must be obtained from a parent or legal guardian. In the event that no formal consent has been sought, once a minor has achieved the age of majority, s/he may then affirm the consent that may otherwise have been implied from the circumstances in which the performance was given.

9.10   Neighbouring rights

Another term that is used in connection with performers is 'neighbouring rights' which are the rights of performers to be remunerated for their performances in connection with sound recordings. For this purpose, performers include singers and musicians. The rights of performers, phonogram producers and broadcasting organisations are internationally protected by the Rome Convention for the Protection of Performers, Producers of Phonograms and Broadcasting Organisations signed in 1961. The WIPO Performances and Phonograms Treaty extended these rights to include the right to licence:

•   the distribution of recordings of their performance for sale or other transfer of ownership, and

- the rental of recordings of their performances, unless there is a compulsory licence scheme in operation and the 'making available to the public' of their performances,

all of which would also encompass the publication of the performances on the internet.

9.11   Performing rights

Performers' rights should be distinguished from performing rights. Performing rights are the rights that give rise to an obligation to pay royalties to the composers and/or publishers of original musical compositions. These payments are made for a licence to perform compositions in public and are payable for live, broadcast and all other performances of copyright compositions in public. The theatrical or cinematic public performances of compositions included in films and shows will generally be covered in annual licences issued to theatres and cinemas by the appropriate collecting societies. In the UK, PRS for Music, (formerly the Performing Rights Society) is responsible for issuing these licences; website: https://www.prsformusic.com Public performances of copyright sound recordings are licensed by in the UK by Phonographic Performances Limited; website: http://www.ppluk.com/ Music is discussed in more detail at section 13.

9.12   Sporting performances

There is much scholarly debate as to whether a sporting performance is protected by performers' rights. There is no protection for such a performance under the Copyright Act. As the law presently stands, judicial commentators do not think that an English court would uphold such a claim. When filming sporting events, filmmakers will inevitably require the permission of those responsible for promoting the event. Admission of filmmakers to the stadium, course or arena where an event is taking place will inevitably be subject to conditions that apply to filming or recording of the event; a licence to film will likely be necessary from those who own or control the venue. Nevertheless, under the law as it stands, a problem may arise in circumstances such as those in which a Premier League footballer is engaged in a kick-about in the local public park with a few of his friends. Can the footballer prevent a filmmaker recording the event from using that recording? The laws of privacy may assist the footballer – though the issue is by no means clear-cut. A discussion on privacy is at section 16.

CONTENT

10   Underlying literary works and options

10.1   Securing permission to use a literary work

Those interested in making a film that is to be based on a pre-existing literary work that is in copyright at the time of the intended production will need to secure the permission of the copyright owner of that work. Once an author has been dead for more than seventy years, permission to make a film based on that author's works will not be required.

Examples

The James Bond books were written by Ian Fleming who died in 1964. Fleming's works will remain in copyright until 31 December 2034. The Sherlock Holmes stories were written by Arthur Conan Doyle who died in 1930. Conan Doyle's works ceased to be protected by copyright at the end of 2000.

10.2   Book publishers may not retain the film rights to all of the works that they publish – particularly novels. However, as digitisation of literary works has eroded traditional revenue streams of publishers, there is an increasing trend for publishers to seek to retain control of – or at least an interest in – the film rights to the works they publish. This is particularly the case with non-fiction and/or works that are commissioned by a publisher from an author.

10.3   Where publishers do not control works, often the best place to start when seeking to clear film rights will be the author's agent or, where the author is deceased, her/his literary executor. An author's agent may also act as one of her/his literary executors.

10.4   Non-fiction works

Filmmakers may query the necessity of clearing copyright works that deal with factual matter that is in the public domain – such as biographies and historical non-fiction. However, when an agent is questioned whether rights to a non-fiction work require to be cleared the answer will inevitably be, 'if you didn't think that you needed to clear the work, why are you bothering to ask me?'

10.5   There may be a fine line between writing a script based on factual material on the one hand and, on the other hand, writing a script based on factual material that has been collated, compiled and interpreted by an author in a particular literary work. If the story to be told in a film may be written on the basis of independent research and independent research is undertaken by or on behalf of the filmmaker, then individual pre-existing works need not be cleared. However, in circumstances where an author has created elements of a story/history based on opinion and/or deduction and/or original research and/or analysis – or where, for example, an author has created characters and suggested personality traits for protagonists and projected scenarios in which the character was involved – then a filmmaker will need to secure a clearance.

Example

Pre-existing historical and literary portrayals of Henry VIII's chief minister Thomas Cromwell typically described him as being calculating and ruthless. In the play, 'A Man For All Seasons', author Robert Bolt's characterisation was that of a thuggish politico, portrayed in sinister fashion by Leo McKern in the screen adaptation directed by Fred Zinnemann. By contrast, in her novel, 'Wolf Hall', author Hilary Mantel paints an alternative picture of Cromwell. Mantel sees him as a pragmatist steering his way through the intrigues and machinations of Henry's court, doing his best to serve king and country against the background of the religious turmoil of the Protestant Reformation. Mantel makes considerable efforts to understand the psychology of Cromwell in what is a more intimate portrait than Bolt's. In the absence of primary sources that delve into Cromwell's psychological makeup, it is apparent that Mantel has created significant, original work in her characterisation in which copyright subsists.

Thus, a filmmaker preparing a feature about Cromwell that relied heavily on Mantel's characterisation would be advised to clear the right to use it. However, the documentary maker contrasting differing views on Cromwell derived from varying sources – of which 'Wolf Hall' is but one– may be able to take advantage of the 'criticism and review' fair use exception addressed in more detail at section 11. The caveat is that use of extensive extracts from either 'Wolf Hall' and/or 'A Man For All Seasons' without clearance would not constitute fair use.

10.6   Life rights

Filmmakers often query whether or not it is necessary to enter into an exclusive agreement with the intended subject of a film to acquire so-called 'life rights'.

'Life rights' is the term given to the rights in a living individual's life and times. The statutes are silent on this matter. There is much written about this issue. However, the current prevailing view of English IP lawyers is that it is not possible to grant exclusive life rights. Nevertheless, filmmakers will often enter into formal agreements to acquire life rights in order to secure the active co-operation of the subject and access to original material that may not otherwise be available. A problem that may be encountered in negotiating such an agreement is the extent to which the subject may want to control the use of the material made available and, more importantly for a filmmaker, a requirement for editorial control over the film's content; the latter, in particular, may erode the filmmaker's creative vision for the film. It is this latter issue and, of course, the filmmaker's objectives that will determine the filmmaker's decision whether or not to engage with a subject in this way and, if so, the terms to which that engagement be subject. An example of an agreement to acquire life rights is at Appendix 2.

10.7   Options: what they are and how they work

Generally, when clearing underlying literary works, the copyright owner will grant a filmmaker an 'option'. In this context, an 'option' is an option to acquire the rights necessary to make a film version of a literary work. In simple terms there are two stages to the process:

•   upon execution of the option agreement the filmmaker will be given a period of time – an option period – during which the film may be developed, a screenplay written, a budget prepared, talent attached and an endeavour made to raise the finance for the film's budget;

•   once a filmmaker is in a position to proceed to production, the option may be exercised at which point the film rights in the underlying literary work will be transferred from the copyright owner to the filmmaker on the terms previously agreed that will include payment of the purchase price.

Options may also be used in acquiring rights from a screenwriter to a completed screenplay in respect of which similar principles to those applying to the acquisition of rights in an underlying literary work will apply.

10.8   The negotiation of film rights options may seem deceptively simple. However, there are a number of matters to be borne in mind that need to be balanced between the negotiating parties that include the following:

- a copyright owner may not want to tie up the film rights to a work for an unreasonably lengthy period; this may particularly be the case with a work that has been recently published and/or which has been successful;

- typically, initial option periods will last for between twelve and eighteen months. Sometimes the copyright owner may agree to one or more extensions to be locked into the option agreement; these may require triggers – such as additional payments by the filmmaker and even demonstrating key milestones in the progress towards funding production;

- whether the option is to extend to prequels, sequels, remakes and anything other than a single film or television series – and, if so, on what basis;

- determining the purchase price to be paid for the rights may be guesswork until the level of the budget and finance has been locked in. Filmmakers will want to pay as little as possible for the option itself and ensure that the option payment will be deducted from the purchase price as and when it is paid. Copyright owners may want option payments to be non-recoupable against the eventual purchase price, especially where there are extensions. Typically, the overall price paid for rights will be somewhere between 1% and 3% of the total budget of a film, depending on a whole host of factors. With a massively popular work, the percentage will likely be higher than that paid for a more obscure work. In relation to certain levels of budget – particularly more lavish productions – the purchase price for the rights may be subject to a cap. Owners of underlying copyrights may also be looking for a share of the net profits from the film and any spin-off income including merchandise;

- maintaining the integrity of the underlying literary work in the realisation of the film, in respect of which the author may wish to assert her/his moral rights; this requirement may need to be balanced with the commercial imperatives by which a filmmaker may be constrained. Any issue will not be resolved by the language of a contract without the parties first reaching a clear understanding as to how the filmmaker may treat the underlying work in the screen adaptation.

10.9 Filmmakers are often concerned not to expend disproportionate resources – time, effort and money – in negotiating the terms of an option. Nevertheless, it is ideally the case that provided the filmmaker has a realistic idea of the scale of the film's budget, the parties should lock into the principal commercial terms and agree the detailed form of assignment of rights before the option is executed. If this is not done, a filmmaker successfully raising a significant budget risks being held to ransom once funding is ready to be committed. The other side of the commercial balance to be weighed is the danger that a filmmaker over-estimates what might be raised to make the film and commits to paying too much for the rights. At that point the solution will necessarily resolve around an endeavour to negotiate a price reduction with the rights owner. As an alternative to negotiating a full-blown option, in recent times there has been an increase in the use of so-called 'shopping agreements' which are considered at paragraphs 10.13-10.14.

10.10   Option agreements

A filmmaker acquiring an option should make certain that the following matters are clearly addressed in the option agreement:

- exclusivity: unless the filmmaker acquires an exclusive right to make the film based on the underlying work, the option will be presumed to be non-exclusive and potentially valueless;

- irrevocable: filmmakers need to know that, once granted an option, they may proceed to develop the project without the risk of losing rights – unless, of course a filmmaker commits a breach of her/his obligations that will then justify termination for cause. An option should therefore be expressed to be 'irrevocable';

- exercise of the option should expressly be required to be made 'by notice in writing'. It is critical when dealing with options to ensure that any notice is properly served in accordance with the requirements of the contract; see paragraphs 25.10-25.11.

A simple form of option agreement is included at Appendix 3; the Exhibit to that option agreement is a form of assignment; see discussion at paragraphs 10.8-10.9.

10.11   Other uses for options

An option may also be used in relation to source material in other media. For example, the filmmaker seeking to raise finance for a movie based on the life and times of a well-known musician may want to option the rights to include some of that musician's original compositions and recordings. One of the terms of such an option could be to secure a period of exclusivity for access to specified works. The use of options is not confined to the acquisition of rights in source material. Options may also be used, for example, by a production company to pick up the services of a director or lead actor, for a broadcaster to pick up another series based on a television format, or where, as part of the consideration for distributing a film, a distributor will be looking at the possibility of acquiring a filmmaker's next project. The principles discussed above at paragraphs 10.7-10.10 will apply to each of these examples.

10.12   Species of options

Species of options with which filmmakers may be faced may include those described in this paragraph. The examples below concern the relationship between a filmmaker and a distributor. In these examples, the rights are made subject to procedures that will require the filmmaker to notify the distributor of the details of a project when it becomes sufficiently developed. Upon receiving the notification, the distributor may decide whether or not it wants to make a proposal for acquiring rights in that project. Although used in the context of a filmmaker/distributor relationship, the following examples may be adapted to other relationships; for example, producer/writer and producer/director. The provisions will generally include designated time periods within which each step of the process requires to be undertaken:

- First Look: the grant of a right to review and consider a given project or a series of projects. During the contractually specified time period, the distributor will have a clear run at considering the filmmaker's project and determining whether it is something in which it may be interested. The distributor will then be in a position to make an offer which will be for the filmmaker to accept or otherwise. The only obligation arising in this situation is the obligation of the filmmaker to let the distributor have a 'first look'.

- Matching Rights: the grant of a right to the distributor to match any offers made by any others who might be interested in the project. The filmmaker will be required under the terms of a matching rights option to notify the distributor of any other offer made to acquire the specified distribution rights and the terms on which the offer has been made. The distributor will then have a given period in which to match the offer already received and, if the distributor does so, then the filmmaker will be obliged to grant the rights in the new project to that distributor.

- First and Last Matching Rights: the grant of a right to the distributor to match the first and last offers made by any other party. These options can become fairly complex and convoluted, not just in the way they may be drafted, but also in the way they operate. In a situation that can turn into an auction, careful consideration requires to be given to the periods within which those making the offers may make them if the process is not to continue for an unreasonably extended time. If the distributor with the last matching right is not prepared to match the last bid made by the 'new' distributor, then it is that 'new' distributor who may then proceed with the project.

10.13   Attachment or 'shopping' agreements

An attachment agreement, popularly referred to as a 'shopping agreement', is one by which a party interested in acquiring rights to a book, a screenplay or other work or project (**Recipient**) is given an exclusive period of time in which to raise finance and to further develop a property to the point at which the Recipient is ready to acquire the rights to produce the project. Other uses of such agreements may include, for example, the acquisition by networks or major production companies from YouTubers of content for development, production and distribution on other platforms or of television formats for development and sale to broadcasters. The form of these agreements varies – some may be no more than a couple of paragraphs, others may include detailed terms, with the emphasis on the requirement to negotiate a long-form agreement in good faith. One common adjunct to such an obligation will be use of language along the lines of 'within customary industry parameters'. The use of this latter term is not necessarily that helpful as there will inevitably be a degree of variation as to what parties may perceive to be 'customary'.

10.14   There has been a recent upsurge in the use of shopping agreements which has inevitably led to some of the forms becoming longer and, in some cases, containing provisions that need to be carefully considered and, in some, if not many, cases, removed before signing. For example:

- there may be an attempt to prevent the underlying rights owner from appointing any other party to attempt to shop the material for a period after the shopping agreement has expired, even if the grantee has failed to secure a deal;

- there may be an attempt to constrict the use of IP developed during the shopping period;

- there may be the inclusion of a turnaround provision requiring payment by the owner to the 'shopper' of various costs before the material may be exploited after expiration of a 'shopping period'.

Some of these provisions may be justified, others may not. Thus, those entering into shopping deals must carefully weigh up the risks associated with potential failure as much as the fruits of possible success. An example of a shopping agreement is at Appendix 4. Turnaround is discussed at paragraph 38.9

11   Third party copyright and other material: fair use

11.1   General principles

As a general principle permission will be required from the owner of a pre-existing copyright work to use it in a film. In certain instances, the right to use an existing work may be controlled by someone to whom an owner has given the authority to deal with a work; for example, a literary agent who acts on behalf of an author. Once a work is out of copyright, permission need not be sought; see paragraphs 5.14-5.19. There are certain exceptions to the requirement to obtain permission, the most important of which are discussed in this section.

11.2   Third party copyright works used by filmmakers may include literary material, photographs, drawings, paintings, illustrations, graphics, tables of information, animation, film clips and other species of audio-visual footage, spoken word recordings and music. The subject of music is dealt with at section 13. In each case the filmmaker will need to find out who owns the copyright work and secure a licence – permission – to include that work in a film. In securing licences, the general principles previously discussed in relation to copyright works and performers' consents will apply; see sections 6 and 9. In other words, the filmmaker should ensure that the licence granted will extend to cover inclusion in the film for all proposed media of exploitation, that there is no territorial limitation that may prove problematic and that, ideally, the permitted use will endure for the life of copyright of the film.

11.3   Notwithstanding the monopoly recognised by the law that enables an owner of copyright to control its use by others, there are circumstances in which fair use may be made of a copyright work without consent. The principal fair use exceptions are:

- Criticism, review, quotation and news reporting

- Incidental inclusion

- Education

- Parody

11.4   Criticism or review

What constitutes 'criticism or review' has been broadly interpreted by the courts. These words are given their ordinary and natural meaning. In simple terms, there needs to be some analysis or comment about the content, qualities, style, substance or other features of a copyright work. Nevertheless, the threshold for what constitutes 'criticism or review' is not a difficult one to achieve. Fair dealing with a work for the purpose of criticism or review of that or another work or of a performance of a work does not infringe copyright in the work, provided that the work has previously been made available to the public and provided that it is accompanied by a sufficient acknowledgement; see paragraph 11.6. If it is impossible for reasons of practicality or otherwise, an acknowledgment is not required. The fair dealing exception for news reporting does not extend to the use of photographs.

11.5   Using an existing work in this way does not give a filmmaker carte blanche to include extended elements of an existing film in a documentary:

Example

In what was promoted as a documentary about the life and work of the iconic comedy sketch writer and performer, Marty Feldman, a filmmaker included a dozen or so complete sketches taken from Feldman's 60s and 70s television shows. Some of the sketches were three or four minutes long, others even longer. The sketches were linked together with the barest minimum of audio-only narration over photos and other visual material. When challenged by the copyright owners of the sketches, the filmmaker was obliged to take the documentary off the market. Use of clips of perhaps ten to twenty seconds illustrating Feldman's style of humour would have been permitted if accompanied by something in the way of a critique or commentary. The documentary maker was unable to avoid the conclusion that, in reality, he had created a DVD 'Best of' without paying to clear the rights of the copyright owners of each of the sketches which, in this instance, were vested in a number of production companies, broadcasters and archives.

Care should be taken when using a number of clips of audio or audio-visual material in the same film from the same source without a clearance in order to avoid any argument that may be made by a copyright owner that the extent of overall use made deprives the work from benefiting from fair use by way of criticism or review. Further, and in any event, the criticism and review fair use exception does not work in the same way in the US as it does in the UK. In a recent US case multiple short clips of a composer's work that were used in a documentary about his life were not treated as fair use and the distributors were required to cease its distribution of the film. With music in particular, especially with well-known and popular composers and artists, the safer course is to seek clearances from the copyright owners of those compositions and recordings sought to be used.

11.6 In order to satisfy the requirement for an acknowledgment, the filmmaker may include the credit either at the end of the film or an in-shot reference. Requisite information includes, as a minimum, the name of the copyright owner of the clip (or, where applicable, other copyright work); adding the © symbol and the year in which the copyright was created is good practice.

Example

In the Marty Feldman case a sufficient acknowledgment for a BBC-owned sketch produced in 1969 would have been 'A day in the life of a stuntman' © BBC Television 1969.

11.7 For the use of literary works for the purpose of criticism or review, the Society of Authors, http://www.societyofauthors.net/quick-guide-permissions/ has suggested the following guidelines to indicate what is the acceptable length of an extract:

- a single extract of up to 400 words or a series of extracts (of which none exceeds 300 words) to a total of 800 words from a prose work;

- extracts to a total of 40 lines from a poem, provided this does not exceed a quarter of the poem.

11.8 Incidental inclusion

Whether or not an existing copyright work has been deliberately or incidentally included in a film should be capable of determination from the circumstances.

Example

In a dramatic feature set in December 1980, John Lennon's 'Imagine' is being sung, live, in the background by a group of extras who accompany themselves on acoustic guitars as two of the principal characters discuss his murder. This discussion is relevant to the story of the film and the recording is deliberately included by the director. This use would not be incidental inclusion. The right to use John Lennon's original composition would need to be cleared. The agreements with the extras would inevitably include performers' consents. The live recording of the musical performance being picked up while shooting the scene, will be treated as having been produced by the filmmaker who will be the first owner of the copyright in the recording.

Example

On the anniversary of John Lennon's death a filmmaker is shooting the introduction to a documentary on the street outside the Dakota Building in New York where Lennon was murdered. In the background, thirty feet away, several mourners with candles are standing by a boom box. While the film's narrator is in full flow talking to camera about aspects of Lennon's murder and the guilty party, Michael David Chapman, and without any intervention by the filmmaker, Lennon's original recording of 'Imagine' starts to play on the boom box. In this instance the filmmaker would be able to take advantage of fair use as it is apparent that the inclusion of the playing of 'Imagine' was incidental.

If the narrator then made unscripted observations about the significance of the song 'Imagine', arguably those observations might constitute 'criticism or review'. The featured use of a short portion of the recording in the film would then be acceptable provided that the filmmaker ensured that there was an appropriate on-screen acknowledgment of each of the copyrights in Lennon's composition and original recording.

If the sound of the recording was mixed to the fore and permitted to run for a couple of minutes without interruption, the benefits of both fair use exceptions – incidental inclusion and criticism/review – would be lost and the rights in the underlying composition and the recording/performance would then need to be cleared.

If the recording on the boom box started during the course of a journalist's coverage on the anniversary of the death, its inclusion in a broadcast of the journalist's piece would be permitted by the fair use extended to including copyright works for the purposes of news reporting, provided accompanied by a sufficient acknowledgement.

In considering these examples, reference should also be made to the subject of music discussed at section 13.

11.9   Research/educational purposes

Certain approved bodies, such as universities, may make copies of copyright works for research or educational purposes. This particular fair dealing exception is unlikely to be of relevance to a filmmaker unless commissioned to make a film for such an approved body. This exception may also assist when third party material is used in student films made as part of a course, provided those films are not used for any other purpose or exhibited outside of the institution in which they are produced.

11.10   Parody

A further fair dealing exception that provides for the use of parody, pastiche or caricature was introduced into the UK in the wake of a European InfoSoc Directive which provides for the limited use of another's copyright work without permission. For these purposes the words 'caricature, parody or pastiche' are given their ordinary dictionary meanings. The guidance note issued by the United Kingdom Intellectual Property Office states:

'In broad terms, parody imitates a work for humorous or satirical effect, commenting on the original work, its subject, author, style, or some other target. Pastiche is a musical or other composition made up of selections from various sources or one that imitates the style of another artist or period. A caricature portrays its subject in a simplified or exaggerated way, which may be insulting or complimentary and may serve a political purpose or be solely for entertainment.'

11.11   This addition to the fair use exceptions under the Copyright Act has yet to be tested in the English courts. There is some concern as to the extent that use as parody etc. may erode the integrity of the original copyrights that are quoted. This, however, is clearly not the intention of the exception and each individual use contemplated must be carefully considered within the boundaries of the rule before being made public. The EU Court of Justice has suggested a two-stage test for assessing a parody: first, it must evoke an existing work whilst being 'noticeably different' from it, and second, it must constitute an expression of humour or mockery. However, this test omitted mention of caricature and pastiche both of which were considered to be 'parody' in the InfoSoc directive.

It may well be that post-Brexit an English court could adopt this test in adjudicating a claim in which the parody defence was raised.

11.12   A film that is a 'pastiche' (i.e. one produced in a style that imitates that of another film or director) might not include any humour; a pastiche may be a tribute and comprise serious content. Thus, the limit to which the 'parody' exception is to extend has yet to be finally determined, which leaves filmmakers in an uncertain position. Additionally

- the exception has no effect on the law of defamation; see section 17;

- the moral rights regime is unchanged, so that, at least in theory, creators are protected from damage to their reputation or image through the use of their works for parody.

11.13   In the US, the use of parody may not constitute an infringement of copyright. Parody, as freedom of expression, is protected by the First Amendment to the US Constitution. There have been a number of cases heard by US courts in which the integrity of copyright has been in opposition to the protection offered by First Amendment rights. The European Court of Human Rights has also been called on to address the extent to which the right to freedom of expression may, in certain specific circumstances, take precedence over the integrity of copyright. However, it is beyond the scope of this Guide to analyse this area of technical legal conflicts.

12   Interviews

12.1   Copyright in an interview

The first owner of copyright in an interview will be the interviewer. It is the interviewer who directs the conversation in an interview by asking her/his subject a series of questions and by responding to the answers with more questions and comments.

12.2   Ownership of copyright in an interview is subject to the same principles and exceptions discussed at section 5. Copyright in an interview conducted by a full-time employee of a broadcaster in the course of her/his employment by the broadcaster, for example, on a news programme, will be owned by the broadcaster. If the interview is conducted by a freelancer, then a filmmaker or broadcaster seeking to own the copyright in the interview will require an assignment which will typically be contained in the agreement or in the letter of engagement pursuant to which the freelancer provides her/his services to the filmmaker. In the absence of an assignment, the filmmaker will have a licence to use the interview, but its uses will be limited to those that were in the reasonable contemplation of the parties at the time the interview was commissioned.

12.3   Interviewee releases

Filmmakers should require every interviewee to provide a written release that enables the filmed/recorded interview to be used for all of the filmmaker's intended purposes, in all relevant media for life copyright of the filmed interview and throughout the world. The absence of a written release may have the result of limiting the potential uses to those that were in the reasonable contemplation of the parties at the time the interview was filmed. A form of interviewee release is at Appendix 13.

Example

A distressed eye witness to a street stabbing is interviewed for television news. No written release is obtained but the purpose of the interview is apparent from the branding on the interviewer's microphone and on the camera used to film the interview, the nature of the questions posed and the visible proximity of the broadcaster's van. The interviewer is a freelancer who has been drafted in at short notice to cover the story. The broadcaster is approached by a filmmaker who wants to use the interview in a low budget slasher movie. In order to make use of the interview in this way, the broadcaster and/or the filmmaker will need to ensure that appropriate releases and/or consents are secured from each of the interviewer and the interviewee.

12.4   One question to which filmmakers might be directed is: when does an interview cease to be an interview? The line to be drawn may be this: a leading poet or an iconic writer is asked in an interview about her/his religious beliefs or philosophy of life. The question may or may not be open-ended but provokes a lengthy, uninterrupted, extemporised exposition of the interviewee's views, whether or not punctuated by further questions. The interviewee may seek to argue that the overall content of the answers constitutes a body of cogent expression of ideas which, by virtue of being filmed and recorded, is thereby reduced to permanent form. The interviewee might not in the ordinary course be the first owner of copyright in the filmed interview even though it includes spoken word material that has effectively been authored by the interviewee. Unless agreed to the contrary, the copyright in the recording/film of the interview will vest in the interviewer. In the absence of anything in writing, the interviewee's ability to use the recording of the material outside of the filmed interview may be limited. The filmmaker's – or broadcaster's – rights, too, would be limited to what was permitted by the terms of the release.

12.5   An interview will not necessarily constitute a performance as such. A performance is generally limited to a person's rendering of a dramatic role, song, dance or piece of music or the other activities mentioned in paragraph 9.1. However, suppose during the course of an interview, the interviewee, a well-known actor, stands up and recites the opening monologue of Shakespeare's Henry IV Part 1, or a pop star sings her latest hit *a capella*? In order to make the position as transparent as possible, clear forms of written consent should be employed by filmmakers to avoid any suggestion by interviewees or others with an interest in the subject matter of an interview that the interview may not be used as required by the filmmaker.

12.6   Filmmakers may be attracted to the use of archive interviews that may be licensed from third party libraries. Before including such interviews into a film, it is important to consider the extent of any limitations set out in the licence and to ensure that what is being licensed is cleared for the purposes intended by the filmmaker.

13 Music

13.1 Introduction

Filmmakers have surprisingly varied attitudes towards music. At one extreme there are those for whom music is not just a key element of a finished film but part of the creative vision from day one. They may hire a composer or seek clearances, in principle, of key third party music during the early days of pre-production, or even in development. There are others who may not bring a composer on board until the start of post-production. There are some filmmakers whose knowledge of what needs to be cleared in order to include third party material – especially musical – is alarmingly deficient. There are also those who underestimate the cost of music and even borrow from the initial music budget to make up a shortfall in other areas. This may result in a problem when the consequences of these actions leave them with a soundtrack in search of musical sound!

13.2 The subject of music rights is complex. Nevertheless, by bearing in mind some simple principles, filmmakers can navigate their way through the mire of these complexities with a degree of impunity.

13.3 Music – itself – is a confusing term to use. For reasons that will become apparent in the rest of this section, it is best avoided unless qualified. In simple terms, rights need to be cleared – or acquired – in three key elements of all of the 'music' that is ultimately heard in a film:

- composition

- performance

- recording

13.4 Compositions

A musical composition is the underlying work which may be reduced to sheet music, what is affectionately known by some as the 'dots'. A composition may include not only musical notation but also lyrics.

13.5 Where an existing composition remains in copyright at the time of it being used in the soundtrack of a film, a licence will be required from the copyright owner.

This will usually, but not always, be a music publisher. The author of the lyrics to a composition may often, but not always, be the same as the writer of the musical element of the composition. Two or more composers of a composition may have their respective interests in a composition administered by different music publishers.

13.6   Performers of compositions

Those who perform a composition have rights in their performances. Those with performers' rights will include not only the musicians and singers but also the conductor of an orchestra. Actors who speak over a musical composition as part of a recording will also be considered as contributing a performance to that recording. In relation to the rights of performers the discussion at section 9 applies to the performance of musical compositions as it does to acting performances. Consents must be obtained from each of those who perform on the recording of any composition that is included in a soundtrack.

13.7   Sound recordings

The individual producer of a sound recording of a performance will usually be the first owner of the copyright in that sound recording. However, if a recording is financed and facilitated by a record company, there will generally be contracts in place whereby the record producer will transfer ownership of the copyright to that record company. Such contracts may also cover situations where a record producer is also a DJ or someone who otherwise contributes elements of performance to a recording by, for example, adding loops, beats and the like.

13.8   When seeking to use existing 'music' therefore, a film producer will need to know that each of the composition, the performances and the recording are cleared. Generally, a record company owning the copyright in a sound recording will have secured the performers' consents and, in the licence granted for the use of an existing recording by a filmmaker, the record company should specifically warrant and represent that it has done so.

13.9   Sync licences

Rights acquired in pre-existing compositions and recordings will generally be granted to filmmakers by way of synchronisation (or 'sync') licences; i.e. licences that permit the synchronisation of these works onto the film's soundtrack. Filmmakers will be concerned to ensure that the ambit of these licences will extend to enable the rights granted in each of the compositions and recordings to be exploited as part of the film's soundtrack by all means and in all media now known or subsequently devised throughout the world for the full life of copyright in the film. Any limitations that may be sought by owners of these compositions and/or recordings – media, territory, period – need to be carefully considered. Filmmakers may need to seek alternative music where limitations will inhibit their intended exploitation of a film; (see also the comments at paragraphs 6.7-6.9). Additionally, when clearing existing works, the filmmaker needs to be absolutely certain that those granting the rights are legally entitled to do so. A short form of sync licence is at Appendix 5.

13.10   Library music

Library music may be available with composition, performances and recording all fully cleared. When acquiring rights to library music filmmakers need to ensure that music selected is available for all of the media, territories and purposes required. Appropriate warranties and indemnities should be obtained from the libraries. Licences for library music need to be carefully checked for any restrictions or limitations attaching to the use of that music.

13.11   Commissioning original soundtrack music

When commissioning the creation of an original soundtrack the above principles should be borne in mind. Filmmakers may engage a single composer/record producer to take responsibility for writing original musical compositions, engaging musicians, hiring sound studios and producing and delivering finished master recordings in a format and to a standard that is suitable for dubbing onto the soundtrack of the film. Equally, it may be the filmmaker who contracts each of the individuals who will collectively provide the component elements of the original musical soundtrack. The following matters are also relevant:

- if the composer is under contract to a music publisher, an appropriate agreement will need to be reached with that music publisher;

- if any one or more of the musicians and/or vocalists are under contract to a record company, appropriate clearance(s) will be required from the record company(ies) in question as well as performers' consents from each of these performers; a form of release is to be found at Schedule 2 to the form of Composer Agreement at Appendix 6;

- the composer/producer who is engaged to take responsibility for delivering finished master recordings should be contractually required to secure written performers' consents from all of the performers whose performances are included in the recordings and to provide these clearances as part of the deliverables. A form of performer's clearance is attached as Schedule 2 to the composer agreement at Appendix 6;

- the commissioned producer of original sound recordings should be required to assign to the filmmaker any copyright interest s/he might claim in the recordings. This requirement may lead to discussions about commercial release of the sound recordings, the outcome of which may depend not only on the commercial potential of the recordings but also on the relative bargaining strength of each of the parties.

13.12   When music is commissioned for a low budget film and for which payment may be limited, the composer/record producer may resist assigning copyright in the commissioned musical works and limiting the grant of rights to the filmmaker to a licence. The discussion that then arises will revolve around the extent to which the composer/record producer may otherwise use the compositions and recordings and the extent of any restrictions (i.e. in time, media) that the filmmaker will require to be imposed on the other uses to be made by the composer/record-producer.

13.13   When commissioning a composer/producer, the general principles relating to contracts that are discussed at sections 24 and 25 should be borne in mind. In addition to the principles considered at paragraph 13.11, particular provisions that filmmakers should endeavour to include in a composer/record producer commissioning agreement will include:

- if possible, outright assignment of copyright in all original compositions and recordings;

- if there are limitations or restrictions on any use of the original compositions and recordings then these should be clearly stated;

- a time period within which the commissioned recordings are to be delivered;

- the length of the music and any specifications as to style, number of individual pieces of music and other required details;

- the fee and any instalments in which it is to be paid;

- the materials and media required for delivery of the finished recordings; if the commission is one for compositions only then whether demo recordings are required in addition to sheet music;

- consideration should also be given to including applicable provisions equivalent to those discussed in relation to screenwriters' agreements at section 27.

A form of composer agreement is to be found at Appendix 6.

13.14   Musical arrangements

If a filmmaker engages a musical arranger to make an arrangement of an existing third party copyright composition for inclusion in a film, the permission of the copyright owner of that existing composition must be obtained. There will be a copyright arising in the new arrangement that will vest in the arranger – unless, in its commissioning agreement with the musical arranger, the filmmaker has required an assignment to it of copyright in all of the musical works created by the musical arranger for the film. However, the copyright in the new arrangement will be a derivative of the copyright in the pre-existing copyright work and dependent upon it. Invariably the copyright owner of the pre-existing work, usually a music publisher, will require the arranger, or the filmmaker, as the case may be, to assign ownership of the copyright in the new arrangement to the publisher. The terms of such an assignment will be negotiable.

Example

A filmmaker decides to use an instrumental version of an Amy Winehouse composition in the soundtrack of a dramatic feature set in Camden Town, London. An arranger is contracted to score the composition for a full orchestra and choir. The late Amy Winehouse's compositions are published by EMI Music, whose permission will be required for the arrangement to be made and recorded for use in the film. Under the terms of the contract by which EMI acquired copyright from Winehouse it may need to seek permission for the arrangement from Winehouse's estate. EMI may require an assignment of the copyright in this new arrangement. There will likely be a discussion about how income from the new arrangement is to be treated, which will be a matter of commercial negotiation.

13.15   Samples

Samples of existing recordings will include an existing composition, an existing performance and an existing sound recording. Assuming that each of these elements is within the period of its respective protection, each will need to be cleared applying the principles discussed above. It is an urban myth that a sample of less than five, or even three, seconds does not need to be cleared – it does.

13.16   Fair use

Use of third party music in films may be subject to the fair use exceptions of copyright that are discussed at section 11. Fair use may apply to some use of music in documentaries, though care must be taken as to the extent of the extracts that are used. Also, see the discussion at paragraph 11.5.

14 Titles, names and trade marks

14.1 Introduction

The use of names in any medium of commerce or creativity is of ever-increasing importance as the universality of the internet enables any brand to become instantly global. Filmmakers will be concerned to ensure they may use a chosen word or phrase as the title of a film or the name of a production company.

14.2 Trade marks

A trade mark is a sign which is used to distinguish goods or services from those of a competitor. A trade mark may include words, logos or a combination of both. A trade mark may also be referred to as a brand, albeit that contemporary use of the term 'brand' may also extend to encompass the values and features that stand behind a trading name.

14.3 Unregistered marks

A trade mark need not be registered to enable its owner to protect it. The owner of an unregistered mark may prevent infringement, though the process is complex and potentially expensive. In pursuing a claim for infringement of an unregistered mark, the owner must necessarily prove that it has established goodwill in its mark and that the mark complained of is sufficiently similar, if not identical, to the extent that it infringes the original mark and is creating, or is likely to create, confusion in the minds of the public.

14.4 Passing off

Many, if not most, claims for infringement of a registered mark will also involve a claim for passing off. Passing off arises when one party in the course of trade misrepresents goods or services to prospective customers or ultimate consumers of the goods or services and which misrepresentation is calculated to injure the business or goodwill of another and which either causes damage to the business or goodwill of the other party or is likely to do so. The most powerful evidence of passing off will be examples of actual confusion.

Example

Nargs Films, producer of a successful cult horror movie, 'The Blood List: Dances with Knives', does not register a trade mark. Shortly after the release of Nargs' movie by Nasty Distribution plc, rival producer, Karkaz Movies, announces the release of a film entitled 'The Blood Mist: Dances with Forks' which, in addition to its title, from all available information, replicates numerous elements of Nargs' original film including, by way of example, certain of the characterisations and scenarios. Unaware that the Karkaz film has no connection with Nargs Films, Nasty Distributors approaches Karkaz with an offer to acquire the European rights in its film for all media. The Karkaz production is clearly designed to trade off the goodwill generated by Nargs' original. The approach by Nasty to Karkaz is evidence of confusion. Even without the evidence of confusion, Nargs may pursue a claim against Karkaz for passing off. There may also be a copyright infringement claim though this will depend on an analysis of the details of the Karkaz film in comparison with the original.

14.5   Trade mark registration

The title of a film – or even a strap-line – may be registered as a trade mark. There are forty-five designated 'classes' in which a trade mark may be registered in most major jurisdictions. Species of goods may be registered in Classes 1-34 and services in Classes 35-45. In addition to single country registrations, there exists a community trade mark or EUTM that provides protection to a mark throughout the European Union.

14.6   At the time this book went to press, the full effect of Brexit on the trade mark regime was not known. The EU and the UK have agreed in principle that there should be a transitional regime that will apply between the projected date of Brexit – 29th March 2019 – until 31st December 2020. During that period EU trade mark law will continue to apply in the UK. However, whether or not the transitional regime will come into effect will depend on the successful negotiation and ratification of the proposed Withdrawal Agreement between the UK and the EU. Nevertheless, the general view of IP lawyers is that EUTMs in existence at the date of Brexit will likely continue to protect marks in the UK until their respective expiry dates. As and when those marks expire their owners will need to apply for protection in both the EU and the UK. Nevertheless, since Brexit was announced in June 2016, those able to afford it have been advised to take a belt and braces approach and make applications for both EUTMs and UK marks. It is beyond the scope of this book to entertain a detailed analysis of the debate surrounding the future of registered marks in the EU and UK post-Brexit, in respect of which contemporary advice will need to be sought as and when required by filmmakers.

14.7   Typically, depending on the nature and scale of the production, filmmakers may consider applying to register marks in some or all the following classes:

Those pertaining to the production and distribution of a film:

9   Compact discs, DVDs and other digital recording media; computer software programmes;

41   Cultural activities; production of television and cinema films; cinema services; television and radio entertainment; videotape editing.

Those pertaining to the promotion and marketing of a film and ancillary activities:

16   Paper, cardboard and goods made from these materials, not included in other classes; printed matter; stationery e.g. DVD packaging;

21   Mugs, water bottles;

25   Clothing, footwear, headgear; e.g. promotional/merchandise items such as t-shirts, sweatshirts and caps;

28   Games, toys, playthings, action figures;

35   Advertising; production of television and radio advertisements; cinema advertising; retail services connected with the sale of goods.

14.8   Before embarking on a programme of registration, the cost and required coverage need to be considered. Makers of low budget films may not have the funds available to finance the cost of registration as and where ideally required. While professional assistance from a lawyer or trade mark agent may assist, marks may be registered online in the UK at: https://www.gov.uk/how-to-register-a-trade-mark; for a EUTM, applications may be made via: https://euipo.europa.eu/ohimportal/en; there are also facilities for international registration that may be accessed via: https://www.gov.uk/government/publications/application-to-register-an-international-trade-mark. Specifically, the Madrid International

Trade Mark System provides a centralised solution for registering and managing trade marks worldwide. This system enables a single application to be filed in one language to provide protection of a mark in up to ninety-five different countries. More information may be obtained at: http://www.wipo.int/madrid/ en/. US trade marks may be registered at the US Trade Mark office. Experience suggests that US registration is a lengthier, costlier and more exacting process than in either the EU or UK and will undoubtedly benefit from the professional assistance of a US trade mark specialist.

14.9   There are a number of technical rules that apply to the registration of trade marks. Not all film titles will be capable of registration. Those titles that are the same as titles subject to a registration in any one or more class in which an existing film has been registered will not be registered in those classes. Titles which are the same as marks used for goods and services other than a film may, in certain cases, be refused registration where the owner of a registered trade mark can show that its goodwill in the mark might be affected.

14.10   Titles that have been used for a number of different films may not be registrable. For example, a quick search of IMDb reveals numerous films under each of these titles: *'I Love You'*, *'The Forest'*, *'You and Me'*, *'The Sea'* and *'Monkey Business'*. No doubt there are many other titles that have been used on numerous occasions. Save in a case where a film under one of these titles may have been sufficiently successful to create substantial goodwill that is uniquely associated with it, there likely will be nothing to stop such a title being used again. Whether it is either creatively desirable or commercially sensible to employ an oft-used title for a new production is a matter for a filmmaker or a distributor to consider.

14.11   Registering a trade mark makes it easier to take legal action against an infringer rather than having to rely on passing off. The mark itself is also an asset that may add to the overall value of a filmmaker's intellectual property assets.

14.12   A filmmaker looking at the possibility of developing a brand – be it a series of films or building a company with a recognisable name – should necessarily check the name in a number of media before making a commitment to it. In addition to existing registered trade marks, searches should also be made of domain names https://www.nominet.uk and the Companies' register https://www.gov. uk/government/organisations/companies-house. It is also worth undertaking some simple internet searches to ascertain whether a chosen name might already be in use in order to prevent a clash with what a filmmaker might wish to use. Simply registering a company at Companies House does not, of itself, give any exclusivity in its name. Additionally, the fact that Companies House permits the registration of a particular name does not, of itself, necessarily make the name impervious to challenge.

14.13   Title searches

When preparing delivery materials for distributors and obtaining Errors & Omissions insurance, filmmakers may be required to obtain a formal title search. One leading provider of such searches is CompuMark, whose website is at: http://www.compumark.com/trademark-searching/title-copyright-entertainment-services/us-full-title-search/; another is The Law Offices of Dennis Angel: www.dangelesq.com

The process of a title search may extend not only to the proposed title but titles that are similar. Searches will also extend to the most well-known and popular entertainment works on a worldwide basis – or, if required, in limited geographical regions. Use is made of a wide range of archives, databases and other sources of information. The more extensive the search that is made, the better informed a filmmaker may be before committing to the use of a particular title for a film or other project. Errors & Omissions insurance is considered at paragraphs 46.5-46.6.

14.14   The question of use on screen of branded goods – those that include a distinctive mark – is examined at paragraphs 19.8-19.9.

15   Confidentiality

15.1   Introduction

Documentary makers and those engaged in reportage may face situations in which they need to address issues of confidentiality and privacy. An obligation to maintain the confidentiality of information may be set out in a written agreement to which a filmmaker is a signatory. Failure to comply with a contractual obligation to maintain confidentiality will render a filmmaker potentially liable in damages and potentially subject to a restraining order. See the discussion about NDAs/confidentiality agreements at paragraphs 7.5-7.9.

15.2   Duties of confidentiality

English law also recognises a duty to maintain confidentiality in circumstances where it is expected that a duty of confidence applies. Obvious examples include a doctor's obligation to maintain confidentiality of a patient's medical records, or the duties of solicitors, accountants or bank managers to maintain the confidentiality of information about their clients. Therefore, the documentary maker endeavouring to expose a politician caught up in a sex scandal ought not to expect disclosure of the politician's bank accounts and tax returns from his professional advisers. An exception may arise if disclosure would be in the public interest; see paragraph 15.6.

15.3   The key questions for a filmmaker to consider before using information that may be considered to be confidential are:

• whether the information has the necessary quality of confidence about it;

• whether the information been imparted in circumstances that import an obligation of confidence;

• whether unauthorised use of information will result in some detriment to the party from whom the information was obtained.

15.4   Permitted disclosure

In the following circumstances, confidential information may lawfully be disclosed:

- where the individual to whom the information relates has consented;

- where disclosure is in the public interest;

- where there is a legal duty to do so, for example pursuant to a court order.

15.5   Consent

Any consent upon which reliance is to be placed should be clear, unconditional and, preferably, in writing and obtained either from the individual to whom the information relies or from a party lawfully authorised to provide such consent; e.g. the parent of someone under 18 years of age. Any conditions should be carefully considered and complied with.

15.6   Public interest

Where a filmmaker seeks to rely on disclosure being in the public interest a clear case will need to be made. Uncovering a conspiracy to assassinate a member of Parliament, exposing the laundering of the proceeds of crime or the manipulation of a local government election would all be matters that are clearly in the public interest. Each of these are circumstances that would properly justify the disclosure of confidential information. However, there may be cases that are less clear-cut where publication or other disclosure of confidential information will be prevented by the courts.

Examples

Volkswagen sought an interim injunction preventing the publication of certain parts of an academic paper which discussed defects in Volkswagen's car immobilisers. The court decided that it was in the public interest to grant the interim injunction as, if the information was published, it would put a new way of stealing cars into the public domain.

Detailed commercial information about Northern Rock was contained in a briefing memorandum being distributed to potential investors. The memorandum was leaked to the Financial Times which made ten pages available on a subscription website to which there was limited access. There was no suggestion that the briefing memorandum contained information that was materially significant that justified it being made public. Consequently, the court concluded that there was no public interest in the publication of the detailed commercial information on the Financial Times website. The court granted a temporary injunction to prevent further publication of the contents of the memorandum.

16   Privacy

16.1   Right to privacy

Albeit that the UK has no codified law on the subject, an individual has the right to protect his or her privacy. The UK is signatory to the European Convention on Human Rights (**ECHR**) which, at Article 8, states that 'everyone has the right to respect for his private and family life, his home and his correspondence'. This right does not extend to companies, government departments or institutions. Being party to ECHR is not dependent upon EU membership and will not be affected by Brexit.

16.2   The individual's right to privacy may be infringed by the publication of information of a private and non-trivial nature; there is a reasonable expectation of privacy in relation to such information. Recent decisions of the courts make it clear that a reasonable expectation of privacy may arise in a public place such as in a park, on a beach or in a restaurant or club.

16.3   Personal private information

Personal private information may include:

- matters of personal identity including photographs;

- details of intimate conversations or revelations;

- personal and sexual relationships;

- details about an individual's state of health, including mental health and details of medical treatment;

- details of an individual's emotional reactions, for example to relationship break-up, bereavement or to illness;

- interaction with others and private disputes, even in a public context, may fall within the scope of private life;

- details relating to an individual's home;

- information about private negotiations.

16.4   Freedom of expression

Whilst editorial convention recognises the right of privacy, that right is balanced, sometimes uneasily, with another right enshrined in the ECHR. Article 10 gives everyone the right to freedom of expression, which includes the freedom to hold opinions and to receive and impart information and ideas. The right extends to enabling expression in any medium, including film; to political expression, including comment on matters of general public interest; artistic expression and commercial expression, particularly when it also raises matters of legitimate public debate and concern.

16.5   Making a judgment about where to strike the balance between these competing rights may be difficult for filmmakers. Nevertheless, some guidance may be obtained by considering the limitations to which the right of free expression is limited by Article 10. Those limitations may be prescribed by law provided they are necessary and proportionate and pursue a legitimate aim, namely:

- the interests of national security, territorial integrity or public safety;

- the prevention of disorder or crime;

- the protection of health or morals;

- the protection of the reputation or rights of others;

- preventing the disclosure of information received in confidence;

- maintaining the authority and impartiality of the judiciary.

The courts will determine the balance between the competing requirements of Articles 8 and 10 on the facts of each specific case.

16.6   The English courts have been asked to consider the law of privacy in a number of cases.

Examples

In 2010, John Terry, then Chelsea and England footballer, failed in an attempt to prevent the publication of details of an affair with a teammate's ex-girlfriend. Terry had previously spoken to the press about the affair. The court decided that Terry's primary objective had been to protect his commercial interests as opposed to his privacy.

In a 2011 case involving News Group Newspapers, the court decided that more harm would be done by allowing publication of details of an affair between two work colleagues than there was a benefit to the public in allowing the publication in the interests of free speech. This was so even though one of the parties' employment had been terminated.

In 2013, the publication of a newspaper article about the birth of a child as a result of an extra marital affair by a politician was considered to have exceptional public interest.

In 2014, acting on a tip-off provided by South Yorkshire Police, the BBC filmed a raid on the Berkshire home of singer Sir Cliff Richard. The raid was part of a probe into allegations of historic child sexual abuse. The police later told Sir Cliff that the allegations were false, prompting him to claim that the BBC had invaded his privacy and 'shattered' his private life. The court ruled that the BBC's reporting had infringed Sir Cliff's rights in a 'serious and also in a somewhat sensationalist way'. The court made a preliminary award of £210,000 in damages and ruled that Sir Cliff was entitled to recover further sums for the financial impact of the legal case, which damages were then to have been assessed at a later date.

16.7   Ofcom has jurisdiction over broadcast regulations which have a direct effect on those making factual and reality programming for UK television. Section 8 of the Ofcom code sets out the framework within which broadcasters may operate to avoid any unwarranted infringement of privacy in programmes and in connection with obtaining material included in programmes. As well as containing a principle and a rule the section includes a number of practices to be followed. Full details are to be found at: https://www.ofcom.org.uk/tv-radio-and-on-demand/broadcast-codes/broadcast-code/section-eight-privacy

Example

*While enforcing a judgment debt against a Miss F, High Court Enforcement Agents (**HCEAs**) using body cameras filmed her inside her parents' house. The footage was included in a Channel 5 programme 'Can't Pay? We'll Take It Away'. Ofcom upheld Miss F's complaint that her privacy was unwarrantably infringed in both the obtaining of the footage and by its inclusion in the* *transmitted programme. During the course of the proceedings, evidence emerged that the body cameras belonged to the programme makers and had been worn for the primary purpose of obtaining broadcast footage and not for what would otherwise have been regarded as legitimate purposes viz. securing evidence of the enforcement proceedings or to protect the HCEAs against unwarranted or false accusations.*

16.8   The closer to the boundaries of controversy that filmmakers tread, the more nimble the path they will need to negotiate through the thorny thicket of privacy, confidentiality and the public interest.

16.9   General Data Protection Regulation (**GDPR**)

GDPR was introduced into law in the UK on 25th May 2018 by the Data Protection Act 2018 (**DPA**). Whilst GDPR has an extensive reach, documentary makers and those making films that include representations of real persons in particular should familiarise themselves with the regulations which, in general, require businesses to protect the personal data and privacy of data subjects for transactions that occur both within and without EU member states. Non-compliance may result in financial penalties that may be substantial. At the time of going to press, it was not expected that post-Brexit there would be any immediate change to UK law and its application of data protection principles; irrespective of this, GDPR will still apply for those engaged in dealing with those based in the remaining 27 EU member states. The DPA 2018, in its adaptation of GDPR for the UK, was calibrated so as to maintain regulatory alignment post-Brexit. More information as to the interaction between data protection rules and Brexit was available at the time of going to press at: https://www.gov.uk/government/publications/data-protection-if-theres-no-brexit-deal/data-protection-if-theres-no-brexit-deal

16.10   GDPR takes a broad view of what constitutes personal data (personal identification information) which includes, but is not limited to:

•   Basic identity information such as name, address and ID numbers

•   Web data such as location, IP address, cookie data and RFID tags

•   Health and genetic data

•   Biometric data

- Racial or ethnic data

- Political opinions

- Sexual orientation

Although not specifically stated to be the case in the GDPR, it is apparent that footage containing imagery of clearly identifiable individuals is likely to be covered.

16.11   Any business based in the EU which processes personal data is subject to the GDPR. Further, any business that stores or processes personal information about data subjects in the EU must comply with the GDPR, even if it does not have a business presence within the EU, where the activities relate to offering goods or services to EU residents (irrespective of whether payment is required) or to monitoring of behaviour within the EU. For these purposes, it is apparent that a filmmaker will be considered as operating a business. Personal data may only be used (i.e. controlled or processed) if a business has lawful grounds to do so. Under the GDPR, it is arguably more difficult for those grounds to be lawfully engaged. It is generally accepted, though not yet tested by the courts, that producing a film that includes personal data will be considered as 'processing' that data.

16.12   Specific criteria determining which businesses are required to comply with GDPR are those

- that have a presence in an EU country;

- that do not have a presence in the EU, but which process personal data of European residents;

- that have more than 250 employees – unlikely to apply to the majority of small production companies;

- that have fewer than 250 employees but whose data-processing impacts the rights and freedoms of data subjects, is not occasional, or includes certain types of sensitive personal data. That effectively means almost all businesses;

- that have fewer than 250 employees; however there is some leniency in internal record keeping obligations unless the processing of data could risk an individual's rights or freedoms or if the data pertains to criminal activity.

16.13   Consent to use data is one of the 'lawful grounds' for use of personal data. Where a film is about a living individual then consent (explicit, informed, unambiguous etc) from that individual should be obtained for all of the purposes contemplated by the filmmaker in producing and exploiting the footage. Filmmakers should note that consent may also be withdrawn. GDPR requires that, at the time of providing their consent, individuals should be made aware that they are able to withdraw consent at any time albeit that this will not render processing on the basis of consent prior to withdrawal to be unlawful.

16.14   A filmmaker, who has gone to the usual fraught lengths of raising finance for the film and then invested considerable resource in filming a subject would, with justification, be horrified at the possibility of consent being withdrawn as apparently permitted by GDPR. Arguably this specific consequence of the implementation of GDPR may not have been intended or even considered by the lawmakers. However, another 'lawful' ground upon which personal data may be used is 'legitimate interest'. Although the GDPR does not include a finely drafted definition of 'legitimate interest', leaving its scope open to interpretation, the question a filmmaker will ask is whether there is a 'legitimate interest' in continuing to process personal data by completing production and thereafter proceeding to exploit the film.

16.15   If relying on legitimate interest, the filmmaker would need to weigh up its own legitimate interest against the interests, rights and freedoms of the individual and only if the balance is in favour of the filmmaker would the filmmaker be able to rely on it. Furthermore, the weighing up exercise would need to be carried out if at any time the individual requested that the processing cease. Where the filmmaker has a written contract with the individual concerning the film, the rights granted etc, a further ground upon which a filmmaker may rely is that the processing is necessary for performance of a contract to which the individual is a party. In such a circumstance if the individual no longer wishes to proceed, s/ he would be in breach of the contract. The disadvantage with relying upon both contract and legitimate interest is that neither will be sufficient in circumstances in which any special categories of data are being processed (such as biometric data, health data, etc); in such a case the individual's explicit consent will be required (see 16.18 below).

16.16   One of the key requirements under GDPR is for a business to demonstrate that it has considered the impact its processing of data will have on individuals, and preventative measures are in place to limit such impact. Thus, it may be that filmmakers should obtain a form of consent that accommodates the 'legitimate interest' ground for 'processing the data' i.e. using the individual's interview. Suggested language is included at clause 8 of the form at Appendix 13. This form has not yet been tried or tested in court and, therefore, its use must be made at the discretion and risk of those seeking to use it. Given the discussion at paragraph 16.15, it is arguable that for significant interviews and performances individually drafted consents should be secured, particularly for potentially controversial content. In any event, if such a consent has not been obtained or if reliance is placed on consents obtained prior to the introduction of GDPR, which may be withdrawn, then to rely on 'legitimate interest' filmmakers should ensure they are able to demonstrate they have considered the grounds on which data will be processed, being that:

- there is a real business interest being pursued in continuing to process the personal data;

- the processing is absolutely necessary in order for the business to pursue that interest (i.e. the interest cannot be pursued in another way which is proportionate);

- the processing is balanced against the impact such processing will have on the fundamental rights and freedoms of data subjects.

16.17   Whether or not 'legitimate interest' will be demonstrated will depend on the particular circumstances of a project and the individual concerned. General questions posed by GDPR require filmmakers to consider the relative impact on the individual of continuing use of the footage as compared to that on the filmmakers themselves. Supplementary questions arising may be many and varied: was the interview originally conducted in the context of a particular political or social situation that has changed? Have the interviewee's views been affected by subsequent circumstances? Can the filmmaker edit the film in such a way as to make changes in attitude clear and explained? What would be the impact financially and/or reputation wise on the filmmaker or interviewee, or both? Are and/or were the parties each acting in good faith?

16.18   The impact of GDPR has yet to be fully assessed in relation to filmmaking activities. However, certain stock footage providers now require all identifiable faces to be blurred out, unless there is a release form, even if the footage is only for documentary-style use and not for 'creative' use.

16.19   Where ancillary data is to be processed (i.e. where a filmmaker acquires a database that may be used to provide information on the subject matter of a documentary) then its use for that purpose will depend on what the data is, how relevant it is, whether any special categories of data are included. GDPR includes a number of 'special categories of data'. These categories are extensive but include, by way of example: establishment, exercise or defence of legal claims, substantial public interest, for the purposes of preventative or occupational medicine, for the assessment of the working capacity of the employee, medical diagnosis, the provision of health or social care. Where no special categories are involved, it will be sufficient for the filmmaker to consider whether it is necessary for its legitimate interests to process the data (viz. include it in the film) and whether any of the individuals concerned would be prejudicially affected by this processing – in which case, whether the filmmaker's legitimate interests would override the rights and freedoms of the individual(s) will depend on an overall consideration of the circumstances. Where special categories are involved, a further condition would also need to be met, which would depend on the purpose of the film, from where the data is being obtained and what information would concerned individuals have about the use to be made of their data.

16.20   Given the potentially wide-reaching effect of GDPR on filmmakers, particularly those making documentaries and other factual-based content, tailored advice should be obtained on the use of data – especially in relation to controversial matter.

17   Defamation

17.1   Disparaging statements/images

Filmmakers, particularly those producing documentaries or current affairs programming, may be concerned to establish the limits within which they may include material that is critical of an individual, company or other body. A statement – or an image or series of images – that 'disparages' any person or any corporate body is defamatory. A 'disparaging' statement or image is one that belittles or discredits its subject. If the statement is spoken it is 'slander'; if it is included in a published work – in any medium – including a film, then it is 'libel'.

17.2   This section of the Guide concentrates exclusively on libel in relation to which English law was simplified in legislation introduced during 2013. The paragraphs that follow include an outline of some of the principal matters that should be taken into account by filmmakers contemplating the inclusion of controversial material that deals with living persons and active organisations. Nevertheless, if a filmmaker is concerned that a film is potentially defamatory, informed advice should be taken on those aspects of that film that are considered to be potentially problematic. This will likely require a filmmaker's adviser to view the entire film in order to assess controversial content in context.

17.3   Publication

A statement is not defamatory unless its publication has caused or is likely to cause serious harm to the reputation of the person making the complaint. For the purposes of filmmakers, 'published' means communicated to the public by way of broadcast, screening or other exhibition, streaming or making available by way of download or via any other medium of communication to the public. Harm to the reputation of a body that trades for profit (i.e. a company) is not 'serious harm' unless it has caused or is likely to cause the body serious financial loss. It follows that financial loss, or the likelihood of financial loss, is not a necessary component to establish libel in a documentary about a charity, trust, hospital, local authority or other public or government body. A dead person cannot be defamed. The 2013 legislation also introduced a 'single publication rule', so that the one-year limitation period for bringing a libel claim runs from the date of first publication of the allegedly libellous material whereas previously that one-year period was renewed each time the words complained of were published (for example, each time they are accessed on a website).

17.4   Innuendo

A statement or image may be defamatory either on the face of what is said or shown – or by inference or by innuendo. An inference will arise where a meaning may be understood from what is stated or portrayed in a film by a viewer without any specialist knowledge of the subject in mind. An innuendo arises when a meaning can be attributed to what has been said or portrayed in a film by those watching it and who have specialist knowledge of it.

Example

An article published in a national newspaper accuses Aidan O'Bett, the head teacher of Brainbox Institute, a school for gifted children in Worthing, of taking a group of fifteen-year-old boys to a pole dancing club in Soho where he treats them all to pints of lager and shots. The allegation is not true and is therefore defamatory on its face.

A Worthing free newspaper reports that the unnamed head of an unidentified local school whose responsibility to intelligent students means that 'he should know better' took a group of gifted fifteen-year-old boys to a pole dancing club in Soho where he treated them all to pints of lager and shots. The allegation is not true. Specialist knowledge is required by those who live in Worthing and/or who read the Worthing paper and/or who are able to identify the head teacher and/or the school in order to show that the article is defamatory by innuendo.

17.5   Defences

Of the statutory defences to defamation those of primary interest to filmmakers are:

- Truth

- Honest opinion

- Publication of a matter of public interest

- Reports, etc. protected by privilege

17.6   Truth

It is a defence to an action for defamation for a filmmaker to show that the imputation conveyed by the statement or, if more than one imputation arises from the statement, then at least the one of which complaint is made, is substantially true. Additionally, if there are two or more distinct imputations and one or more is not substantially true, the truth defence can still succeed if the imputations which are not substantially true do not seriously harm the complainant's reputation. In making a film on a controversial topic, filmmakers are advised to maintain comprehensive records of all interviews and source material. Where potentially controversial and/or defamatory allegations are made by those contributing to a film, their sources should be verified. Information provided to and obtained by a filmmaker should be recorded in a suitable medium – writing, photographs, film – so that it may subsequently be produced in any action as evidence in support of the defence of 'truth'.

17.7   Honest opinion

It is a defence to an action for defamation for a filmmaker to show that the statement complained of was a statement of opinion provided that:

•   the statement complained of indicated, whether in general or specific terms, the basis of the opinion and

•   an honest person could have held the opinion on the basis of any fact which existed at the time the statement complained of was published.

The defence will fail if it can be shown that the filmmaker – or the person included in the film making the statement – did not hold the opinion. There are other technical aspects to this defence that relate to certain species of privileged statements. Privilege is briefly discussed at paragraphs 17.10-17.12. If a filmmaker is working on controversial topics in which individuals are named and criticised then specific advice will undoubtedly be required to consider the extent to which privilege, and any other defences, may apply to contentious material to be included in the film.

17.8   Publication of a matter of public interest

It is a defence to an action for defamation for a filmmaker to show that the statement complained of was, or formed part of, a statement on a matter of public interest and that it is a reasonable belief that to make the film available for broadcast or distribution is in the public interest. The rules that apply to determine whether the public interest has been served are technical and not easily summarised. However, the overriding principle is that in assessing the public interest all the circumstances of the case must be taken into account.

17.9 In deciding whether publishing (or broadcasting) a statement was in the public interest, an omission of the filmmaker to take steps to verify the truth of the imputation conveyed by it may be disregarded. Allowance will also be made for a degree of editorial judgment. As these rules were only made part of English law in 2013, the full extent of their application has yet to be determined by the courts. Once again, tailored advice should be sought for a film that may include defamatory material but in which a public interest is claimed.

Example

*Economou v De Freitas was the first case in which this defence was considered. In 2013, the defendant's daughter, Eleanor De Freitas, accused Alexander Economou of rape. The Crown Prosecution Service (**CPS**) decided not to bring charges. Economou then started a private prosecution against Eleanor. Economou claimed that Eleanor had made a false claim and had therefore endeavoured to pervert the course of justice. The case was subsequently taken over by the CPS. Eleanor, who suffered from bipolar disorder, committed suicide three days before she was due to stand trial. In the aftermath of her suicide, her father, in a number of statements, raised concerns about the role and conduct of the CPS and its decision to prosecute his daughter. Economou argued that these statements were defamatory of him as they imputed that he had falsely prosecuted Eleanor when the truth was that he had raped her. In his defence, Mr De Freitas told the court that he reasonably believed that his statements were made in the public interest, pointing out that Economou was never identified or named in any of the statements. The court held that Mr De Freitas had published in good faith, for proper purposes, taking aim at the CPS not at Economou; further, De Freitas had sufficient factual basis for writing what he did.*

17.10 Privilege

There are two levels of privilege – absolute and qualified. Including material in a film that is protected by absolute privilege is a complete bar to a libel action. To invoke the protection of 'absolute' privilege, the publication requires to be as close in time as is possible to the events in question.

17.11   Species of absolute privilege include:

- Reports of proceedings in public before the UK courts, the European Court of Justice, the European Court of Human Rights and certain international tribunals. It is believed that these defences will not be affected by Brexit.

- Statements made in Parliament and official reports of parliamentary proceedings (includes select committee proceedings but not statements made by MPs outside Parliament).

- Statements or complaints of criminal behaviour made to the police.

Example

Businessman, Sir Philip Green, succeeded in obtaining an injunction from the High Court to prevent publication by The Daily Telegraph of allegations that he was said to have repeatedly engaged in sexual harassment and bullying of employees. Shortly after the injunction was granted, Peter Hain MP disclosed Green's identity during the course of a speech in Parliament. Hain's speech was protected by absolute privilege; reports of the speech were protected by qualified privilege; see paragraph 17.12 below.

17.12   Qualified privilege

Qualified privilege attaches to three main groups of published material:

- Otherwise defamatory statements made under a social, moral or legal duty to a person who has a corresponding interest in receiving them.

- Reports of certain proceedings referred to in the Defamation Act 1996. These include fair and accurate reports of public proceedings in legislatures, courts, and international conferences anywhere in the world.

- Reports of parliamentary and judicial proceedings.

  Qualified privilege may only be established in the absence of malice, albeit that malice may be difficult to establish.

17.13   Malicious or injurious falsehood

A malicious or injurious falsehood is an untrue statement that is made maliciously. The party responsible for making the statement knows it to be false (or did not take proper care to check whether it is true or not) and the statement is calculated to cause pecuniary damage to the party who is the subject of the comments. The courts have decided that 'calculated' in the phrase 'calculated to cause pecuniary damage' means 'more probable than not' rather than 'something which is a possibility'.

17.14   The differences between defamation (libel/slander) and malicious or injurious falsehood are that in malicious falsehood the claimant must prove all of the following:

- the statement is false;

- the statement has been published maliciously;

- actual loss or damage has arisen as a consequence of the publication of the statement.

17.15   The laws of defamation vary from one jurisdiction to another. Broadcasters in different territories may or may not have sufficient resources to review every controversial documentary for defamation before it is shown. Other exploiters of films, especially documentaries, may rely on exhaustive warranties from filmmakers that a film is not defamatory. Thus, those making films that court controversy will inevitably need to take specific advice on potentially problematic content in the course of production and/or once a film is complete.

18   Rights of publicity

18.1   General

Under English law an individual has no right to protect her/his image. Historically, rights of publicity and the right to commercialise celebrity have been eschewed by domestic courts. This contrasts with the position in the US where a right of publicity has been long established by which *'a man has a right in the publicity value of his photograph i.e. the right to grant the exclusive privilege of publishing his picture'*. Statutory rights are also in existence in a number of EU member states including France, Italy, Germany and the Netherlands, that provide for an individual to protect her/his image.

18.2   Use of IP laws

In the UK, other IP rights have been employed to protect an individual's image, such as trade mark registration of names or signatures. The law of passing off has also been used to prevent the unauthorised use of a person's name and image as part of product/service endorsements. The requirement to obtain permission for use of an image in this way extends not only to a photographic image of a person but also a caricature.

18.3   Passing off

The law of passing off, discussed above at paragraph 14.4, has been used to protect the rights and interests of persons in the public eye.

Examples

In 1999, Talksport, a UK specialist sports radio broadcaster, engaged in a promotional campaign to support its rebranding from Talk Radio. It distributed a flyer bearing a photograph of Eddie Irvine, a well-known Formula One driver. The original photograph, which showed Irvine with a mobile phone, had been photoshopped so that a radio replaced the mobile phone. The words 'Talk Radio' had been added. The court decided that the distribution of the flyer falsely implied that Irvine endorsed Talksport and, as a consequence, was an actionable passing off. The court further stated that Irvine had 'a property right in his goodwill' which he could 'protect from unlicensed appropriation consisting of a false claim or suggestion of endorsement of a third party's goods or services'.

In 2012, Topshop started selling a T-shirt featuring a photograph of globally known pop star Rihanna. The photograph had been licensed from the photographer who had taken the photograph. No licence had been obtained from Rihanna. The court agreed with Rihanna, who contended that the sale of the T-shirt without her permission infringed her rights. The court accepted that many fans would buy a product because they would think Rihanna had approved of it, even though she had not and that others would do so because of the value of what they perceived as being Rihanna's authorisation of the item. In both situations the court took the view that Rihanna's fans will have been deceived by the use of the image on the T-shirt.

18.4   Advertising Standards

Consistent with the court decisions referenced at paragraph 18.3, The Advertising Standards Authority Code of Conduct includes specific provisions regarding the use in advertising of individuals' images and/or statements attributed to them.

18.5   Trade marks

An individual may endeavour to protect the right to exploit her/his image for commercial gain by applying to register trade marks and in doing so prevent others from making the unauthorised use of her/his image. Trade marks may be registered that include or consist of a person's name, signature, nickname, slogan, voice or likeness, though it is celebrities' names that are most often registered.

Examples

Former footballers David Beckham and Alan Shearer have registered their names as trade marks. In Beckham's case his mark seeks to protect a range of goods including perfume, hair care and cosmetics; Shearer has registered his image in relation to goods such as clothing, bags and sports articles.

Nevertheless, there may be difficulties in registering a 'celebrity' mark where the celebrity's reputation has not been established in the goods and services for which an application may have been made.

Trade marks are considered at section 14.

18.6   Copyright

If an individual owns the copyright in a photograph in which s/he appears then in given circumstances it may be possible for publication of the film/photograph to be prevented; see the discussion on copyright at sections 5 and 6.

18.7   Misuse of confidential information

See the discussion on confidentiality at section 15.

18.8   Misuse of private information

See the discussion on privacy generally at section 16.

18.9   Data Protection

The Data Protection regime may be used by any individual to prevent the processing of her/his personal data. For these purposes, personal data may include photographs or film. This right now also includes the 'right to be forgotten', where an individual may request a search engine to prevent links to information appearing in search engine results. There is an exception in connection with journalistic purposes, where those responsible for publication of such photographs or other information believe it is in the public interest to do so. Also see the discussion about Data Protection at paragraphs 16.9-16.20.

19   Sponsorship and product placement

19.1   Product placement

The Audiovisual Media Services Directive 2010/13/EC provides that product placement is permitted:

- in cinematographic works, films and series made for audio-visual media services, sports programmes and light entertainment programmes (but not children's programmes);

- where there is no payment but only the provision of certain goods or services free of charge, such as production props and prizes, with a view to their inclusion in a programme.

19.2   Theatrical features

There is no prohibition on products being placed in theatrical feature films nor is there any current regulation that prevents a commercial enterprise from sponsoring the production of a movie.

19.3   Television

The UK's Ofcom Broadcasting Code (**Ofcom Code**) contains rules in relation to commercial references in television designed to ensure editorial independence, protect audiences from surreptitious advertising and prevent unsuitable sponsorship.

https://www.ofcom.org.uk/tv-radio-and-on-demand/broadcast-codes/broadcast-code

https://www.ofcom.org.uk/__data/assets/pdf_file/0005/100103/broadcast-code-april-2017.pdf

19.4   The Ofcom Code applies to all programmes broadcast on channels licensed by Ofcom - Channel 4, STV and Channel 5. Although Ofcom does not licence the BBC, all programmes made by the BBC must be free of product placement. The Ofcom Code makes broadcasters primarily responsible for compliance. Programme makers who require guidance on applying this Code should, in the first instance, talk to those editorially responsible for the programme and to the broadcaster's compliance and legal officers. Nevertheless, a working knowledge of the Ofcom Code is important for programme makers.

19.5   Restrictions are imposed in relation to each of the following four categories:

- Species of products

    Cigarettes/tobacco, prescription medicines, all other medicinal products, alcoholic drinks, food and drink high in fat, salt or sugar, baby milk, electronic or smokeless cigarettes, cigarette lighters, papers or pipes; products that may not be advertised on i.e. guns, weaponry, escort agencies;

- Species of programmes

    News and current affairs programming, consumer advice programmes or children's programming. Children's programming is defined as '*a programme made for a television programme service or an on-demand programme service, and for viewing primarily by persons under the age of sixteen*'. Thus, product placement is only permitted in the following television genres: films (including films made for cinema), series made for television/other audio-visual genres, sports programmes and light entertainment programmes.

- How products may be seen and/or referred to

    Thematic placement is prohibited. Editorial content must not be created or distorted so that it becomes a vehicle for the purposes of featuring placed products. The placement must be relevant to the programme and there must be sufficient justification for its inclusion.

    Product placement must not impair the broadcaster's independence and must not influence the content and scheduling of a programme in a way that affects the responsibility and editorial independence of the broadcaster.

    Programmes may not give a product too much prominence nor promote it e.g. by claiming how good it is.

- Indicating product placement

    Product placement must be signalled clearly by means of the requisite 'P' logo and universal audio signal. The logo should appear:-

- ➤ at the beginning of the programme in which the placement appears;
- ➤ when the programme recommences after commercial breaks;
- ➤ at the end of the programme.

The 'P' logo should appear for a minimum of three seconds. The signalling requirement does not apply when a broadcaster acquires a programme containing product placement, in circumstances in which the broadcaster has neither produced nor commissioned the programme.

19.6   Sponsorship

Sponsored programming is that which has had some or all of its production costs paid by any public or private undertaking or individual with a view to promoting their products, services, brands or activities. The Ofcom Code provides that sponsorship must be clearly identified by means of sponsorship credits, making clear both the identity of the sponsor by reference to its name or trade mark and the association between the sponsor and the sponsored content.

19.7   Credits must be broadcast at the beginning and/or during and/or end of the programme. Credits may also be broadcast entering and/or leaving a commercial break during the sponsored programme. With the exception of the sponsorship credits, any reference to a sponsor appearing in a programme as a result of a commercial arrangement with the broadcaster, the programme maker or a connected person will be treated as product placement and must comply with the product placement rules. Sponsored credits must be distinct from editorial content and advertising. There are further detailed requirements that pertain to credits broadcast around and/or during sponsored programmes to be considered, primarily by broadcasters

19.8   Prop placement

Unpaid prop placement occurs when a product is included in a programme/film with no significant value and the provider has not been paid for its inclusion. Unpaid prop placement will not come within the definition of product placement in the Ofcom Code. To determine whether a product has 'significant value' the price of the prop in relation to the overall budget of the programme needs to be considered.

19.9   Brands

Consideration should be given by filmmakers as to whether consent should be sought from brand owners for the inclusion of their products in a film/TV programme where their inclusion is intentional, even though no payment is made. There may be circumstances in which, without such consent, the IP rights of the product owners, for example in distinctive labelling, could be infringed. Consideration should also be given where branded products are seen on screen in circumstances where they may be disparaged. Trade libel per se has been developed more extensively in the US, but there are circumstances that may give rise to claims under English law. Defamation is considered at section 17. Trade marks are considered at section 14.

20   Locations

20.1   Location licences

When filming at premises owned by a third party or at an outside location it is generally necessary for a filmmaker to obtain formal permission to film from the owner or leaseholder of that location. Proceeding without permission may create more difficulties than simply dealing with the red tape that may be encountered in obtaining the permission.

20.2   Matters to be covered by a location licence may include some or all of the following:

(a)   authorisation for the premises/location to be depicted in the film;

(b)   clearly defined areas in which filming may take place;

(c)   the extent to which the filmmaker will have the exclusive use of the location;

(d)   confirmation that copyright and all other rights in the footage shot at the location will vest in the filmmaker for life of copyright and for use in all media;

(e)   the dates on which the premises may be used and when filming may take place, including the precise times of day on each date;

(f)   how and when access may be obtained;

(g)   parking availability, where applicable;

(h)   any particular facilities/utilities required/to be provided;

(i)   a warranty that the signatory to the licence is authorised to enter into the agreement;

(j)   a warranty that the premises are in a safe condition;

(k)   details of who is to provide security at the location and on what terms;

(l)   an option to return to the location if required by the filmmaker – and the terms for so doing;

(m)   an obligation on the filmmaker to make good any damage or compensate owner for the same;

(n)   provisions as to which liabilities are to be covered by insurance and to identify the party responsible for putting that cover in place;

(o)   payment provisions: (i) amount; (ii) when and in what instalments (iii) deposit and terms for release;

(p)   credit for the location/its owners;

(q)   confidentiality.

An example of a location licence is to be found at Appendix 7.

20.3   Where a filmmaker requires to use a public building as a location, it is apparent that filming will likely not be tolerated and actively prevented without the management of that building being formally approached for a licence. The same is true for venues at which sporting or other events take place.

20.4   Buildings and structures used as background

Filmmakers will often include in the background of shots images of buildings and, in some cases, well-known buildings or structures for which no location licence is sought or obtained. Copyright is likely to be protected as an artistic work in buildings originally designed by architects or designers who are still alive or who have not been deceased for more than 70 years. The London Eye or the new Wembley Stadium fall into this category whereas Buckingham Palace or the Tower of London do not.

20.5   However, under a principle often referred to as 'freedom of panorama', the UK copyright in a building is not infringed by making a photograph or film of it nor will UK copyright be infringed by putting on the world wide web a photograph or film of a building.

20.6   Technically a copyright claim may arise not in relation to a building itself but in relation to the architect's plans for the building. The existence of such a claim is considered to be an unintended loophole in the UK copyright legislation, though it is not known how frequently, if at all, it has been used as the basis of a claim against filmmakers; additionally, the quantum of damages that might be awarded in such a case may make the pursuit of a claim an uneconomic proposition.

20.7   The same principle does not apply in all countries. For example, under French and Belgian copyright law there are more restrictions on showing images of buildings. Where there are genuine concerns as to how a building may be portrayed on screen, tailored advice should be sought, especially in those countries in which the relevant building(s) have been filmed.

20.8   Where a particular building is featured in a film and treated in a disparaging way consideration may need to be given to applicability of the laws of defamation; see section 17.

20.9   Filming in public places

Filming in so-called public places can sometimes be problematic. At one end of the spectrum, low- and no-budget filmmakers shooting on city streets with a small crew are known to take chances and not seek the formal permission of the applicable local authority. Nevertheless, permission should be sought – and this will necessarily need to be the case when a sizeable crew and support vehicles are required. The same principles apply to rural locations.

20.10   Other matters to be taken into account when filming on the streets include: obtaining consents from interviewees: see paragraph 12.3; but bear in mind issues of data protection and the possibility of consent being withdrawn: see paragraphs 16.9-16.20; also consider the discussion around incidental inclusion of third party copyright material: see paragraph 11.8.

20.11   Filming on the streets may inevitably mean that members of the public will be caught on camera not having given consent to be filmed. Reference should be made to the discussion at section 16 in relation to privacy. The UK has no codified law of privacy so it is not possible for an individual to prevent her/ himself being filmed, assuming that a filmmaker is not in breach of any other legal obligation, for example trespassing or filming in a place without a licence. Nevertheless, the principles at paragraph 16.3 should be borne in mind when individuals are filmed and shown on screen without consents.

21   Documentaries

21.1   General considerations

The creative process employed by documentary makers will generally be very different to that followed by the producer of a theatrical drama. A documentary will not necessarily start with a script. The outline may be sketched in a treatment, the detailed narrative may only emerge as the component parts of the documentary are assembled and, subsequently, edited. Nevertheless, the legal framework within which creatives and crew are hired and the manner in which the component elements of a documentary are bolted together by contracts will be much the same as for any other production. Many, if not most, of the topics covered by this Guide will apply to documentaries. There are, however, questions that documentary makers frequently ask that are covered in the succeeding paragraphs of this section.

21.2   Use of existing literary copyrights

Concerned with facts as they are, the first question documentary makers often ask is whether or not it is necessary to clear the rights of books or other literary works that address the subject matter of their proposed documentaries. In some situations the answer may be less than clear-cut. Anyone can undertake independent historical research into a particular person or event and make a documentary about it. However, if sources are used in a documentary whereby the author of the source has created original input, the filmmaker necessarily needs to consider whether a clearance may be sought. In this regard see the discussion at paragraphs 10.4-10.5.

21.3   Researchers' work

Researchers and other contributors will generate original work that will concern the subject matter of the documentary. Filmmakers should ensure that they acquire from researchers ownership of the copyright in all of the original material they create for a documentary by way of written assignment. The assignment may be included in the agreement by which a researcher is contracted. The form of commissioning agreement at Appendix 17 may be adapted for the engagement of researchers.

21.4   Criticism or review

When commenting on or critiquing copyright works, documentary makers will inevitably make use of the 'criticism or review' exception to the requirement to clear third party copyrights; see paragraphs 11.4-11.7; in relation to the use of third party copyrights see section 11 generally.

21.5   Filming 'on the street'

Filmmakers endeavouring to capture live events – including unscheduled occurrences – may need to move quickly. They may shoot first and only afterwards be in a position to consider legal issues arising from the footage they have captured and whether or not it may be used as they intend. There are no special rules governing such filming but regard should be had to general principles, the discussion at 20.9-20.10 and the particular matters listed at paragraph 21.6

21.6   A number of topics covered by this Guide will be of relevance to a documentary maker – not only to footage shot *ex tempore* as mentioned in the previous paragraph but other content, too – and may include:

(a)   life rights (paragraph 10.6);

(b)   interviews (section 12);

(c)   music (section 13);

(d)   confidentiality (section 15);

(e)   privacy (section 16);

(f)   defamation (section 17);

(g)   the extent to which a person's name and likeness may be used (section 18);

(h)   locations (section 20).

21.7   Legal compliance

Those who are the subjects of documentaries who believe they have been defamed and who have the resource may have recourse to the law to attack a film and sue those responsible for its production and distribution. As a general rule, before a documentary is exhibited, its maker will have the film reviewed for legal compliance which will include consideration of any matter that disparages or may be considered to disparage its subjects. Broadcasters may undertake such a review – particularly where documentaries have been commissioned by them. Licences to broadcasters and other distributors will inevitably require documentary makers to warrant that their films do not contain any defamatory material nor that any third party copyrights or other rights have been infringed.

22   Animation & VFX

22.1   Animation – legal requirements

Aside from the absence of humans on screen, the legal requirements of filmmakers working in animation are no different from any other species of film. The general principles pertaining both to the underlying intellectual property comprising an animation and the contracts that are required for an animated film employ the same principles as those for any other production. Contracts commissioning outside animators may comprise the structure suggested at section 41.2. An example of a short form of commissioning agreement is to be found at Appendix 17.

22.2   Artwork

Those creating the original artwork upon which an animation is based will be the first owners of the copyright in that artwork. The filmmaker producing a film based on a pre-existing cartoon strip or other underlying material will need to acquire the right to do so from the owner of the copyright in that cartoon strip. Animations based on pre-existing literary works that are still in copyright will require to be cleared; see sections 6 and 10. Actors providing voice-overs will necessarily be required to provide their performers' consents; see section 9. For the use of music see section 13.

22.3   Animators

Where the entirety of an animation is created by an in-house team comprising employees of a production company, that production company will be the owner of the copyright in the resulting film. Where an outside animation studio is used, that studio must, in terms, either warrant that its work is either undertaken by full-time employees or, if outside contractors are used, that such contractors have assigned or will assign all of the copyright and any other rights in all of the work they each create to the animation studio so that, in turn, it may assign copyright in that work through to the filmmaker.

22.4   Filmmakers who commission outside animators to work on a film will necessarily need to include a licence enabling the animators to use the underlying copyright works and other assets relating to the film for the limited purpose of making the animation and which licence will prevent all and any other use of the underlying works. Commissioning is covered at paragraphs 6.2-6.3 and at section 41.

22.5   VFX

Contracting post-production houses and VFX providers is a not dissimilar process to that of commissioning other outside creatives to provide original work in which copyright will subsist. Reference is made to the requirements made for animation (paragraphs 22.1-22.5). The key issues for post-production and VFX providers include a clearly stated specification of the work required to be delivered to the filmmaker, delivery times and milestones, description of media in which the work is to be delivered and payment provisions.

22.6   In addition to the above, of particular importance for a VFX supplier is a change request procedure. Frequently, a filmmaker's needs in relation to VFX alter – and often expand – as production and post-production evolve. In order to protect the best interests of both the filmmaker and the VFX provider, a clear process is required to determine the cost and the timing for delivery of any additions and alterations to the initial schedule of VFX requirements. Additionally, VFX providers will want provisions in their agreements with filmmakers to protect themselves in the event that a filmmaker's requirements may not be accomplished technically.

22.7   The general principles for commissioning work from third party contractors, which includes VFX houses, are covered in more detail at paragraphs 6.2-6.3 and at section 41.

23 Virtual Reality

23.1   Introduction

For some time, filmmakers have been exploring and adopting the use of Virtual Reality (**VR**) which provides a new way for audiences to experience film. Whilst the commercialisation of VR within a movie context is still developing, there are already film festivals dedicated to VR or that include VR programming. This section is limited to considering legal issues affecting VR content and its production and not the technology by which VR is created and consumed.

23.2   VR employs technology to capture and project content in real or imaginary environments and to simulate a three-dimensional experience within which a user may be immersed and interact generally by using a screen or headset – a head-mounted display (**HMD**). Given the overall potential offered by VR, and particularly the extent to which user interaction is possible, the new medium is attracting not only established filmmakers but also those previously working in the games industry.

23.3   Production agreements

Some of those entering VR production from the world of games have tried structuring production-finance arrangements on the basis of the milestone model used in the games industry; in simple terms, a game's development is broken down to a number of stages against delivery of each of which a distributor will make a milestone payment. Typically, such stages may include 'first playable version', 'alpha' – when key gameplay functionality is implemented and, later on in the process, 'code release' – when bugs are fixed and the game is made ready for distribution. Such stages are calibrated to demonstrate a game's technical progress and playability. However, evidence suggests that this model does not work in the production of VR content in which the filmmaking elements – at least for the present – are more pertinent in budgeting a production than the technicalities. A VR content producer needs to know that the budget may be drawn down in accordance with a production schedule that will typically cover the traditional stages of pre-production, principal photography and post-production and within which the technical requirements for the production will be accommodated. The general principles discussed elsewhere in this Guide apply to the creation and inclusion of content in VR productions, as they will to the process of contracting with creators and talent.

23.4   Nevertheless, as commercialisation of the new medium becomes increasingly successful, there will inevitably be issues that will require resolution; what these may be is open to speculation, as are the solutions – but a few initial reflections are included in the following paragraphs.

23.5   Content

Confusion may arise in relation to the use of existing third party content so that those seeking rights to make VR works of existing copyright material will need to ensure that previous grants of film/television rights or games rights were not drafted in such a way as to preclude a VR producer from using the rights for a VR production. Further, given the current proliferation of distribution media and the rapid pace at which VR is developing, rights owners will want to carefully evaluate and define the precise extent of those rights they may grant to VR producers so as not to limit the possibility they may have to grant rights to others in creative and distribution media not yet developed and/or those that are also broadly available.

23.6   VR content owners (**VRCO**) may want to make it clear in their terms of use that rights in user-generated content within a VR world are to belong to the VRCO even where, on general principles, the user employing the VR device in question might otherwise seek to make a claim to authorship.

23.7   Authors of third party copyright content imported into VR productions may be concerned to address situations where the treatment of their works within a VR environment may be considered to be derogatory and thus an infringement of their moral right of integrity. Waivers of the right to object may be effective under English law but ineffective in other jurisdictions. The moral right of integrity is considered at paragraphs 8.5-8.8.

23.8   Product placement

Issues relating to product placement and use of brands will, in the first instance, be assessed by reference to the principles applying to regular productions; see section 19.

23.9   VR exhibition

VR exhibition presently falls, broadly, into two areas being firstly location-based, in which a room scale experience is enjoyed by multiple users and secondly, direct distribution to individuals via headsets, mobile apps and in web-browsers. Models of contracts in use for each of these primary media adopt tried and tested formulae for the licence and use of content comprising IP.

23.10   Third party liability

Some commentators have raised the issue of claims being made by users against VR producers for personal injuries suffered in the real world whilst using an HMD. When wearing HMDs, users are unable to see the real-life environment in which they are situated, leading to the possibility of tripping, falling, walking into sharp inanimate objects and even falling down stairs or out of windows. This narrative continues with the possibility of users suffering from psychological trauma, nausea and so on. Although VR producers will make significant disclaimers endeavouring to shift risk to the user, under English law it is not possible to exclude or even limit liability for personal injury or death. The question that may then occupy courts is whether there is a sufficient link of causation between a VR production and the injury/effect allegedly suffered by the user while experiencing that production who then claims compensation?

23.11   Even though unable to exclude liability altogether, VR producers and exhibitors will undoubtedly seek to reduce or even extinguish liability for injury by pleading contributory negligence and/or *volenti* – a common law doctrine which states that if someone willingly places themselves in a position knowing that some degree of harm might result, such a person may not bring a negligence claim against the other party. Some distributors have already considered the issue by including in their terms of use the requirement that VR end-users should remain seated while wearing an HMD.

CONTRACTS: OVERVIEW

24   Preliminary considerations

24.1   Elements of a contract

English law recognises that binding contracts may be made orally or in writing. In order to be enforceable, however, any contract, whether oral or written, needs to contain certain elements:

- offer

- acceptance

- consideration

- intention to create a legally binding relationship

Example

During a meeting in a restaurant, Darius, a filmmaker, offers the opportunity to Edward to write the script for a film, 'Project X', that has been commissioned by a television broadcaster. A first draft is required within six weeks. Darius shows Edward the broadcaster's letter that sets out some of the key terms of the commission. Darius agrees to pay Edward a fee of £5,000. £2,500 is to be paid prior to the writer starting on the project and the balance on delivery of the first draft. Darius indicates that Edward will be given a single-frame credit in the front-end roller of the film. Edward agrees to the proposal.

Although not in writing:

- there is a clear offer;

- there is a clear acceptance;

- the consideration moving from the filmmaker is £5,000 and the agreement to provide the front-end credit; the consideration moving from the writer is undertaking to write and deliver the script; the concept of consideration is reviewed at paragraph 25.6;

- there is a broadcast commission in existence and the circumstances of the meeting demonstrate the seriousness of the parties' intentions so that both may consider themselves legally bound to perform their respective obligations.

24.2   Implied terms

The ability to enforce an oral contract may be diminished where key terms are not certain. In the above example no mention is made of many of the details that would ordinarily be included in a written agreement such as ownership of copyright, extent of rights granted, required interaction with the director, requirements for second and subsequent drafts and polishes, back-end payments, the language in which the script is to be written, when and how payment is to be made and so on. (Writers' agreements are considered in more detail at section 27.) In the absence of express terms, English law may imply terms into an agreement. An implied term is one that is required to address an obvious omission from the express terms of a contract. In order to determine the application of implied terms, an examination of all relevant facts and matters needs to be made. Where the discussions between parties break down, or where there is disagreement as to what was intended, a resource and energy-sapping dispute may loom, if not a potentially expensive court battle.

24.3   Contracts by email

Recognising the realities of instant communications, which are a key part of the way in which the early twenty-first century filmmaker operates, the tools for avoiding, or at least minimising, areas of potential dispute are immediately available. Even in circumstances where a full-blown written agreement has not been prepared in advance by a lawyer, parties may reduce the uncertainties surrounding their arrangements by exchanging emails or other text-based messages which provide an instant record of what has been said between them.

Example

In the example at 24.1, if Edward, the writer, is keen to be contractually bound, following the lunch he might send an email to Darius, the filmmaker, along the following lines:

Dear Darius,

Further to our meeting of today I am writing to confirm the principal terms of the agreement that we reached whereby you engage me to write the script for 'Project X' for which you will pay me £5,000.

As soon as I have received the initial agreed payment from you of £2,500, I will start work in order to deliver the first draft by no later than six weeks from my receipt of the said sum of £2,500. You will pay me the balance of the fee due, being a further £2,500, upon my delivering the first draft to you.

I confirm that I will negotiate in good faith the balance of the detailed terms that will apply to our agreement upon receiving a draft from you or your lawyer. In the meantime, I will proceed on the basis of the above.

Yours sincerely

Edward

Once sent, the date of the email will automatically establish when the agreement was made.

24.4   To the extent that further detail has been discussed and agreed, there is no reason why the writer should not include it in the email. Putting something in writing immediately will facilitate the filmmaker's response and provide her/ him with the opportunity to add vital details or, equally importantly, to clear up any misapprehensions. The above is a simple example of just one relationship that will exist in the course of production of a film. Nevertheless, the principles discussed above may be used to address the relationships between co-writers, producer and director, owner of underlying material and producer, producer and talent agent, producer and financier and, indeed, any others. If a proposal is discussed in principle and key terms agreed and the parties wish to be bound, then there is no reason why those agreed terms may not be instantly recorded in writing; where the parties do not wish to be bound consider the discussions at paragraphs 24.6-24.14.

24.5   With the proliferation of digital communication, filmmakers increasingly use other media in which to communicate. Evidence of the terms of an agreement may be determined by considering the content of messages exchanged via Facebook, Twitter, WhatsApp etc.

Example

Sam, a Hollywood-based producer, meets Janet, a British filmmaker, at AFM, where Janet is pitching her project entitled 'Enchanted Evening' which she has conceived as a US-UK co-pro. Janet has raised development money. Following AFM, Sam and Janet speak a couple of times, agree to co-produce and then exchange extensive WhatsApp messages – both written and audio – in which various details are discussed. Upon the faith of Sam's messages that include a promise that his attorney is drawing up a formal contract to record the agreed terms, Janet transfers $50,000 to Sam's account to cover her share of the development budget. After a couple of weeks Sam's contacts become increasingly intermittent and no contract is ever received. Janet hires lawyers who, using the WhatsApp messages, are able to piece together a clear course of dealing and a set of agreed terms that enable them to file a claim at court that results in Sam paying back Janet's money.

24.6   Subject to contract

However, in order to consider being bound, one or other of the parties may require more detailed terms and/or the consent and/or approval of persons not at the meeting referred to. If that is the case, then it will be necessary for those conditions or approvals to be referred to in the email and for what has been agreed in principle to be made 'subject to contract'.

24.7   'Subject to contract' is the expression used to indicate that while terms have been negotiated in good faith, no binding arrangement may come into force between the parties until such time as all of the terms have been agreed unconditionally; the medium for so doing will generally be a formal written contract or exchange of letters setting out all of the agreed terms.

Example

In the example given at 24.1 and 24.3, the filmmaker might respond as follows:

Subject to contract

Dear Edward,

Thank you for your email which accurately reflects our discussions. However, as I did explain, before I can proceed to formally engage you and pay the first instalment of your fee I will need to get board approval. Additionally, in order to release the payment I will need you to sign a writer's agreement in our standard form. That being the case, at this stage, all of our discussions will remain subject to contract.

Yours sincerely

Darius

24.8   Pre-contract considerations

An exchange of emails may beg one or other of the parties to clarify its position in further correspondence and to protect it by making it clear that the arrangement under discussion is 'subject to contract'. Nevertheless, for low/ no-budget productions where the parties are investing creativity and trust with a view to demonstrating their abilities as filmmakers, use of email can be helpful for setting out principles. In the next example, although emails may help, short forms of signed documents will generally be more effective.

Example

A filmmaker is planning her first solo project which is a documentary about a community of westerners living on a remote island in the South Pacific. The community was established in the late 1960s by Americans escaping the Vietnam War draft. The community members are now in their late sixties and early seventies. One of them has a cache of many hours of unedited Super 8 footage shot between 1969 and 1981. The filmmaker agrees to take the footage back to the UK and have it converted to a digital format before commencing an edit. The filmmaker agrees to cover the cost of the digital conversion and to supply the community with a complete copy of the footage on DVDs. In return, the community members, including all of those who shot the film and who appear in it, agree that the filmmaker may use the footage for all of the purposes of the documentary.

24.9   In this example, before incurring the cost of converting the footage, the filmmaker should ensure that her position is clear and that there is no mismatch of expectations. She should obtain simple forms of release from each of the relevant persons confirming that:

•   they each consent to the use of film that they respectively shot for all of the purposes of the documentary and for the full life of its copyright – which may include using parts in a teaser to raise production funding and/or to attract distribution, editing and use in the final film and for promoting it;

- they each consent to their on-screen appearances being used and included by the filmmaker and acknowledge that the filmmaker may exploit the appearances in the finished film by all means and in all media now known or hereafter invented for the life of copyright of the film;

- they each acknowledge that copyright in the finished film is vested in the filmmaker;

- they each agree that the filmmaker may exploit the documentary (and, ideally, all of its component footage) by all means and in all media (now known or hereafter invented) throughout the world for the life of copyright in the documentary.

24.10   The filmmaker should also include in her arrangements with the community members written confirmation of the key terms, being:

- her undertaking to procure and pay for digital conversion of the footage;

- her obligation to deliver a digital copy of the footage to the community;

- any other significant detail – i.e. the credits she may be proposing for the community and its members.

24.11   Terminology in common use

Filmmakers may be presented with documents bearing a variety of different headings. Some of these include:

- Memo(randum) of Understanding (**MoU**)

- Heads of terms

- Deal Memo

- Deal terms

- Letter of Intent (**LoI**)

- Contract proposal

- Contract summary

- Offer letter

- Without prejudice

24.12   When considering the terms mentioned at 24.11, the principles discussed at 24.1 apply. Thus,

- if a document contains key terms that both parties have agreed, and

- the key terms, including consideration, are sufficiently clear and complete to be enforceable, and

- there is a clear intention to be legally bound,

then the parties may each be in a position to rely on the document and enforce their respective rights against the other party. It is this last matter on which filmmakers should focus and ask themselves a simple question: do I want to be bound at this point or not? If the answer is 'no' – for whatever reason (i.e. other interested parties on the horizon, concerns about the other party's status, resources etc) then the document should be marked and referred to, clearly, as 'subject to contract'.

24.13   Letter of intent

In the absence of language indicating whether the arrangement is to be 'subject to contract' or not, in order to determine whether or not there is a binding agreement consideration should to be given to:

- the overall terms of the document;

- the precise language that has been used;

- the context in which the document has come into being.

Examples

If a Deal Memo issued by the in-house lawyer of a broadcaster is clearly marked 'subject to contract', then no binding terms will come into effect without further documentation and/or terms being agreed.

If a LoI states that 'pending the negotiation of a long-form agreement the parties will proceed with the project on the basis of this Letter of Intent', then the parties will be bound on the basis of the terms included in the LoI; problems may arise if there are differences of opinion or disputes about detailed aspects of the arrangement that have yet to be negotiated and recorded in writing.

If a MoU provides that 'the parties agree to continue to develop the project with the above principles in mind' then, in the absence of any additional language, the position may be unclear and a review of the overall circumstances in which the MoU came into being will need to be examined to determine the extent of any legal rights and obligations arising.

It will be more problematic, disruptive and, likely, expensive to unravel an unclear position. If intending to be bound, the parties should state clearly at the outset that they are each proceeding in reliance upon the terms of the MoU or LoI having legal force and effect.

24.14   Heads of terms

Irrespective that they may be stated to be 'subject to contract', heads of terms may be useful to those responsible for preparing a contract, i.e. the lawyers or business affairs executives who may not have been involved in the original discussions between the principals. Being provided with a clear list of key commercial terms that have been agreed is generally a more efficient and cost-effective way to negotiate a detailed contract than to debate complex amendments to a long-form agreement. Ticking off key points on a checklist will help. Reference to the headings of the clauses considered at section 25 may assist in listing some of the variables to be agreed, for example those at 25.3, 25.6, 25.7, 25.10, 25.13, 25.14, 25.19 and 25.29. In addition, reference should be made to the various species of agreements considered at each of sections 27-35 that cover the individual requirements of a writer, a director and so on.

24.15   Part performance

Where no formal agreement has yet been concluded but steps are taken in furtherance of a project, in order to determine whether parties are contractually bound, the substance of what has been agreed and the context within which those steps have been taken need to be evaluated. Of particular importance will be any written evidence, including email exchanges. Using clear, simple language, that states either that there is or is not an intention to be contractually bound, will remove any doubt. Consideration should also be given to those situations in which the principle of part performance may apply.

Example

Continuing with the scenario described at paragraph 24.1, Darius, the filmmaker, decides to produce a sequel to 'Project X'. Darius offers the opportunity to Edward, to write the sequel, entitled 'Project Y', that Darius says will 'likely' be commissioned by the television broadcaster. Edward has been in regular contact with Darius since the successful broadcast of 'Project X' and has read in the trades that the broadcaster is intending to commission the sequel, albeit that no contracts have yet been signed between Darius and the broadcaster. Darius tells Edward that a treatment is urgently required and needs to be delivered within a week and a first draft six weeks later. The agreed fee is £7,000, of which £3,500 is to be paid immediately upon delivery by Edward to Darius of the treatment. The balance will be paid on delivery of the first draft. The filmmaker indicates that the writer will be given a single-frame credit in the front-end credits of the film. Edward agrees to the proposal. There is no exchange of email. The following day Darius makes the first payment. Edward starts work on the treatment but stops and refuses to continue when he reads in the trades that the broadcaster has stated in public that it is no longer commissioning outside productions and all current projects are to be abandoned. Darius may validly assert that Edward is in breach of contract. Darius has performed his required obligations thus far, has part-performed the agreement and is willing to pay the rest of the fee as and when Edward delivers the script, irrespective that the original broadcaster has dropped out of the project. Edward's failure to deliver is a breach of contract for which he will be liable in damages, albeit the quantum may not be easy to assess.

24.16   Estoppel – going back on your word

Another rule of English law may be of relevance in situations where, in common parlance, one party to an arrangement seeks to go back on her/his word. An estoppel may arise in circumstances where Party A has said or done something and Party B, to her/his detriment, then acts in reliance upon Party A's words and/or actions. This doctrine is technical but may be simply illustrated by adapting the example at paragraph 24.15. In the US the doctrine is sometimes referred to as 'detrimental reliance'.

Example

Darius tells Edward that he must start work straight away, deliver the treatment within a week and the script six weeks later. Edward informs Darius that he will be unable to do this as he has been asked to go to Hollywood the following week to spend ten days providing script editing services for Ordinary Productions Inc. Ordinary will be paying Edward $5,000 plus all of his expenses and offering the possible bonus of well-paid ongoing work if Ordinary's project is picked up by a US network. Not put off, Darius ups his offer to Edward. Darius will pay Edward £1,500 for the treatment and £7,000 for the script of which £5,000 will be paid on delivery of the treatment and £3,500 on delivery of the script. Edward turns down the Hollywood job and delivers the treatment within a week. Consequent upon the broadcaster pulling out, Darius's refusal to pay will be met by Edward with the assertion that Darius is estopped from denying his obligations to Edward. Edward has acted to his detriment in turning down the Hollywood job and has lost out on paying work and the opportunity to earn more. At the very least Darius will be obliged to pay Edward his agreed fee and will likely also be liable for other damages.

24.17   Without prejudice

The term 'without prejudice' does not strictly belong in a situation where an arm's length commercial negotiation is in progress. The term is usually used in the circumstances of a dispute between parties who want to make suggestions, proposals, disclosures or concessions 'without prejudice' to their strict legal position. If, as a consequence of negotiations and exchanges of written information and proposals that are made without prejudice, no agreement is reached, the material that was disclosed and the proposals made under the umbrella of 'without prejudice' discussions may not be viewed by a judge or arbitrator subsequently appointed to decide the subject matter of the dispute. Thus the judge or arbitrator will not be influenced by the extent of the concessions that either party had been willing to make during the course of their attempts to resolve their differences before the dispute comes to trial.

25   Constructing a contract

25.1   Approaches to entering an agreement

In an ideal world, every filmmaker's budget would be sufficient to enable all of the relationships engendered in the production of a film and for the rights thereby created to be formally documented by those both qualified and experienced to do so. For many filmmakers the ideal world does not exist. Some follow the Blue Peter principle of adopting something that has been used previously. Others put together home-made agreements. There is nothing wrong, in principle, with using DIY contracts. However, without the benefit of legal training and/ or previous experience of drafting and construing contracts, there are numerous traps that lie in wait for the unwary. In this regard see the discussion of the role of the lawyer at section 53. There are a series of precedent agreements in the Appendices to this Guide which may be of use to filmmakers whose budgets do not make provision for legal representation and advice. Nevertheless, great care should always be taken in using any precedent. A precedent should be regarded as a guideline to what may be required for inclusion in an agreement – it should not be regarded as holy writ to be slavishly followed. The particulars of every arrangement are likely to be variable. In addition to the contract forms included in the Appendices to this Guide, PACT (formerly Producers' Alliance for Cinema and Television) provides a library of documents for its members. More information may be found at http://www.pact.co.uk/

25.2   The following are some general comments that may be of assistance – not just to those endeavouring to put a contract together, but also to those who are in receipt of a contract from another party, irrespective of whether it has been professionally drafted or not. At sections 27-36, consideration is given to some of the specific provisions that are required in contracts for various of the key participants in a film.

25.3   Parties

The precise legal name and correct address should clearly be stated for each party to a contract. If a contracting party is a limited company that should be made clear and its registered office and registered number included as well as its trading address (if different to the registered office).

Examples

For a limited company

ABC Film Productions Limited of 47 Dean Street London W1H 4BZ and whose registered office is at 11 Oxford Place, Norwich, NO9 5KU (registered number 06345789)

If the individual has a stage name then use both the legal/birth name and the stage name:

Algernon Emanuel Tibbs (pka Snudge Ratface) of 97 Railway Cuttings, East Cheam, Surrey KT6 9EU

*pka = professionally known as

Remember that a limited company has a separate legal personality to that of the individual, or individuals, who set it up. There will therefore be situations in which an individual will need to enter into an agreement with her/his own company. For example, the writer/producer who decides to produce a film through a production company will need to assign the rights in the screenplay to the company that s/he establishes.

25.4   Recitals

Including recitals at the beginning of an agreement may often be of use in explaining the background to a deal, for example where there has been a series of events that have led to an agreement being put in place. This may often be the case where a project has been through a number of developments before being funded. Recitals may be used to explain the passage of rights from one producer to another or where, for example, different writers have contributed to the creation of the script.

Example

Recitals

(A)   *Producer has developed, shot and prepared a rough-cut of an original motion picture feature film entitled 'Circular Image' ('Film') based on an original Screenplay written by Hugh U Kidding ('Writer')*

('*Screenplay*') *pursuant to a writer's agreement made between Producer and Writer;*

(B)   *Bannockburn Finance plc has funded production of the Film in the sum of £500,000 (five hundred thousand pounds) which arrangement was evidenced by a loan agreement dated 27 October 2014 and secured by way of a fixed and floating charge over the Film;*

(C)   *The Film remains unfinished and requires further funding to enable it to be completed;*

(D)   *Bannockburn has agreed to providing additional funding to complete the Film on the terms and conditions of this Agreement.*

Further examples of recitals may be found in various of the agreements in the Appendices including Exhibit A to Appendix 3 and in Appendices 9, 10 and 17.

25.5   Definitions

If particular terminology is frequently used in a contract then it is common to have a definitions section at the beginning. The number of definitions in a contract may vary enormously.

Examples

Delivery   *delivery of the final cut of the Film to be made in accordance with the provisions of Clause XX of this Agreement;*

Film   *the motion picture feature film provisionally entitled 'Circular Image' to be directed by Arty Martsmart and based on the Screenplay;*

Financier   *Bannockburn Finance plc whose registered office is at 19, Cypress Avenue, Shady Hollow SC1 5SM registered number 070531933;*

Materials   *all physical properties and chattels and all negative and positive material relating to the Film, including the original film and sound negatives, internegatives, interpositives, and other material whether on film, disc or tape including without limitation the items listed in the Schedule;*

Screenplay   *the original screenplay, 'Circular Image', by Hugh U Kidding;*

Schedule   *the schedule to this Agreement*

Term   *the term of this Agreement as more particularly defined at Clause XX.*

25.6   Consideration

Consideration is an essential component of a contract to make it binding under English law. There are exceptions to this rule in relation to what are known as 'deeds'. However, in order to be valid, a deed must be drafted and signed in a specific way. Best practice is for the consideration – or promises – being provided by each party to be clearly stated.

Examples

Producer will pay Screenwriter the sum of £9,000 as to: (a) £3,000 upon signature of this agreement; (b) £3,000 upon delivery of the first draft of the Screenplay; (c) £3,000 upon acceptance by Producer of the final shooting script for the Film. Producer shall also procure that Screenwriter is accounted for and paid a sum equal to 2% of Producer's Net Profits as that term is defined in the principal finance and production agreements for the Film. Producer will procure that Screenwriter is given a single-frame credit in the form 'Screenplay by [insert name of Screenwriter]';

Screenwriter will deliver a first draft of the Screenplay by no later than 1st February 20++ and, after discussions with the Producer, a final shooting script by no later than 1 March 20++

In this example, the consideration moving from the Producer is (a) the promise to pay £9,000, (b) the promise to account for the profit share and (c) the undertaking to provide a credit; any one or more of these acts of consideration would be sufficient to make the contract binding. The consideration moving from the Screenwriter is the promise to write and deliver the Screenplay. Profit participations and royalties are considered at section 47.

Part of the payment made to those contributing to a film may be subject to a deferral. Many low and no-budget films are dependent on the goodwill of contributors and participants who agree to defer their payments to the point in time when – or if – the film makes a profit.

Example

Producer shall pay to Director a fee of £10,000 (ten thousand pounds) of which £5,000 (five thousand pounds) shall be paid within seven days of the completion and signature of this agreement and of which £2,500 (two thousand five hundred pounds) shall be paid within seven days of the completion of principal photography and of which the balance of £2,500 (two thousand five hundred pounds) shall be deferred ('Deferred Fee') and be paid in accordance with the recoupment schedule for the film.

Recoupment schedules, or payment waterfalls, are considered at paragraph 40.3.

25.7   Rights

The details of the rights being created, transferred or licensed under a contract should be clearly stated. If the arrangement is one whereby Party A is commissioning Party B to create or to contribute to the creation of a copyright work for which Party A is paying Party B a fee, then the contract should clearly state whether or not Party A is acquiring the copyright or merely a licence. If the arrangement is for a licence only, there should be a clear explanation of what media, for what period and in what territories the copyright is licensed as well as any applicable restrictions on use of the copyright being required by either party of the other.

Examples

Assignment – or transfer of copyright in the case of a filmmaker commissioning a composer to compose and record an original soundtrack:

Composer hereby assigns to Producer copyright in and to the musical compositions and sound recordings for the life of copyright of the musical compositions and the sound recordings and throughout the world.

Licence – where a synchronisation licence is being acquired to use an existing sound recording:

Gynormous Records hereby grants to Producer by way of licence the right to synchronise the original sound recording 'Temperature's Rising' ('Recording') by The Hot 5 for all of the purposes of the Film so that the Producer and those deriving rights and/or title in the Film from the Producer may exploit the Recording as part of the soundtrack to the Film by all means and in all media now known or hereafter invented for the life of copyright of the Film and throughout the world.

25.8   Warranties and representations

Warranties are statements made by each party as to facts and circumstances upon which the other party will rely in entering into a legal relationship.

Examples

Screenwriter hereby warrants that the Screenplay will be Screenwriter's own original work and will not infringe the copyright or rights of any other party.

Director warrants that during the Term she will not be committed to any other production that will prevent her from performing her obligations to the Producer as required by this agreement.

Often the subject matter of a warranty may also be made a 'representation'.

Example

Screenwriter hereby warrants and represents [emphasis added] that the Screenplay will be her own original work and will not infringe the copyright or rights of any other party.

The significance of making a statement a representation as well as a warranty lies in the remedy for breach. A breach of warranty will result in the party responsible for the breach being liable for the damages that flow from that breach; i.e. the losses actually suffered by the party not in breach. However, if circumstances are misrepresented and the statement is made recklessly or knowing it to be untrue, then the party who suffers as a result may be able to exercise the additional remedy of rescinding the contract – cancelling it – as well as claiming damages, the quantum of which may extend beyond simply those that directly flow from the breach.

In the body of an agreement, a party to it may warrant and represent the accuracy of the recitals. If, subsequently, the matter contained in a recital is found to have been misrepresented, a party who relied on the representation and who suffers a loss as a consequence will have a claim against the party who made that representation. So, in the example at paragraph 25.4, if, in truth, the Producer has not run out of funding, but has instead diverted money intended for 'Circular Image' to another project, upon discovery of this fact Bannockburn would have a claim against Producer for misrepresentation and might seek to rescind its agreement to make additional funding available to complete the film.

25.9   Good faith

Unlike the law in various of the United States, an obligation of good faith (*bona fides*) is not implied into contracts by English law. Adopting the ordinary and natural meaning of the terminology, requiring parties to act in good faith obliges them to commit to a sincere intention to be fair, open, and honest, regardless of the outcome of the interaction. Raising the performance standard to 'utmost good faith' (*uberrimae fidei*) requires the parties to act towards each other as if in a fiduciary capacity and reveal all and any information that in any way impacts upon the respective performance of their obligations in the contract in question. Resistance to including a good faith obligation may say something about the party who does the resisting.

25.10   Time limits

The time period within which an obligation is to be performed should be clearly stated; if possible, dates should be specific – although that is not always possible. Consider the following:

Examples

Producer requires Director to commence pre-production on 3 April 2016.

Producer requires Director to commence pre-production twenty-one days after Producer notifies Director in writing that the Budget for the Film is fully funded.

Note that if a contract provides that 'time is to be of the essence' of an obligation, then that time period will be strictly construed so that failure to perform in due time will render that party in breach.

Example

In consideration of Director making himself available to start work on pre-production of the Film on 3 April 20++, Producer shall pay first instalment of Director's fee in the sum of £10,000 by no later than 15 March 20++, time being of the essence of the Producer's payment obligation.

In this example, failure to pay by the due date will automatically put the Producer in breach. Depending on how the contract has been drafted, the Director may be in a position to terminate as soon as the payment date has passed with no payment having been made. In any event, all contracts should provide for the basis upon which they may be terminated for breach and for what is to occur consequent upon a breach being committed; see paragraph 25.15-25.16.

25.11   Notices

Every contract should contain a clear notice provision setting out how, when, to whom and where any formal notification required under that contract be given. When serving a notice, the requirements of the notice provision should be followed precisely in order to ensure that a notice is valid and may subsequently be relied upon in the event of a dispute.

Example

Any notice under this agreement shall be in writing and delivered by hand, by facsimile or by other print-out communication mechanism including but not limited to email or sent by prepaid recorded delivery first class post (air mail equivalent if posted to another country) to the recipient of the notice at its address above stated at the head of this agreement or such other address if notified in writing and shall be deemed to have been served immediately if hand-delivered, faxed or emailed during business hours (or otherwise when the next business day starts) or, if posted, on the second business day after the date of posting (the fifth if posted to another country).

25.12   Examples of situations arising in the course of film production where one party may need to give *formal notification to the other of a requirement under a contract include the following:*

- *The holder of an option to acquire film rights in a book raises the finance for the production and wishes to notify the owner of the copyright in the book that he wishes to exercise that option; see the discussion at paragraphs 10.7-10.12 in relation to options generally.*

• *A producer wishes to notify an actor on a 'first call' agreement that the first day of principal photography has been arranged and her presence on set from that day is required; see the discussion at paragraph 28.1.(c) in relation to 'first call'*

• *A director wishes to notify the producer that payment of part of her/his fee has not been made in due time.*

• *Where a party has committed a breach of an agreement and the other party requires that breach to be cured; see paragraph 25.15.*

25.13   Delivery materials

The materials to be delivered by a filmmaker should be carefully considered and agreed as part of a production or any other agreement that provides for delivery of materials. Filmmakers should never accept a schedule of materials included in an agreement just because the other party (or its lawyers) say that the list is standard. Failure to deliver precisely what is included in a schedule may result in a filmmaker being automatically in breach with one consequence potentially being that a distributor or other recipient of the materials may be contractually able to withhold payment. Lawyers, sales agents and executive producers may not always be sufficiently knowledgeable or qualified to take a view as to whether a schedule is either appropriate or accurate. Someone with knowledge of the technicalities employed in the production and post-production process of the project and who properly understands the technical detail of the requisite delivery materials in question needs to review the schedule and amend it in order that it is consistent with what a filmmaker is able to make available for delivery.

25.14   Delivery and acceptance

Where a filmmaker is engaged to deliver a film to any other party – a distributor, a financier –the procedures for both delivery by the producer and acceptance by the third party should be clearly set out in the contract. Effective delivery and acceptance may be the key to triggering payments to the filmmaker and/or release and distribution obligations.

Example

Producer shall deliver the Materials to Company at its offices at 99c, Dean Street London W1 or otherwise as Company may hereafter notify Producer in writing. Company shall have seven days in which to notify Producer of any defects in any of the Materials failing which the Materials shall be deemed accepted.

25.15   Breach, cure and termination

The basis on which a breach of an agreement may be notified to a party in breach should be included as well as a period in which such a breach may be cured. Breaches that are incapable of being remedied should be stated to justify termination of the agreement, assuming that is the intention of the parties. Making provision for breach and its consequences will be critical in many situations; for example, a director who repeatedly turns up drunk on set and, as a consequence, is incapable of performing her/his duties effectively or at all. The ability to terminate that director's involvement in a production within the bounds of a written agreement may save a problem unfolding where the position is unclear.

Example

Either party shall have the right to terminate this agreement by giving written notice to the other in the event of (a) a failure to remedy a breach of this Agreement within five days of the date of receipt by it of a notice in writing identifying the breach and, assuming such breach is capable of remedy, requiring it to be remedied or (b) forthwith by notice in writing in the event that the other party commits an irremediable breach of this agreement.

Clause 15.1(d) of the director's agreement at Appendix 9 is a provision that may be used by a producer to terminate a director's appointment for continually turning up drunk on set with the consequences provided for at Clause 15.4 of that agreement.

Additional provisions entitling a party to terminate will usually include situations where the other party becomes insolvent or ceases to be in business.

25.16   Consequences of termination

Depending on the nature of the agreement in question, a provision explaining what will happen upon termination should be included.

Example

Forthwith upon termination of this agreement by the Producer, the Director shall leave the set and be relieved of her/his obligation to provide any further services. Producer shall not be required to make any further payment to the Director [or as the case may be] and may replace the Director.

25.17   Suspension and force majeure

Many film contracts will provide for the right of a party to suspend the operation of a contract in given circumstances. Examples of specific instances that may give rise to a producer to suspend the operation of an agreement with a director or actor may include;

•   refusal or neglect to perform an obligation as required by the producer in the course of production;

•   incapacity rendering the actor/director incapable of performing her/his obligations;

•   an act of force majeure making it impossible for a production to continue.

Events of force majeure may include Acts of God; war; accident; fire; strikes; riots; civil disturbances; terrorism; power failures; ongoing failure of the internet or other technical issues; natural disasters; transportation problems; death, disability or disfigurement (with respect to cast members); inability to obtain health insurance for a principal member of the cast or the director or inability to obtain visas, labour permits or other governmental licences for any such persons; or any other cause not reasonably within the filmmaker's control which hampers the development or production of a film.

25.18   Suspension of an engagement will generally last for as long as the event giving rise to it plus such further period as may be reasonably required by a filmmaker either to prepare to resume production or until such time as there are grounds for the filmmaker to terminate. The suspension provision will need to address issues such as payment and the obligations of each party during the period of suspension. The maximum length of the period of the suspension may also be stated. To initiate a period of suspension will require the filmmaker to serve a written notice.

Example

An example of a suspension provision and its effect will be found at Clause 14 of the director's agreement at Appendix 9.

25.19   Credits

Ensuring that a participant is properly credited for her/his contribution to a film is an important part of any film contract. The worth of a credit for the purposes of securing future involvement in other productions may be significant. In order to minimise the possibility of disappointment and argument when a film is finally edited and completed, the wording, position and size of credits should be negotiated and included in applicable agreements.

Examples

Producer shall accord the Artist a [single-frame] credit on screen on all copies of the Film in the main titles of the Film which may appear at the beginning or end of the Film above or before the title of the Film in a size of type no smaller than that used for the credit of any other cast member in [first]/[second]/[third] position on a separate card.

Company shall procure that Producer and its contributing personnel shall receive customary end title credits and in major paid advertising details of which shall be delivered by Producer to Company within a reasonable time after principal photography has concluded.

25.20   Assignment

A filmmaker will likely want – and may need – to freely assign and otherwise deal with the rights in a film. From a filmmaker's point of view, best practice requires a broadly drawn right to assign in every agreement made in connection with the development and production of a film. However, the expectation of being able to assign needs to be balanced with the requirements of each of those granting rights to a filmmaker or who otherwise participate in the production of a film to know that payment and other obligations passed on to third parties may be enforced. Without this requirement, the individual participants will have no direct contractually enforceable rights against an assignee, what is known in English law as 'privity of contract'.

25.21 Under English law a filmmaker should be obligated to require those to whom rights are assigned ('**assignee**') to enter into a direct covenant with each of the contributors to a film. In this way the assignee will be required to agree with each of the contributors to perform all of the filmmaker's obligations to them. These obligations will include the obligation to account for and pay participants what they are each due under the terms of their respective contracts. Any individual presented with an agreement that permits its unconditional assignment by the other party with whom s/he is contracting (i.e. a producer) should insist on an obligation by the producer to procure that an assignee should covenant directly with that individual. This process is known in English law as novation. Without such an obligation, the ability of an individual to effectively enforce his or her entitlements under the agreement may become materially diminished.

Example

Company may assign this Agreement subject to the Writer's consent which may not be unreasonably withheld provided that Company shall first procure that its assignee shall enter into a direct covenant with the Writer to observe and perform all of Company's obligations under this Agreement including the provisions of this clause as if such assignee was primary obligor thereof.

25.22 The significance of failing to ensure that such a covenant is not only included but also enforced is something that unfortunately arises far too often. In many of these cases an actor's or director's agent may have negotiated the contract with a production company without legal input and without appreciating the effect of the assignment clause.

Example

*A highly successful television drama series was co-produced by companies based in three different countries. The three co-production partners had incorporated an English company as a special purpose vehicle (**SPV**) to undertake the physical production of the programmes. The SPV contracted with all of the actors and crew line-producing the programmes. Lead actors were contracted to be on a share of the producers' net profits of the programmes.*

*Consequent upon completion of the production, copyright and all exploitation rights in the programmes were assigned by the SPV to a separate rights-owning company incorporated in an off-shore tax haven. The assignment contained no obligation on the SPV to procure that its assignee directly covenant with the actors to account for and pay their respective net profit shares. There was no collection account management agreement (**CAMA**) put in place to facilitate a third party collecting income from the programmes and accounting and making payments to profit participants. The actors' only redress for non-accounting and non-payment was to pursue the SPV which had no assets and was ultimately dissolved.*

CAMAs are discussed below at paragraph 48.5.

25.23   Confidentiality

The parties should mutually agree to maintain the confidentiality of their dealings and of commercially sensitive information that pertains to a project.

Example

The Parties shall keep this agreement and its terms confidential and shall not disclose the same to any person other than their professional advisers or as required by law.

Confidentiality is discussed in more detail at section 15.

25.24   Covenant for further assurance

A useful provision to include in any agreement where there may be a subsequent need for the delivery of additional documentation or the performance of additional obligations is set out below.

Example

The parties shall each do such further or other things and/or enter into such further or other deeds and documents as may reasonably be required to give effect to the terms of the agreement.

Additional language may be required to address issues of costs and time periods within which performance of this obligation may be required by one party of the other and the consequences of non-compliance. Agreements may provide for the party requiring the additional document to be treated as if having been granted a power of attorney to execute the required documents on behalf of the other party.

25.25   Indemnities

The general position under English common law is that a party in breach of an agreement will be liable to the other party for the damages that flow from that breach. In film production agreements, parties tend to expand this common law entitlement to a full indemnity. Unless qualified or limited in some way, an indemnity for breach will require the party committing the breach to fully compensate the other party for all and any costs, expenses and damages that arise from the breach. This latter formulation will give the party suffering from the breach a more extensive remedy than that to which they might otherwise be entitled under English common law.

Example

An actress is hired by a producer to appear in a film, 'Dark Steps', for which she is to be paid a total of £20,000. The initial payment of £10,000 is made on the first day of principal photography; the balance is contracted to be paid in four equal instalments over the four weeks of the shoot. After two weeks of shooting the first two instalments have not been paid. A couple of days later filming is stopped as it emerges that the producer has not raised sufficient funds to complete the film. The producer will therefore be in breach of the agreement with the actress who may properly claim the balance owed to her. If the agreement provides for an indemnity, the actress may also be able to claim other losses, such as the amount of the fee she might otherwise have earned for another part that she turned down in order to work on 'Dark Steps'– after giving credit for the amount of any sums actually received by her from the producer of 'Dark Steps'. In the event there is no money available to pay, then the indemnity will be worthless.

Ultimately, warranties and indemnities are only as valuable as the underlying financial worth of those who stand behind them.

25.26   In certain circumstances, insurance may be sought to cover liability under an indemnity. Inevitably the limits of indemnities may be subject to detailed negotiations whereby parties may seek to cap the possible extent of an indemnity to, perhaps, the maximum amount payable under the contract or to the maximum amount of a party's insurance cover or to some other formulation.

25.27   Remedies

Film contracts frequently include a provision that if a production company is in breach of any of its obligations the rights and remedies of an individual – such as an actress/actor or director – will be limited to the right to make a claim for damages and in no circumstances will the individual be entitled by reason of any such breach to restrain the distribution, exhibition, broadcasting, promotion or exploitation of the film. As a matter of English law, the right to claim an injunction – a restraining order – is a discretionary remedy that only a court can grant. Although the point is not yet believed to have been considered by an English court, it is doubtful that a judge would consider her/himself to be bound by an attempt to contractually restrict the grant of a discretionary remedy. Opinions taken from lawyers in both California and New York have, in the past, suggested the courts of those states might be inclined to a similar view. Nevertheless, inclusion of such a provision remains commonplace in film contracts and, indeed, in other entertainment contracts and is asserted by some lawyers as evidence of the parties' intentions in the event that a dispute was ever to come before the courts.

Example

Producer's sole and exclusive remedy for any breach of this Agreement by Company shall be money damages and in no event shall Producer be entitled to terminate or rescind this Agreement or to prevent the exercise of any of the Rights or any other right granted hereunder or to seek to apply for any form of injunctive or equitable relief against Company and/or the Rights and/or the Film.

25.28   Entire agreement

An entire agreement provision will usually be included in film contracts that will provide, in terms, that the agreement replaces, supersedes and cancels all previous arrangements between the parties and constitutes the entire agreement between the parties and that no variation of the agreement may be made unless in writing and signed by the parties. By including such a provision, the parties exclude the uncertainty that may otherwise be introduced into their relationship by admitting pre-contract email exchanges and other materials.

Example

This Agreement replaces supersedes and cancels all previous arrangements understandings representations or agreements between the parties whether oral or written. No variation of any of the terms or conditions hereof may be made unless such variation is agreed in writing and signed by each of the parties hereto

Even allowing for the inclusion of an entire agreement provision there are circumstances where additional terms may be implied into a contract even though they have not been specifically expressed; (see paragraph 24.2). The interplay between these two concepts is complex. If a dispute arises in which a filmmaker believes that a term should be implied into an agreement that includes an entire agreement provision then bespoke advice should be sought.

25.29   Governing law and dispute resolution

Filmmaking is an activity that frequently involves participants and intellectual property originating from various countries as well as the sourcing of finance, physical production and distribution. Typically, filmmakers will feel most comfortable when a contract is made subject to the law and governed by the courts of a country with which they have a genuine connection. However, that may not always make the most sense.

25.30   Deciding the most appropriate governing law and dispute resolution procedure for an agreement may become a battle of wills between those advising the contracting parties. There are no hard and fast rules. While no-one goes into an agreement contemplating a dispute, disputes may – and do – arise. Before deciding on which governing law should apply, some thought should be given to the court or other forum in which it is most appropriate for any dispute to be resolved:

•   Financing agreements will likely be governed by the law of the jurisdiction in which the provider of the finance is domiciled. Nevertheless, if the financier is domiciled in an off-shore tax haven such as the British Virgin Islands or Jersey, it may make more sense for the governing law and forum of jurisdiction to be the domicile of the borrower. It may be easier for a financier to enforce its rights against a borrower – and a film – using the laws and courts where the borrower is located and/or where the ultimate owner of the IP in the film is located.

- Agreements providing for the engagement by a filmmaker of the principal cast and crew may most effectively be governed by the law of the jurisdiction in which the principal producer is located. There may be situations where locals engaged solely to perform on location in a particular country should have their contracts governed by the law of that country.

- Agreements dealing with the provision of goods and services for a shoot may best be governed by the law of the jurisdiction in which the shoot is taking place, or, depending on the nature of the goods and services, the jurisdiction in which the provider of the goods or services is located.

Example

Equipment for a shoot taking place in Braganza, Portugal is supplied by a Spanish company that is located in Leon, Spain. The extras on the shoot and the local crew are all Portuguese. The agreement for the supply of the equipment is most appropriately governed by Spanish law; the contracts for the extras and crew may best be covered by Portuguese law.

- Distribution agreements and licences for exploitation will arguably be most easily enforced in the courts and pursuant to the laws of the country in which the exploitation is taking place. However, filmmakers and rights' owners in jurisdictions where there is established expertise in dealing with complex copyright and contractual issues with a media flavour will often not want to rely on what may be less well developed jurisprudence and expertise in countries where there is little in the way of precedent for addressing such disputes. In such cases, the parties may opt for the law and courts of a jurisdiction where the experience and expertise in dealing with media disputes is well developed.

- The courts of one jurisdiction may be required to apply the law of a second jurisdiction. As and when this does occur external input by lawyers from the second jurisdiction will be required – which can become messy and expensive.

- An agreement may provide for the appointment of an independent mediator. Mediation is an efficient method of resolving disputes where the mutual will of the parties is to resolve a dispute and is often a preferred way of so doing. However, where there are entrenched positions mediation may simply not work.

- The Independent Film and Television Alliance (**IFTA**) provides an arbitration service specialising in the film and television industries. Its procedures are relatively straightforward and its established panel of arbitrators comprises experienced film and television lawyers. International arbitrators are accustomed to working on disputes that may involve consideration of the laws of more than one jurisdiction. Arbitration using the IFTA procedure may often be quicker and simpler than using the courts – particularly with regard to disputes that concern copyrights and technical subjects such as royalty computations and accounting procedures, disputes over the delivery materials, credits and so on. More details may be found at http://www.ifta-online.org/ifta-arbitration The panel currently includes arbitrators from nineteen countries http://www.ifta-online.org/ifta-panel-arbitrators

25.31   Signed and dated

Agreements should be dated and where possible signed. Many contemporary agreements are signed in different locations and the signature pages scanned to the other parties so that original 'wet ink' signatures do not necessarily appear on the same physical page. This is a valid practice. Agreements may be valid even if not actually signed; see examples at paragraphs 24.1, 24.3, 24.15 and 24.16. There are also available a number of services that provide for electronic signature of documents. Leading providers include DocuSign https://www.docusign.co.uk/learn/how-electronically-sign-document and eversign https://eversign.com/ Nevertheless, an assignment of copyright or an agreement that includes an assignment of copyright must be signed by the party transferring the copyright in order to be enforceable.

CONTRACTING THE TEAM

26   Introduction

26.1   Experience demonstrates that no two deals are identical. Every contract will have certain specific requirements. Nevertheless, the following suggestions may be helpful to bear in mind when negotiating the principal deal points with various of the contributors identified below. The matters set out in the following sections are not intended to be a comprehensive statement of every matter that requires to be addressed in each species of the contracts considered – but a guide to the key issues.

26.2   In addition to the particular matters covered in the following sections, depending on the nature of the contract, most, if not all, of the general provisions described at section 25 ought to be included in agreements for each of the team. Specific requirements for a composer's contract are addressed at paragraphs 13.11-13.13.

26.3   The forms of agreement included in the Appendices are varied in length and complexity and therefore do not necessarily include each and every provision described at sections 27-36.

27   Writer

27.1   The principal provisions for inclusion in a writer's agreement may include:

(a)   determining how many drafts, revisions and polishes of a screenplay are required and the language in which the screenplay is to be written;

(b)   structuring a timeline for delivery of each of the drafts, revisions and polishes by the writer and their review by the filmmaker. The writer's other commitments will need to be taken into account. The filmmaker may require the writer's exclusivity during key writing periods;

(c)   determining a payment schedule that balances (i) the need of the writer to be paid as s/he progresses with a project (ii) the project cash flow (iii) the filmmaker's need to hold back some payment pending delivery of an acceptable final shooting script;

(d)   confirmation by the writer that s/he is an independent contractor and will be solely responsible for her/his income tax and provide an indemnity to the filmmaker in that regard;

(e)   agreeing whether the writer should receive a share of the film's profits and, if so, the percentage of those profits and how they are to be calculated;

(f)   considering what requirements of the writer there may be as a project evolves, i.e. as a director and/or co-producers come in or drop out of the project;

(g)   ensuring that copyright in all of the writer's output is assigned outright to the filmmaker. The filmmaker will require free rein to do whatever may be required with the script and any other work created by the writer in the course of performing her/his obligations under the agreement;

(h)   determining the details of the writer's credit, including its size and position. Assuming the filmmaker seeks a waiver by the writer of her/his moral rights, the writer will need to ensure an appropriate credit obligation; (see section 8);

(i)   providing for what is to happen as a consequence of the writer's work being unacceptable and the right of the filmmaker to bring in other writers and the consequences arising;

(j)   providing for the possibility that the writer may need to work with other creatives on the project, i.e. the director, other writers – and how, and on what basis;

(k)   an option in favour of the filmmaker to engage the writer to work for the filmmaker on any prequel, sequel, remake or spin-off project and the principal terms to apply;

(l)   whether it is necessary to restrict the writer from working on directly competing projects – even for a limited time period – and, if so, on what terms;

(m)   arrangements for and payment/reimbursement of travel, subsistence and accommodation costs as necessary;

(n)   use of writer's (approved) name, likeness and biography in connection with the promotion, marketing, advertising and distribution of the project;

(o)   provision to the writer of DVDs or other copies of the finished film;

(p)   invitations to premieres and other promotional events and activities;

(q)   termination provision with specified consequences.

27.2   The general matters addressed at section 25 will also need to be included in a writer's agreement. An example of a writer's agreement is to be found at Appendix 8.

28   Director

28.1   Principal provisions for inclusion in a director's agreement may include the following:

(a)   Defining the extent of the director's commitment to the project as it may be required during each of pre-production, principal photography and post-production. In particular, filmmakers may want a director's input on the script from an early stage.

(b)   The director may seek a pay-or-play provision; this will require a filmmaker to guarantee a payment to the director in order that the director clears his schedule of other commitments for a given period so as to be able to start work once the producer has finished financing the film and made the necessary arrangements to start pre-production. The payment so guaranteed will be made even if, through no fault of her/his own, the director is subsequently released from the contract. Examples where this might happen include: failure by the filmmaker to raise all of the finance for the film so that it is not made at all or, perhaps, where financiers insist on a different director being engaged as a condition of putting up their investment.

(c)   The filmmaker may require a 'first call' entitlement. During a given pre-agreed period, the filmmaker will have first call on the director's services. The director will be contractually bound to turn down any other offers of work that require the director's services to be provided during the period when the filmmaker has first call, (unless otherwise agreed by the filmmaker).

(d)   The director's involvement in casting.

(e)   The extent of the director's input required in preparing the budget, final shooting script and the shooting schedule.

(f)   The obligation to direct the film to the best of her/his ability in accordance with the script and as per the agreed budget and to deliver a cut of the film in an agreed format to a given location by a particular date.

(g)   The extent of any creative or other approvals that the director may require and any cutting rights. Producers will typically deny a director final cutting rights. This is a privilege that tends to be restricted to well-established name directors. As a general rule, experienced financiers and producers will not agree to a director having 'final cut'.

(h)   The extent of the requirement of a director to assist in promoting the film, attend premieres, festivals, interviews and events.

(i)   The right of a filmmaker to suspend the director where there is a breach of contract and the consequences arising.

(j)   The right of the filmmaker to take out life and other insurance during the term of the director's engagement.

28.2   Many of the requirements that a filmmaker has of a writer will apply equally to a director. When including the following provisions in a director's agreement, the language employed in a writer's agreement may need adapting to address the specifics of a director's engagement and may include each of the provisions referred to at the following sub-paragraphs of paragraph 27:

(c)   payment;

(d)   independent contractor;

(e)   profit shares;

(f)   ongoing requirements;

(g)   assignment of copyright;

(h)   credit;

(j)   collaborating with other creatives;

(k)   options for sequels/other projects;

(l)   restrictions regarding competing projects; (m) reimbursement of expenses; (n) use of name and likeness;

(o)   provision of DVDs;

(p)   promotional activities;

(q)   termination provision.

28.3   A producer may need to have some regard to the director's moral right of integrity notwithstanding it will likely be the producer who will want to have approval over the final cut; also see section 8.

An example of a director's agreement is at Appendix 9. This example is in loan-out form. See section 36 for a discussion of loan-out agreements.

29   Producer

29.1   The primary obligation of an individual producer will be to take overall responsibility for managing the production of a project on budget and to deliver the finished film to a specific location by a designated date. A production company will engage one or more individual producers for a film. The obligations that are considered in this section exclude those accorded credits as 'executive producers' and others known as 'producers'. There are those who may play no active part in the physical production of the film, but who have been accorded a producer or an executive producer credit by virtue of their investment in the film or for some other reason.

29.2   In addition to the general contractual requirements discussed at sections 24 and 25, provisions equivalent to many of those included in each of the writer's and the director's agreements will likely be required. When including the following provisions, the language employed in the writer's and director's agreements may need adapting to address the specifics of a producer's engagement. A producer's agreement will likely need to include some or most of the following:

- provisions equivalent to those mentioned at the following sub-paragraphs of paragraph 27:

    (c)   payment;

    (d)   independent contractor;

    (e)   profit shares;

    (f)   ongoing requirements;

    (g)   assignment of copyright;

    (h)   credit;

    (j)   collaborating with other creatives;

    (k)   options for sequels/other projects;

    (l)   competing projects;

    (m)   reimbursement of expenses;

    (n)   use of name and likeness;

    (o)   provision of DVDs;

    (p)   promotional activities;

    (q)   termination provision.

- provisions equivalent to those mentioned at the following sub-paragraphs of paragraph 28.1:

    (a)   extent of commitment during project;

    (b)   pay-or-play;

    (c)   first call;

    (d)   casting;

    (e)   preparing the budget, shooting script and shooting schedule;

    (g)   approvals;

    (h)   promotional activity;

    (i)   suspension;

    (j)   life insurance.

An example of a producer's agreement is at Appendix 10.

30   Featured cast

30.1   The forms of agreement used for featured cast vary. Inevitably the scale and budget of a production and its principal media for exploitation – viz. theatrical or television – will inevitably affect the nature and extent of detail required. Featured cast may include cameos and voiceover artists. In addition to the matters covered at paragraph 30.2, regard should be made to the general contractual considerations discussed at sections 24 and 25 as well as those at the following sub-paragraphs of paragraph 27: (d) independent contractor; (e) profit shares; (n) use of name and likeness; (o) provision of DVDs; (p) promotional activities and 28.1 (j) life insurance.

30.2   Key factors to be considered for featured cast – referred to below as 'artist' will include:

(a)   the period during which the artist will be exclusively committed to the project – including rehearsal and principal photography. The amount of the artist's time to be spent on a project per day/week may be specified – including the time required for breaks/days off;

(b)   the granting by the artist of her/his performer's consent and all and any other rights in and to her/his contribution to the film to enable the filmmaker to exploit the film by all means in all media for the life of copyright of the film throughout the world;

(c)   commitment to premieres, festival appearances, interviews and other promotional activity and the payment/reimbursement of the expenses occasioned;

(d)   obligations to comply with the reasonable requests of the producer(s) and director;

(e)   remuneration and arrangements for and payment/reimbursement of travel, subsistence and accommodation as necessary. Depending on the status of the actor/ress there may be extensive rider requirements for particular food, accommodation and other perquisites;

(f)   pay-or-play/first call provisions; also see paragraphs 28.1(b) and (c);

(g)   credit requirements; see paragraph 27.1(h);

The Filmmakers' Legal Guide

(h)   wardrobe/hairdressing obligations (of the filmmaker to the artist);

(i)   provision of DVDs or other copies of the finished film;

(j)   insurance of the actor for the duration of her/his involvement in the production;

(k)   nudity/sex: agreements may include detailed provisions about the requirements for filming of scenes in which an artist is to be shown nude and/or performing sex or other acts of intimacy. Such detail may address when, where and how the scenes are to be filmed, who may be on set, the extent of activity and nudity portrayed, restrictions on how the footage may be used and on the use of stills taken from that footage;

(l)   use of doubles and stunt actors and the ability to dub the artist's voice in other languages;

(m)   depending on the status of the artist, approvals may be sought over a whole host of matters, including co-stars, the subject matter of sub-paragraph 30.2(k), choice of hair and make-up artists, use of name and likeness etc.;

(n)   an option in favour of the filmmaker for a commitment from the artist to prequels, sequels, further series;

(o)   the artist should render services to the best of her/his ability;

(p)   right of a filmmaker to suspend or terminate engagement of the artist where there is a breach of contract and its consequences;

(q)   lead artists may require 'favoured nations' status. In essence this means that a producer will be required to advise an artist of the financial and other terms offered to other leads in the film if those terms are better than those agreed to the 'original' artist and increase them to match those of the 'new' actor/actress.

Example

Zippo Media hires Darlene Delaney to appear as lead in its upcoming feature 'Ides of Doom' for which she is to be paid £25,000. She is also given £100 per diems and a return Premium Economy flight from London to Johannesburg where the film is being shot and a luxury room in a five star hotel. Darlene's contract includes a favoured nations clause that is applicable to the terms offered the male lead. Only after signing Darlene is Zippo able to secure Max Mydosh to be the male lead. Max's agent negotiates a fee of £30,000, £125 per diems, Business Class travel and a suite in a five star hotel. As a consequence of its favoured nations' obligations, Zippo will have to increase the benefits of Darlene's contract to match those of Max. Accordingly, Darlene, too, will be paid a fee of £30,000, £125 per diems and be provided with Business Class travel and a suite in a five star hotel.

An example of a performer's agreement that may form the basis of an agreement for featured cast members is at Appendix 11.

31   **Minor cast & extras**

Shorter forms of agreement may be used provided that, at the very least, the key elements described in the following paragraphs of section 30.2 (Featured Cast) are included

(a)   commitment period;

(b)   performer's consent;

(d)   comply with producer/director requests;

(e)   remuneration;

(g)   credit;

(h)   (possibly) wardrobe/hair;

(j)   insurance;

(k)   nudity etc;

(l)   doubles/stunts, and

(o)   standard of performance.

Depending on the circumstances, others of the provisions applicable to the featured cast may also be required of minor players.

A short form of performer's consent is at Appendix 12.

32   Presenter/talking head

A presenter provides similar services to that of an actor albeit that, in certain cases some, or perhaps much, of the presenter's contribution will not be scripted. Accordingly, the principal provisions of a presenter's agreement may be in a similar form to that of a featured actor. Account will need to be taken of the nature of the project and the specific circumstances of the presenter's involvement.

33   Interviewees

The key requirements regarding interview releases are discussed at paragraphs 12.3-12.6. In order to use an interview for all purposes intended by a filmmaker, a release in writing signed by the interviewee should be obtained. By agreeing to be filmed, an interviewee implicitly consents to the interview being used. A properly drafted written release addressing the filmmaker's requirements will put the matter beyond doubt.   Attention should also be focussed on an interviewee who provides photographs and other items that may be included on camera or otherwise used for the purposes of a film.

A form of interviewee release is at Appendix 13.

34   Children

34.1   In addition to ensuring that the contract itself contains the provisions addressed at sections 30 or 31, there are specific requirements in relation to engaging children to act in films. Where a filmmaker wants to film a child who is of compulsory school age the filmmaker is obliged by law to apply to the local council for the area in which the child lives to obtain a licence prior to filming. Failure to do so can lead to a filmmaker's prosecution and, if convicted, a fine and a maximum two year prison sentence. Individuals are considered to be of compulsory school age until the last Friday in June in the school year in which they reach sixteen, which means some sixteen-year-olds will require a licence.

34.2   Those of sixteen or over are able to give their own consent to participate in many circumstances. However, if the proposed participant is still at home and/or still in education, filmmakers are advised to obtain parental consent or consent from those who are *in loco parentis*.

34.3   The filmmaker will need to complete a form that will be supplied by the applicable local authority. At the time of writing, the completed application form must be accompanied by two identical passport sized photos of the child taken during the six months preceding the date of the application, a copy of the birth certificate of the child, a medical certificate or doctor's letter stating that the child is fit to undertake the performance, a copy of the agreement by which the child's services are contracted by the producer and a school permission letter. The place of performance or rehearsal must be approved by the local authority. A child may only work for eight hours a day including travel time.

34.4   Serious consideration should always be given as to whether a young person should be accompanied by a parent/guardian or chaperone. Experienced filmmakers will generally make this a contractual requirement – especially in circumstances where a child is particularly young. If a child with any kind of handicap is to be engaged, the relevant agencies must be contacted.

34.5   More detail about engaging children in films may be found at https://www.gov. uk/child-employment/performance-licences-for-children

35   Crew

35.1   Many low- and no-budget filmmakers will engage friends and ask for favours when hiring people to work behind the camera and to undertake other production roles. The best advice is that everyone who participates in the production of any film should sign at least a short form of letter of engagement, release or agreement confirming the basic terms of their respective arrangements and acknowledging that ownership of copyright and all other rights in the film belong to the filmmaker which said rights may be unconditionally exploited by the filmmaker and those deriving title from the filmmaker.

35.2   Irrespective that many crew members will not create original work subject to copyright protection, there are those who may and actually do. For example:

    (a)   the art department members who design props and sets will create copyright in their sketches, drawings and other artwork; design rights may attach to props and other physical objects created for a film;

    (b)   the director of photography may lay claim to a copyright in the images that he is responsible for shooting;

    (c)   a crew member drafted in to appear as an extra will have a performer's right.

35.3   Principal matters to address in a crew agreement will include the following:

    (a)   period of engagement;

    (b)   duties to be undertaken;

    (c)   remuneration;

    (d)   an assignment to the production company of copyright in all and any of the crew member's contribution and consent to use the same by all means and in all media for life of copyright in the film throughout the world;

    (e)   a warranty that the crew member is self-employed and an undertaking that s/he is personally responsible for payment of income tax on the payment made to him/her which is to be paid gross;

(f)   confidentiality;

(g)   governing law.

Regard may also be had to the general contractual requirements discussed at sections 24 and 25.

A form of crew agreement is at Appendix 14

35.4   The original copyright work of crew members who are full-time employees of a production company will vest in that production company. Nevertheless, it is worth ensuring that each of the matters mentioned at paragraph 35.3 are included in a company's employment agreements.

35.5   Filmmakers should note that employment law is itself a complex and technical field. This Guide does not address the law of employer and employee. Where filmmakers have any concerns about the detail of employment contracts, specialist advice from an employment lawyer or HR adviser should be sought.
.

36   Loan-out agreements and inducement letters

36.1   Many individuals – producers, directors, writers as well as performers and other crew members – may elect to provide their services through the medium of a loan-out company. In simple terms, a loan-out company is a limited company by which an individual is employed. Individuals may be advised to establish loan-out companies for tax reasons and/or to limit the extent of personal liability to which an individual may be exposed.

36.2   From a purely practical point of view, before engaging any personnel, a filmmaker should always ask the question whether the services will be provided personally or via a loan-out company and prepare the contract accordingly. Having asked the question and then prepared a tailored contract for an individual it is a time-consuming and irritating task then to have to convert it to a contract in favour of that individual's loan-out company that will also require an inducement letter to be drafted.

36.3   Where a filmmaker enters into an agreement with a loan-out company the following matters should be observed:

(a)   the loan-out company should warrant that it has an agreement in force with the individual creative/performer for her/his services and that the loan-out company therefore has the right to enter into an agreement with the filmmaker, and

(b)   either

(i)   the individual counter-signs the agreement and confirms, in terms, that in the event that the loan-out company is no longer able to provide the individual's services then the individual will provide those services directly,

or

(ii)   more usually, the individual will sign an inducement letter addressed by her/him to the filmmaker representing that the loan-out company has the right to provide her/his services to the filmmaker and that if the loan-out company is no longer able to provide the individual's services, then the individual will provide those services directly to the filmmaker and be personally responsible for performing them.

Example

The director's agreement at Appendix 9 is in loan-out format to which a form of inducement letter attached as a schedule. The inducement letter and loan-out language of the agreement may be adapted for use with other contributors who provide their services through a loan-out company; language equivalent to that of Clause 4.1 of the director's agreement at Appendix 9 should be included in the body of the contributor's agreement as follows:

Company shall provide the services of [Contributor] to take primary responsibility for performing all of the Company's obligations set out in this Agreement and shall procure that Contributor executes the Inducement Letter which Company shall deliver to Filmmaker upon execution of this Agreement.

CONTRACTING THE PRODUCTION

37   Chain-of-title

37.1   Introduction

The chain-of-title to a film comprises all of the agreements and other documents that, together, demonstrate that a filmmaker has acquired all of the rights required to produce and exploit a film.

37.2   Even the most modest of films made on the smallest of budgets likely comprises a host of elements for the inclusion of which a filmmaker needs to secure consents. The most effective way of doing this is for a filmmaker to ensure that as each new element of the film is added and each new member joins the team, the applicable provider/individual signs a formal contract or confirms the basis of her/his/their contribution by way of letter, release or other suitable document.

37.3   Importance

The crucial importance of chain-of-title is demonstrated by the following:

(a)   if made subject to a challenge, the filmmaker can show that the entitlement to exploit the film or the rights that have been made subject to challenge have been properly acquired or cleared by the filmmaker;

(b)   the ability of a filmmaker to satisfy an investor, distributor or a party subsequently seeking to acquire outright ownership of the film that the rights are clear so that the agreement to invest in, exploit or acquire the film will not be undermined by a third party claim.

37.4   The chain-of-title often starts with the agreement by which either a screenplay has been acquired or a screenwriter commissioned to write a screenplay. If the film is based on a pre-existing literary work the chain will start with the agreement by which the right has been acquired to commission a screenplay based on the pre-existing work. Remember that a limited company has a distinct legal personality which is separate from that of an individual, even if the individual is the founder and initial sole shareholder in the company. Accordingly, an individual establishing a limited company to be the vehicle for production of a film will need to formally assign to the company all and any rights s/he has created or acquired before the company has become involved in the production.

Unless the individual becomes an employee of the company, s/he will also need to put in place the appropriate contract(s) to cover contributions made once the company is up and running.

37.5   The chain continues with each of the agreements by which other rights are acquired (e.g. music) and personnel are engaged to provide input: producers, directors, lead talent, composers etc.

37.6   Review

Of particular importance is the need to continually review the completeness of the chain-of-title where (a) additional/alternative production companies become involved and/or (b) creatives come into a project and/or (c) additional investors/financiers make contributions in cash and/or in kind. Transfers of ownership of rights must also be properly documented. Each of these events requires the parties to confirm the details of the arrangements in writing and to set out clearly the particulars of ownership and other interests in the film, its copyright and in its shares of income and profit.

37.7   Maintaining the integrity of the rights in a finished film where different individuals and entities have made creative and other contributions can be challenging for a filmmaker unless each of these contributions is collected, by way of the appropriate contract, into a single rights-owning entity. Where different contributions have been made by different parties, the simplest solution is for each of these contributions, including the benefits under any agreements, to be assigned in writing into the rights-owning vehicle.

37.8   Keeping track of all of the chain-of-title agreements is an important administrative task. Filmmakers are advised to establish and maintain a complete file or series of files – in digital and/or physical form – of all of the agreements and other key documents evidencing the creation and acquisition of all rights and other contributions in and to a film as well as its financing and, subsequently, its sales and distribution. This will facilitate the ease with which any investor, distributor or other interested party may interrogate the chain-of-title.

37.9   Dissolved companies

If any one or other of the companies involved in the creation and/or ownership of rights in a film ceases to be involved with the film and it is proposed to dissolve that company, then, before dissolution, filmmakers must ensure that any rights that may have been created and/or vested in such a company are assigned in writing to the intended owners of the copyright in the finished film. Failing to do this will invariably lead to complex problems that are often difficult and potentially expensive to solve. For comments on the use of limited companies generally see section 52.

38 Development Agreements

38.1 Introduction

When two or more parties co-operate in the development of a project in advance of production or with a view to raising production finance, there are a number of matters that should be clearly agreed at the beginning of the parties' dealings. Some of the key issues are considered in this section.

38.2 Special purpose vehicles

The parties may establish a 'special purpose vehicle' (**SPV**) in the form of a limited liability company that is intended to own the rights in the film and which develops the project and ultimately produces the film. There are a number of matters to consider before establishing an SPV. Proper thought requires to be given to the respective shareholdings to be allotted to each of the developing parties and to how and by whom the SPV is to be managed and controlled. The SPV's decision-making process on all creative, commercial and financial matters needs to be agreed and clearly set out either in a shareholders' agreement or in the development agreement itself. Provision should also be made to address the respective roles and obligations of each of the parties participating in the SPV. For additional considerations relating to the use of a limited company in which to house rights or via which to undertake a production see section 52.

38.3 Whether or not an SPV is necessary in the early stages of a project may depend on the nature and scale of the project, the stage reached in its development, the respective standing – and legal status – of the collaborating parties and even the amount of funding available for seed development. In the event that the parties decide to proceed without an SPV, the development agreement should, as a minimum, address the matters discussed in the rest of this section.

38.4 Ownership of rights

One or other of the parties (**Producer 1**) may already have acquired an option to an existing literary work. The collaborating parties may wish collectively to hire a screenwriter to write the screenplay. Agreement will need to be reached as to the basis upon which Producer 1 continues to deal with the owner of the underlying rights and whether, for example, the other party (**Producer 2**) should acquire a legal interest in the option.

38.5   Development funding

Producer 1 may already have spent money on acquiring the option and in some initial development work – perhaps a draft of the screenplay that needs more work and perhaps input from another writer. That expenditure and all and any subsequent expenditure by each of Producer 1 and Producer 2 should be provided for. The parties may agree a development budget and commit to the amount each is to make available and how these sums are to be reimbursed or otherwise dealt with once the film is financed.

38.6   Development work

Typically, during the development period, the length of which will, too, be a matter for agreement, the parties will aim to do some or all of the following: commission a bankable script, develop a full-blown budget and a shooting schedule, attach a director and other key crew and talent – especially lead actors – identify locations and also put together a financing structure (often referred to as a 'finance plan') and strategy. In the course of taking these steps costs may be incurred as other parties become interested in the project. Each of these processes and relationships should be carefully documented and provided for, not only in the development agreement itself, but also in the arrangements negotiated with each of the other parties who become involved in the project.

38.7   A framework may also be agreed between the parties for their continued development of the project and to establish the extent of the further financial commitments each may be committed to make in the event that certain milestones are achieved. Trigger provisions may also be included for each party to terminate its respective involvement in the event that given milestones are not achieved.

38.8   The development agreement should provide for what is to happen in the event that one or more of the parties no longer wishes to proceed, leaving the other(s) to continue. In the example at paragraph 38.4, it may be that after a couple of years and having invested cash and resource, Producer 2 decides to leave the project and enable Producer 1 to continue on its own. Perhaps there is an additional payment to be made to extend an option on the underlying rights to which Producer 2 does not wish to contribute. In dealing with what is to happen in the event that Producer 1 succeeds in financing the project, Producer 2 will want to ensure that its position is protected. It may be appropriate for Producer 2 to be paid a premium or interest on monies advanced by Producer 2 (but arguably not both). Consideration will also be needed to determine to whom the rights to 'existing' development work may be assigned and on what basis. In addition to a screenplay, there may be other of the elements as described at paragraph 38.6 to be assigned or novated.

38.9   Turnaround

A project will be in 'turnaround' where some or all of those responsible for acquiring rights and commencing the development of a film project elect not to continue, and enable the project to be acquired by others on the basis of a predetermined formula. Turnaround provisions may be included in various species of contract including, for example, screenplay options where the option is not exercised but where the grantor wishes to acquire the benefits of a grantee's development work.

Examples

Continuing with the example at 38.4, an applicable turnaround provision in the termination agreement signed by Producer 1 with Producer 2 could be:

1   *Notwithstanding termination of the co-production agreement, Producer 1 shall have the right to continue to seek production finance and shall have an exclusive option to purchase all of Producer 2's rights in the Project.*

2   *If at any time after the date of this Agreement Producer 1 succeeds in raising production finance it shall notify Producer 2 in writing of the date upon which Producer 1 may be in receipt of sufficient funds to pay to Producer 2 the sum of £25,000 being a full reimbursement of Producer 2's investment in the Project together with simple interest thereon from the date of this agreement to the date of payment calculated at a rate of 3% above Barclays Bank Base Rate for the time being in force (**Transfer Payment**).*

3   *Upon receipt of the Transfer Payment Producer 2 shall execute an assignment of all of its right title and interest in the Project to Producer 1 or as Producer 1 may direct.*

4   *Producer 1 shall procure that:*

(a)   *Producer 2 [may nominate one of its principals to] [shall] receive an executive producer credit in the opening credits of the finished Film;*

(b)   *Producer 2 shall be accounted for and be paid one per cent of the Net Profits of the Film (as the term 'Net Profits' is defined in the principal finance and production agreements for the Film) and that Producer 2 shall be a direct beneficiary of the CAMA for the Film.*

39   Film finance

39.1   The nature of the arrangements by which one party will put up money to fund a film's budget or even part of it are infinite. Some examples include the following. Many, if not most, films will require more than one and often several sources of funding, of which the following are examples:

(a)   loans or gifts from family and friends;

(b)   angel investment;

(c)   grants by recognised film funding bodies;

(d)   individuals investing in the production and/or rights-owning company(ies) for which those individuals will be issued shares;

(e)   investment in a production company with a slate of films under the SEIS/EIS schemes;

(f)   development funds that may become repayable once the production budget has been raised;

(g)   reimbursement of the production tax credit on UK spend;

(h)   arrangements that require production spend to be made in a particular territory to obtain tax credits or other benefits offered to those who produce in that territory;

(i)   tax driven arrangements that may involve off-shore structures;

(j)   cash provided by way of a personal or commercial loan to a filmmaker or production company to be repaid from budget funds raised and/or receipts or profits;

(k)   equity investment in a film with repayment from receipts and a share of the back end;

(l)   pre-sales that generate recoupable advances from distributors or broadcasters that involve the granting to them of certain rights of exploitation in the film;

(m)   crowd-funding;

(n)   deferrals of fees by individual participants or those providing services and/or supplies to the filmmaker in return for paying what is otherwise due from the receipts of the film and/or a share in the producer's share of net profit from exploitation of the film; deferrals may include a filmmaker's own entitlement to a producer fee;

(o)   investment from providers of post-production services;

(p)   provision of gap finance on a last-in and first-out basis.

Quite apart from the above, filmmakers will, themselves, often make cash investments into their own films.

39.2   Complex arrangements may need to be made as between the various investors and others providing funding in cash and/or in kind in order to determine their place in the 'waterfall' of income generated by a film's sale. Investors may become parties to a CAMA; (see paragraph 48.5). Although this Guide does not deal with the intricacies of film finance, some general comments about investment agreements follow at section 40. For the purposes of this discussion the terms 'investor' and 'investment' are used but the terms may equally refer to other categories of those who make funding available for a film.

39.3   Since publication of the first edition of the Guide, the rules concerning SEIS/EIS investment into film have been materially changed. By way of the briefest of summaries, these schemes may no longer be used for companies established for a single project but only for those set up to engage in the business of developing and/or producing and/or exploiting a slate of films.

40   **Finance agreements and charges**

40.1   General

In its simplest form, an agreement to finance a film will be put in place between the party putting up the money and the filmmaker – which may be an individual or a production company. Regard should be had to the general requirements for a contract discussed at sections 24 and 25.

40.2   Key provisions

The key provisions in an investment agreement should include:

(a)   recitals setting out the background to the arrangement;

(b)   the amount of money being made available;

(c)   when and how the money is to be released to the filmmaker – including details of any instalment dates and/or triggers;

(d)   details of any conditions precedent to be met before funds are released. Perhaps the investment has been made on the basis that a given director is to be hired and release of funds is made subject to the director signing his contract with the filmmaker. Perhaps, too, the investment is made subject to a given level of pre-sales being reached. The bigger the investment the more the number of likely conditions precedent or 'CPs';

(e)   filmmaker's warranties and representations as to the amount of the film's budget and other elements of the production;

(f)   how and when the investment is to be repaid;

(g)   whether the investment is to bear interest or a premium and, if so, at what rate and how and when it is to be accounted for and paid;

(h)   what, if any, share of producer's net receipts are to be paid to the investor and where in the payment waterfall that share will be placed;

(i)   any credit entitlement.

A simple form of investor agreement is at Appendix 16.

40.3 Payment waterfall

The payment waterfall will be reflected in a formal schedule, also termed a 'recoupment schedule' that will set out the order in which each of those contributing to the financing of the film, directly or indirectly, and each of the net profit participants will be paid from the proceeds of a film. There are no hard and fast rules as to the order in which payments will be made from a film's income. The more participants there are the more complex the negotiations may become.

Example

1. *To the collection manager appointed to collect and administer such receipts and expenses in accordance with the CAMA for the Film in payment for its fee and set up cost.*

2. *To sales agent in payment for Marketing and Distribution Expenses up to £7,500, including marketing cost in the first market.*

3. *To sales agent in payment of its Sales Commission calculated at 15% of all receipts throughout the world.*

4. *To Producer 1 in recoupment of its payment of Additional Funding of Budget a sum not to exceed £40,000.*

5. *To Producer 1 and Producer 2, in recoupment of their respective contributions to the Budget, up to 100% of such sum.*

6. *To sales agent in payment of its remaining Marketing Costs.*

7. *To all deferrals as follows and in such waterfall order:*

   First, pari passu, Director: £10,000, Producer: £15,000 and Writer: £5,000

   Second, all the actors as below pari passu

   (i)   Actor 1 £7,500

(ii)   *Actor 2 £6,000*

(iii)   *Actor 3 £5,000*

(iv)   *Actor 4 £4,000*

(v)   *Actor 5 £4,000*

(vi)   *Actor 6 £3,000*

8.   *All further sums shall be deemed net profit and shall be divided as follows:*

     60% to Producer 1

     40% to Producer 2

40.4   Escrow

Requirements may be made to put money into 'escrow'. An escrow account is one in which funds will be held by the escrow holder subject to designated terms and conditions. Once the conditions are satisfied the escrow holder may release the funds to the payee.

Example

Enchanted Productions is developing a feature film budgeted at £1.2m. Gulliver Finance has agreed, in principle, to put up half the budget. On the strength of the script and the proposed investment, award-wining Hollywood director, Johnny C Lately, signs an agreement to direct the film provided that:

(a)   *the rest of the budget is available in cleared funds within 90 days of his signature, and*

(b)   *the first half of his agreed fee of £40,000 is paid to him unconditionally no later than 100 days after the date of his signature.*

With the director's commitment made in principle, Offramp, a gap funder agrees to make up the rest of the budget; it puts its contribution into escrow at a bank. Enchanted is authorised by Offramp to draw down the gap payment in three tranches subject to Enchanted procuring that Gulliver pays its contribution into the account within 30 days of the deposit being made by Offramp. Provided Gulliver complies with this condition, Offramp's payment may be released by the bank from escrow in the tranches agreed between Offramp and Enchanted. Enchanted will then be in a position to make the first payment of Lately's fee.

40.5   Charges

Some investors will look to secure their investment by way of a charge over the assets of the production company and/or the copyright and other rights in the film and/or the income streams flowing from exploitation of the film. A charge over a production company's assets operates in a similar way to the mortgage of a residential property. In the charge document, the production company will grant a security interest in favour of the investor. The investor's investment in the film therefore becomes protected.

40.6   Assuming the production company is registered as a limited company or as a limited liability partnership in England & Wales, any charge may be registered against that production company at Companies House. It means that unless permitted by the terms of the charge or otherwise agreed by the investor, the production company will not be able to deal with the rights in the film without the charge-holder's consent. A charge of this type will usually also attach to the materials comprising the film as well as the income streams to be derived by the production company from its exploitation of the film. As a consequence, the rights in a film made subject to such a charge will be subject to the investor's interest until such time as the terms of the investment agreement have been satisfied that will enable the charge to be released.

40.7   Where there is a default by a filmmaker in performing obligations that are secured by a charge, or the charge itself, depending on the way the charge is drafted, it will be possible for the investor to take over the copyright and other rights in a film and to deal with them accordingly.

40.8   Deed of priorities/inter-party agreement

Where there are two or more investors in a film – whether or not seeking charges – negotiations between each of them will be necessary to establish the priority of their respective investments. The resulting arrangements will be documented in what is generally known as either a deed of priorities or an inter-party agreement.

40.9   For tutorials and information about film finance there are a number of dedicated resources. Good starting points for UK based filmmakers include:

https://www.bfi.org.uk/sources-funding-uk/sources-funding-uk-filmmaker

http://www.weareukfilm.com/sources-of-funding

41   Commissioning agreements

41.1   Introduction

In its most frequently used sense in the film and TV industries, the term 'commissioning agreement' will refer to an agreement by which a television broadcaster will commission a production company to produce programmes or films for television broadcast. The term is also used in a more general sense to refer to an agreement by which one party commissions another to undertake work on its behalf.

41.2   Commissioning copyright work

The contractual framework for the commissioning of a work that includes copyright or other species of IP may include most or all of the following:

(a)   the general principles for constructing a contract discussed at sections 24 and 25 will apply;

(b)   a clear description and, where applicable, a properly drawn specification of the work that is required as well as a statement of the standard to which the work is to be undertaken;

(c)   from the commissioner's point of view the agreement should include an assignment to the commissioner of any copyright that the contractor may create for the life of copyright of that work for use by the commissioner throughout the world. Reference is made to the matters discussed at paragraphs 6.2-6.3;

(d)   if there is a reason why copyright may not be assigned, then the agreed terms of the licence that will apply should take into account the matters discussed at paragraphs 6.5-6.8;

(e)   the commissioned contractor must, in terms, warrant that any copyright work is original. If the contractor is using others to provide input on the project then it should further warrant that the work being provided to the commissioner is being undertaken by full-time employees. If, in turn, the contractor is using outside sub-contractors, the contractor should warrant that the sub-contractors have each assigned or will assign all of the copyright in all of the work they each create to the contractor so that, in turn, it may assign copyright in that work through to the filmmaker;

(f)   a timeline for delivery with milestones where applicable;

(g)   a payment schedule;

(h)   details of the materials required to be delivered and the media via which they are to be delivered;

(i)   credit provisions;

(j)   change request procedure – if applicable; see, for example, the comments at paragraph 22.7;

(k)   a provision for the reimbursement of expenses.

An example of a short form commissioning agreement is at Appendix 17.

41.3   The requirements for commissioning music are discussed at paragraphs 13.11-13.13.

41.4   The key principles for contracting with a post-production house to work on a film are no different to those for commissioning any other party. The discussion in relation to VFX at paragraphs 22.5-22.7 applies.

41.5   Broadcaster commissions

The requirements for a filmmaker commissioned by the principal UK broadcasters to produce and deliver programming are set out in some considerable detail on their respective websites. Many of the detailed requirements of the broadcasters, including those that refer to technical standards, clearances, health & safety and so on, are given contractual force by the framework agreements which networks will require production companies to enter. Outside of these detailed requirements, the main provisions of a broadcaster's commission will include the matters discussed at paragraph 41.2 as well as those addressed at section 42 in relation to production agreements.

41.6   The particular requirements of the principal UK networks may be accessed via the following URLs:

http://greenlight.broadcastnow.co.uk/commissioning-editors

http://www.bbc.co.uk/commissioning/

http://www.bbc.co.uk/commissioning/tv

http://www.itv.com/commissioning

http://www.channel4.com/info/commissioning/4producers

http://about.channel5.com/programme-production/

http://www.sky.com/shop/__PDF/3D/Sky_3D_Production_Pack_Apr_2011_v2.pdf

41.7   Care must be taken when reviewing network commissioning arrangements to the extent that production and delivery requirements, provisions as to rights and the like may be contained in a number of resources and documents – all of which may apply to the subject matter of particular commissions.

42   Production agreements

42.1   Introduction

The term production agreement may be used to mean different things at different times. Broadcast commissioning agreements (see paragraphs 41.5-41.7), production services agreements (see section 43) and co-production agreements (see section 44) are all species of production agreements. One production company may appoint another to assist in making and delivering a film; the agreement by which it does so may be called a production agreement.

42.2   Key characteristics

The key characteristics of a typical 'production agreement' will require the producer to produce the film within a framework which will likely include the following elements:

(a)   the general principles for constructing a contract discussed at sections 24 and 25;

(b)   the film/programme(s) will be described and/or reference made to specific scripts and/or other elements as may be applicable;

(c)   ownership and use of the copyright requires to be addressed; if copyright is not to be assigned then terms of the licence that will apply should take into account the discussion at paragraphs 6.5-6.8;

(d)   the production company must warrant that, subject to any licence that it is granted by the party commissioning it to use any underlying copyright work, all of the work created by the production company during the production term will be original;

(e)   the production company should further warrant that:

         (i)   either the work is being undertaken by full-time employees (see paragraphs 5.5-5.8), and/or

         (ii)   if the production company is using freelancers and/or other outside contractors, that all of these freelancers and contractors have assigned or will assign all of the copyright in all of the work they each create to the production company. This will enable the production company, in turn, to assign copyright in the film to the party who has commissioned the production company; see paragraphs 5.9, 6.2-6.6 and 41.2(e);

Of course, it is possible that a production company will use a mix of full-time employees and freelancers.

(f)   provisions will be required to determine agreement to:

*   a detailed production budget;

*   pre-production, shooting and post-production schedules;

*   timeline for delivery;

*   detailed cash flow and payment schedules.

(g)   a schedule of the materials required to be delivered and the media via which they are to be delivered with applicable technical specifications;

(h)   credit provisions;

(i)   payment, including any net profit participation;

(j)   other detailed requirements will depend on the nature of the film or programme – whether it is drama, musical, documentary or animation. The producer will necessarily need to enter into contracts with a whole range of personnel to which various of the agreements and matters covered elsewhere in this Guide will apply.

43   Production services agreements

43.1   Purpose

Filmmakers, particularly producers of theatrical features or large scale television programming, may undertake the physical production of a film using a company that is specifically incorporated for that purpose and which stands apart from the entity that owns the rights in the project. The arrangements between the two will be set out in a production services agreement (**PSA**) – which may also be referred to as a production agreement. The primary purpose for separating the functions of production from rights ownership is to ring-fence the IP rights in the film against any legal liabilities that might arise during and as a consequence of production. Contracts with cast, crew as well as the providers of goods and other services for a film may also be made by the production services company (**PSC**).

43.2   Licence of rights

The PSA will contain a licence from the rights owner (**RO**) to the PSC granting to it the right to produce the film. In return the PSC will assign to the RO ownership of the copyright and other IP it creates or acquires in the film it produces or in any of its underlying elements.

43.3   Principal provisions

The PSA may also include provisions that deal with cash-flowing the budget, a timeline for the various stages of pre-production, production, post-production and delivery of the finished film. The delivery schedule itself will include a list of the materials required to be delivered by the PSC to the RO upon completion of the film. A PSA will also be used where an outside producer is brought in to make a film for which the PSA effectively constitutes an agreement for the commissioning of the production and delivery of a finished film based on a script and in accordance with the terms of a designated budget.

43.4   Once a production has been completed and the copyright and all other IP assigned to the RO, the PSC may be wound-up and thereafter dissolved.

43.5   In addition to provisions that address the formal commissioning of the PSC as referred to at paragraphs 43.1-43.3, the principles explained at section 42 will apply. The general provisions of sections 24 and 25 will be relevant as will various of the provisions equivalent to those required for an individual producer that are applicable and which are discussed at section 29.

44   Co-production agreements and international treaties

44.1   Concept

At its simplest, the term 'co-production agreement' (or 'co-pro') denotes an agreement between two or more filmmakers who contract to produce a film together. In such an agreement, key provisions will address:

(a)   the principal responsibilities and obligations of each producer during the development and production process;

(b)   responsibility for creative and other decision making;

(c)   ownership and control of the rights in the finished film;

(d)   financial contributions and profit sharing arrangements;

(e)   location and process of principal photography and post-production;

(f)   marketing, sales and distribution process.

In negotiating the detailed provisions of a co-production agreement, regard may be had to the general principles and considerations described at sections 24, 25 and 42. The most basic form of 'co-production' is the collaboration between two or more parties on a low/no-budget film of which one may be the writer, one the director and a third the producer.

A simple form of such a collaboration which is suitable for entry level producers is at Appendix 18.

44.2   International co-productions

Co-productions may be undertaken between filmmakers located in different countries. Even though this may be the case, qualifying as a British film under one of the UK's official co-production treaties provides a number of advantages including eligibility to apply to the BFI Film Fund and also for Film Tax Relief (**FTR**); (see section 45). More details of certification for FTR as a co-production may be found at http://www.bfi.org.uk/film-industry/british-certification-tax-relief/co-production

44.3   UK bilateral co-production treaties

The United Kingdom has current co-production treaties with the following:

- Australia
- Brazil
- Canada
- China
- China (TV)
- France
- India
- Israel
- Jamaica
- Morocco
- New Zealand
- Occupied Palestinian Territories
- South Africa
- South Africa (TV)

44.4   European Convention on Cinematographic Co-production

The UK is one of many countries that is a signatory to the European Convention on Cinematographic Co-production (**ECCC**).   More information about this convention may be found on the Council of Europe website http://conventions. coe.int/Treaty/Commun/QueVoulezVous.asp?NT=147&CL=ENG   This treaty provides an umbrella arrangement under which it is possible for any two or more producers from signatory countries to collaborate and take advantage of the tax and other benefits that may be available in their respective home territories.

44.5   At the time of writing it was not thought that Brexit would have any effect on the legal ability of UK companies to contract with companies from other ECCC countries.

45   Film tax credits

45.1   General

It is not within the ambit of this Guide to provide an in depth analysis of film financing and tax credits. Filmmakers are advised to engage specialist film accountants and/or tax advisers for that purpose.

45.2   Film Tax Relief

Filmmakers working in the UK should be aware of the existence of Film Tax Relief (**FTR**) or Film Tax Credits (**FTC**) introduced in April 2007 by the Government. This tax concession has been a significant driver for investment in the British Film Industry. For a film to qualify for FTR/FTC it must comply with the following requirements:

(a)   it must qualify as a British film; in order to be British, a film must either pass the cultural test or qualify as an official co-production (see paragraph 45.3). Cultural Test guidelines may be found at http://www. bfi.org.uk/sites/bfi.org.uk/files/downloads/bfi-revised-cultural-test-for-film-guidance-notes-2015-03.pdf

(b)   the film must be intended for theatrical release;

(c)   films, including those made under official co-production treaties, must reach a minimum UK spend requirement of 25% of the film's budget;

(d)   tax relief is available on qualifying UK production expenditure (a) for films with a total core expenditure of £20 million or less, the film production company (**FPC**) can claim a cash rebate of up to 25% of UK qualifying film production expenditure; (b) for films with a core expenditure of more than £20 million, the FPC can claim a cash rebate of up to 25% of the first £20 million of qualifying UK expenditure, with the remaining qualifying UK expenditure receiving a 20% tax credit;

(e)   the FPC needs to be within the UK corporation tax net;

(f)   the FPC must be incorporated before the start of principal photography and be responsible for pre-production, principal photography, and post; it must also be actively involved in planning and decision making with regard to the film and be directly responsible for negotiating the contracts and paying for the rights comprising the film.

More information may be found at http://britishfilmcommission.org.uk/plan-your-production/tax-reliefs/

45.3   To qualify as an official co-production, a film must be made pursuant to:

(a)   one of the UK's official bilateral co-production agreements (see paragraphs 44.3); or

(b)   The European Convention on Cinematographic Convention (see paragraph 44.4).

45.4   Other tax reliefs

Additional information with regard to the relief for High End television production and animation may be found at https://www.bfi.org.uk/film-industry/british-certification-tax-relief/about-tax-relief#television-animation

45.5   There are innumerable tax credits, reliefs and incentives offered in a whole range of territories, regions and countries (**Territories**) in various parts of the world. These reliefs and benefits are generally dependent on either shooting and/or spending significant percentages of production budgets in such Territories. It is beyond the scope of the Guide to analyse them. Some information on comparable reliefs may be found using the following resources:

https://nofilmschool.com/2016/07/film-production-incentives-tax-incentives-movie-rebates

https://www.mazars.com/Home/News/Our-publications/Surveys-and-studies/Study-of-tax-systems-and-tv-and-film-production

46   Insurances

46.1   General

Filmmakers should consider taking out various species of insurance in connection with their productions. Inevitably the scale of a production and the size of its budget will dictate the nature and extent of cover that will be sought and obtained. Working with a broker experienced in arranging insurance in the film and television industries will enable a filmmaker to identify and obtain suitable policies that are tailored for the particular requirements of a production.

46.2   Public liability insurance

Public liability insurance will cover the filmmaker for liabilities incurred to any third party during the course of production. The risks to be covered will necessarily need to be evaluated on a case-by-case basis. In addition to protecting the cast and crew from the consequences of accidents or death occurring during production, filmmakers take out public liability cover in the event of injuries or death caused to members of the public as well as damage to property.

46.3   A production company that is engaged in ongoing productions should ensure that it has suitable cover for its employees as well as public liability insurance. Particular attention should be paid to the need to ensure that cast and crew are fully covered for accidents or death.

46.4   Completion bonds/guarantees

Completion bonds or completion guarantees (**Bond(s)**) will generally be required by those financing or underwriting the budgeted cost of larger scale productions. A Bond is, in effect, an insurance policy stipulating that if a project runs over budget, the completion guarantor will provide funds to complete the production. The cost of a Bond will generally be within the range of 1.5%-2.5% of a film's budget. Prior to issuing a Bond, the provider will review the script, the shooting schedule and the budget for the production. The object of the review is to ascertain whether the project is feasible. Feasibility will not only involve assessing whether the quantum of the budget is realistic but also whether the designated producers and director are sufficiently expert and experienced to be able to deliver the project in accordance with the budget and within the projected time frame. The Bond company will then set out its terms and any conditions attached. One of the leading providers of Bonds is Film

Finances, from whose website more may be learned; http://www.filmfinances. com

46.5   Errors and omissions

Filmmakers will often be required to obtain an Errors & Omissions policy (**E&O**) before distributors will finalise an agreement to exploit a film. E&O cover will also be required by television networks. E&O insurance will provide an indemnity against claims that may arise from the content of a production that may include copyright infringement, defamation, malicious falsehood and infringement of a title, slogan, or trade mark.

46.6   Larger organisations may have E&O insurance in place that covers all of the films they distribute, exhibit or broadcast but will need filmmakers to provide evidence that they have taken all reasonable steps to check and clear all of the third party content included in a film. That content will include underlying literary rights, the performances and other creative elements provided by all of the contributors to the film, third party clips, stills, musical compositions and sound recordings. Production lawyers may be required to undertake a libel review of the script and the finished film and to certify that no living person has been defamed. This process will be particularly relevant to documentaries and other films that include depictions and/or references to living persons. Copyright and title searches will also likely be required; see respectively paragraphs 5.26-5.28 and 14.13. E&O cover will need to be obtained before commencement of distribution and not after.

EXPLOITATION

47   Profit participation and royalties

47.1   Introduction

For a filmmaker to negotiate a deal that includes a participation in the profit of a film is always promising. If the promise is to be met by reality there are a number of notes of caution for a participant to heed in order that the contracted share of profit of a financially successful film is paid through.

47.2   More often than not, participation will be defined in terms of a percentage share of 'producer's net profit' (or similar terminology). In the vernacular, the term 'points' may be used to mean 'percentage profit points'. In many cases references to profit percentages or points will be supplemented by the additional language 'as that term is defined in the principal financing and distribution agreements for the film'. So far so good.

47.3   Using the term 'net' means three things:

•   that there is gross income from which

•   there are expenses and deductions to be made in order to determine

•   the amount of the 'net'.

47.4   Expenses

The nature and extent of the costs and expenses that may be deducted by an accounting party should be carefully considered, defined and explained. The net profit participant should not automatically accept a contractual provision for extensive deductions without evaluating whether they are both justified and appropriate. Whether any one individual participant will have enough commercial bargaining power to persuade a monolithic accounting party to negotiate the detail of deductions is questionable. All of this is stating the obvious, but stating it is worthwhile because it is remarkable how often the commercial consequences of what is a simple equation viz. $N = G - E$ (where N means net, G means gross and E means expenses) become lost in the mire of the agreements that collectively provide for the financing, production and distribution of a film.

47.5   The bigger the budget and the greater the number of profit participants, the more complex the contractual web that will be woven. The filmmaker with the original idea and a resulting interest in the 'producer's net profit' may become two and three and even more stages removed from the income generating centre of the project. Agreements may be put in place into which a net profit participant has no input. The computation of net profits may become increasingly watered down as various parties in the chain of exploitation inject different levels of expenses and other deductions from gross. There is a point at which it may become difficult, or even impossible, for a filmmaker to exercise much control over the way that the details of exploitation contracts are written and thus keep a close eye on how those costs and expenses to be deducted from gross are to be defined and dealt with. In these circumstances, the filmmaker's best position is to require that, in each of the agreements providing for the production and distribution of a film, there is an obligation to give the filmmaker copies of all of the applicable agreements – or at least the most important ones – so that s/he can directly consider how the profits are contracted to be divided.

47.6   Having established a right to participate in the net profit of a project (or an entitlement to a royalty) the participating parties, be they producers, writers, directors, cast or others, will each want to ensure they are being accounted to and paid their due share. There are five elements involved in the accounting process which apply equally to the calculation of both net profit shares and to royalty accounting which are (a) record keeping (b) accounting/reporting (c) payment (d) inspection and (e) audit.

47.7   Record keeping

Those responsible for accounting for any of the financial aspects of producing or exploiting a film should be required to maintain complete and accurate records of all of their dealings that relate to that film. Record keeping obligations should not be limited to accounts and computations of sums to be paid through but should also extend to the source material on which those records are based. The records should include not only those of income but also those of expenditure and costs. An auditor may need to review the underlying arrangements from which accounts have been derived to include contracts, invoices and even relevant correspondence.

47.8   Accounting/Reporting

Those accounting for payments and receipts should have an enforceable contractual obligation to do so. Accounting may typically be required either semi-annually or quarterly. Reporting dates are usually defined to be within forty-five, sixty or ninety days of the calendar quarter days; (30 June and 31 December for semi-annual accounting and, in addition, 31 March and 30 September for quarterly accounting). Some online media companies are able to account more frequently and some contemporary online distribution agreements even provide for monthly accounting.

47.9   Accounting statements should be required to provide sufficient detail of all income and properly deductible expenditure as will enable the recipient to effectively evaluate the completeness and accuracy of what is being reported. Standards used vary immensely. Some companies are able to provide lengthy line-item breakdowns that run to multiple pages (or screens); others provide not much more than headline figures that beg as many questions as they purport to answer.

47.10   There is no gold standard for the form of an accounting statement. The advice that is generally given is that where a film is apparently achieving commercial success and generating material amounts of income, there will likely be merit in undertaking an audit; see paragraphs 47.15-47.21. The more extensive the contractual record keeping obligation, the more comprehensive the range of material will be available for an auditor to review and from which to draw an accurate conclusion.

47.11   Payment

The party in receipt of accounting statements will also require to be paid. Obvious? Of course, but there are innumerable examples of contractual language that talk about accounting but fail to mention payment. There are other clauses that talk about money being payable (not paid) or a recipient's entitlement to be paid but not who is actually supposed to be doing the paying. Whilst this all may seem to be obvious in the context of the clauses in question, some very simple and unambiguous language will put the matter beyond argument – and where there are apparent ambiguities, there will always be those prepared to argue shades of meaning.

47.12   Ideally, the payment provision should state something along the lines that '*Y shall pay to Z all sums shown to be due on each accounting statement*'. The provision should also indicate whether payment is to be made (a) with delivery of the accounting statement (b) within a given number of days of delivery of the accounting statement or (c) within a given number of days after receipt by Y of Z's invoice for the amount shown to be due on each accounting statement.

47.13   VAT

Where a payment under any contract is subject to the addition of Value Added Tax (**VAT**), the agreement must provide, in terms, that '*all payments under this Agreement are exclusive of VAT which, where applicable, will be added subject to delivery of a valid VAT invoice*'. This requirement applies to every species of contract and that includes commissioning agreements and writers' agreements as well as distribution agreements or licences. If the position is not clear or if similar language is not included in the contract then the payer is entitled as a matter of law to treat the payments being made as inclusive of VAT.

Example

A contract is silent on the question of VAT. A writer provides his services through a loan-out company that is registered for VAT. The writer's contract provides for payment of a fee of £7,200 for writing a script. If the writer asks for payment of VAT, the filmmaker paying the writer is entitled to pay that writer £6,000 plus the VAT, which, at the rate in force, currently 20%, will be £1,200; the total therefore paid will be £7,200 as provided for by the contract.

However, if the writer's intention is to be paid £7,200 plus VAT of £1,450 making a total of £8,650, then, simply, the contract should provide for payment of £7,200 plus VAT subject to delivery of a valid VAT invoice.

47.14   Inspection

Inevitably the inspection of a paying party's books and records will be bound up with an audit. However, the two processes are different and should each be addressed in the agreement. An inspection is the flip-side of the record keeping obligation (paragraph 47.7). An audit is concerned with checking that the accounting for payments and expenses is accurate. The audit – or checking – process will inevitably unearth questions that make it necessary to inspect underlying records, contracts and other information.

47.15   Audit

Ensuring that a profit or royalty participant is provided with an audit right is only the first step. Careful consideration of the wording of audit provisions is essential as accounting parties may try and restrict the right in a number of ways. Very often, in participation provisions, there will be attempts to curtail the right in the following ways:

(a)   the payer will provide that, unless challenged within a given period (often two but sometimes even one year from delivery), an accounting statement may not be made subject to inspection and audit. The provision may then continue by providing a cut-off date by which a statement made subject to a challenge must be audited or the audit right will be lost;

(b)   the payer may provide that unless a claim is brought on a disputed statement within a given period – again, perhaps two years from the date when the statement was delivered – the payee may not bring such a claim.

Example

1   *In the event that Producer enters into a collection account management agreement, Producer shall procure that Contributor shall be made a party thereto.*

2   *Producer shall maintain and shall procure that those deriving rights in or to the Film from Producer shall maintain true and complete books of account containing an accurate record of all data necessary for the proper computation of payments hereunder, and Contributor shall have the right by itself or its duly authorised representative to examine such books at all reasonable times (but not more than once in each calendar year) for the purpose of verifying the accuracy of the computations rendered by Producer. Upon reasonable advance notice, such examination shall be made during normal business hours at the principal place of business of Producer. If such examination reveals that statements furnished by Producer were inaccurate by more than 5% and that amounts in excess of those paid to Contributor are due, such sums shall be paid to Contributor forthwith following such examination and the cost of such examination shall be borne by Producer and Producer shall pay Contributor's costs of and occasioned by the said audit. Additionally, Producer shall pay Contributor interest on all underpayments calculated at the rate of 3% above Barclays Bank*

Base Rate for the time being in force effective from the date upon which each underpayment should have been paid up to and including the date of actual payment, such interest to be compounded annually.

47.16   Filmmakers and other profit participants should resist unrealistically short periods within which they may audit and/or bring claims based on accounting statements. It may take two years and even more for a film to generate sufficient income to make an audit worthwhile. If the periods within which audits require to be undertaken or claims must be brought are unrealistically short, then profit/royalty recipients may need to consider at least putting payers on notice of a challenge if that will keep their rights alive. Whether this will work will depend on the precise wording of the clause in question. Once an audit notice is served, difficulties may arise when contractual time periods start running and the auditing party does not then take the necessary steps within the requisite time period.

47.17   Under English law there is a limitation period that prevents a claim being brought for breach of contract more than six years after the breach is committed. On its face, failing to properly account for a payment due under an agreement would constitute a breach of contract. The argument is, therefore, that imposing restrictive periods in English law contracts is pointless unless the main objective is to dissuade a dissatisfied participant from either (a) undertaking audits and/or (b) pursuing claims through the courts for sums found due after an audit, because even if denied the right to audit, a dissatisfied royalty payee will not be prevented from suing for breach of contract and an account where there is evidence to suggest there may be significant under-accounting. Such proceedings may be brought at any time within six years of the date on which the dissatisfied filmmaker may show that the breach of the accounting obligation was first committed by, for example, an underpayment. A determined and well-funded filmmaker may thus succeed in having the court order the paying party to account for a period going back to the date of the alleged breach. This is a convoluted and expensive process which may be avoided by omitting the sort of restrictions on audit and payment claims that are commonly seen in accounting clauses.

47.18   Limitation periods under English law will not apply in cases of fraud. In order to prove that a paying party has acted fraudulently, the profit participant making such a claim needs to show that the paying party had acted with dishonest intent. The burden of proving fraud is placed upon the person making the allegation and is not an easy burden to discharge.

47.19   In the event that an audit reveals an underpayment, the payer should be obliged to do the following:

(a)   pay the amount of the underpayment within a given period without any deduction; the period should be very short – ideally no more than seven days following the determination of the amount of the underpayment;

(b)   pay interest on the amount of the underpayment from the date(s) the amount should have been paid;

in the UK, judgment rate of interest is currently 8% per annum. Potential payers of interest will often try and push back on this rate and instead seek to establish a commercial rate that might be 2% or 3% above bank base rate. Some potential interest payers will try not to be obligated to pay any interest at all. There is no commercial –or moral – justification for a party in default of a payment obligation to resist paying interest. Legislation addresses the issue of interest on outstanding monies due and provides statutory redress for those who are late in paying commercial debts. Under-accounted profit participants should not be treated as the providers of interest-free finance;

Example

For an example of interest payment language see paragraph 47.15(b): Example 2

(c)   reimburse the payee's audit fees;

in order to trigger a reimbursement, payers will seek to impose a threshold – perhaps a minimum amount of underpayment found by the auditor or a percentage being the amount that the discrepancy bears to the amount that has been previously paid for the period(s) being audited. Further, a cap may be sought on the amount of the audit fee to be imposed.

Example

If the examination establishes that the total amount of profit share actually paid to the Producer in respect of the accounting periods covered by the examination falls short of the amount which should have been paid by ten per cent (10%) or more, or at least five thousand pounds (£5,000) (whichever is the greater), the Distributor shall pay the reasonable costs of the accountant conducting the examination provided that the costs payable by the Company shall not in any event exceed five thousand pounds (£5,000) and shall not be taken into account in computing the extent of any underpayment.

The details for these provisions are all matters for negotiation.

47.20   There are other limitations that a paying party may seek to impose on the audit right that may relate to the identity of the auditor; rejecting the appointment of an auditor already working for another payee (even on an entirely unrelated matter); making it impossible for an audit to be undertaken while any other (again unrelated) audit is taking place. All of these proposed restrictions should be carefully considered in the context of the substance and standing of the payer and the overall negotiating strength of the parties. Experience suggests that, despite oft-made protestations to the contrary, there is little credible commercial justification in practice for any of these restrictions.

47.21   Having worked with royalty auditors on many dozens of audits across a range of film, television, music, computer games and other IP assets, in no single instance was there a case in which the writer of this Guide was involved where an auditor failed to uncover some significant discrepancies. In only one of those cases was the amount uncovered insufficient to require the paying party to reimburse the costs of the audit as per contract. In that case, the threshold figure for triggering reimbursement of the auditor's costs had been set at an unusually high level.

48   Sales agents

48.1   Initial considerations

A good sales agent may become a film's best friend, a bad one can become a filmmaker's nightmare. Deciding who to appoint and the extent of authority to be conferred can be as critical a decision as appointing a director or casting lead performers. Filmmakers are encouraged to undertake as much due diligence as they can on the standing of an agent. Reputations go a long way in the industry and that is no more relevant than to those of sales agents.

48.2   As digital exploitation of films becomes ever more commonplace, some of the conventions that have typically been adopted by sales agents are continually being challenged. The requirement made by sales agents for excessively lengthy terms – 15 and even 25 years – may make commercial sense where the agent is delivering substantial pre-sales that generate the hard cash necessary to fund a sizeable budget for a guaranteed international multi-screen theatrical release. However, the requirement of an agent to tie up the destiny of a lower budget independent film for a lengthy period where that film may find its biggest audience online, on niche television channels and on DVD and with little in the way of pre-sales may be harder to justify.

48.3   Appointing a sales agent

In considering the appointment of an agent, the filmmaker is encouraged to ask as many key questions as possible; these may include:

- What other films in this genre has the agent represented and with what success?

- Is the agent currently representing any other films that might conflict with and/or derogate from the agent's ability to provide effective representation?

- What is the agent's current corporate and financial standing – as best as can be ascertained? Filmmakers are encouraged to undertake at least some due diligence on sales agents which may include searches at Companies House and making enquiries of others whose films have been represented by the agent under consideration.

48.4   Requirements

One matter that continually comes back to haunt filmmakers – even those with years of experience – is the practice in the film and television industries whereby some sales agents contract with distributors and licensees as principals and not as agents; see discussion at paragraph 48.6. This is not a practice which producers and rights owners should accept just because the agent 'has always done it this way'. This is especially so where the profit participants in a film do not appoint an independent collection agent pursuant to the terms of a properly drafted and negotiated CAMA. Experience suggests that as good as a sales agent may be at sales, not all of them have an equivalent level of expertise in either contract law or how to act in a fiduciary capacity. Similar comments also apply to distributors.

48.5   Collection Account Management Agreements

A collection account management agreement (**CAMA**) provides for all of those participating in the income from a production to appoint the collection agent to collect all of that income and then to pay it out to the participants in accordance with the agreements they have each reached between themselves. The sales agents and distributors are contractually required to procure that all payments arising from exploitation of the film or programmes are paid to the collection agent. Notwithstanding this, it is accepted that there will be cases where the scale of a project and its likely income may make a CAMA seemingly expensive. Nevertheless, there is no reason why arrangements for collecting income from productions other than feature films, including television deals that involve co-production and/or multi-party interests in back end shares, might not use a CAMA managed by an independent collection agent. By way of examples, each of Freeway and Fintage, are well-established collection agents with proven records as both effective and trustworthy. Further details may be obtained from their respective websites as follows:

Freeway   https://www.freeway-entertainment.com/

Fintage   http://www.fintagehouse.com/

48.6   Agents contracting as principals

In some instances, sales agents (or principal distributors) will enter into contracts with overseas distributors, broadcasters and other licensees and when they have done so, the named party to the agreement is that sales agent or principal distributor; the filmmaker or rights owner in the film is not made a party to the agreement and may not even be mentioned, in terms, as a profit participant. The sales agent or principal distributor then assumes the obligation of collecting the income from the distributors and licensees and passing it on to the filmmaker. However, what happens if the sales agent or principal distributor runs into financial trouble and/or goes out of business altogether?

Example

*A programme maker (**Producer**) had an exclusive tie-up with a UK broadcaster. The Producer was permitted by the terms of its broadcasting commission to sell the programmes overseas. The Producer entered into an agreement with a London-based sales agent (**Agent**), whose standard form agreement provided that it was granted the exploitation rights in the programmes outside of the UK in all media on a ten-year term and on an exclusive basis.*

In accordance with the terms of the sales agency agreement, the Agent was granted extensive and unfettered rights to deal with the programming in question. The record keeping and reporting obligations in the sales agreement were sparse, the audit and accounting provisions inadequate. Further, it was the Agent's responsibility to collect the income from its licensees around the world and, after deducting its commission, to account for and pay the balance through to the programme maker. No CAMA was put in place.

In addition to its sales activities the Agent was also co-producing some of its own programming. It did not keep the money it was collecting on behalf of third party film and programme makers separate from its own production funds.

The Agent's production activities were not successful; it became tangled up in a widely-woven web of financial difficulties and went into administration. The Agent had received significant monies from its licensees that it has not passed on to the Producer and to other filmmakers it was representing. The Producer was offered little protection under the terms of the sales agency agreement. Equally problematic was the fact that the Producer had no privity of contract (i.e. direct contractual relationship) with the licensees of its rights (see discussion at paragraphs 25.20-25.22). Worse still, the Producer had not even been provided with copies of the agreements signed between the Agent and its licensees.

Having terminated the sales agency agreement, the Producer faced an uphill task in endeavouring to secure payments from licensees which the licensees had contracted to pay to the Agent. The administrator of the Agent took the view that the monies it collected from the Agent's licensees should be paid into its collection account for allocation to all of the Agent's creditors pro rata. In addition to losing its income streams, with no direct contractual relationship with the end licensees, the Producer had no easy way of protecting its underlying rights in the programmes. Had there been a CAMA in place, the licensees would have been contractually committed to pay income into the CAMA and the Producer's income stream would have been protected.

48.7   Unlike solicitors, accountants, banks and even estate agents there is no regulatory framework within the UK that obliges film sales agents to keep their principals' money separate in the equivalent of a clients' account. Albeit that a fiduciary obligation is arguably implied from the nature of a principal-agent relationship, the agreement referred to at 48.6 failed to mention anything of the sort. Better to have a specific obligation spelled out in an agreement than to rely on what the law should or might imply.

48.8   Limiting an agent's authority

In any event, rights owners and producers should be careful about enabling their agents to collect money directly unless a satisfactory arrangement can be guaranteed for safe-guarding that money. The sales agent's interest is to ensure that its commission is paid and its expenses reimbursed. In the absence of a CAMA, there is no reason why a licensee or distributor may not be required by contract to account for each of the rights owner's share and the agent's commission directly.

48.9   In the white heat of MIPCOM or AFM, it is easy for an agent scenting a sale that might otherwise escape, to have conveniently short forms of agreement that licensees and distributors may quickly agree and sign. That is no reason for the agent not to be obliged to have the form of that agreement approved in principle by the filmmaker and the extent of the agent's authority clearly set out in the sales agency agreement. Additionally, wherever reasonable, a signature copy of all agreements signed by an agent should be sent to the filmmaker as a matter of course.

48.10   Clear controls need to be included in the sales agreements that cap the extent to which sales agents may run up expenses and charge them to the rights owner. Additionally, it is advisable to provide that a sales agent may not grant terms of exploitation to distributors and licensees that extend beyond the end date of the agent's term of appointment. This will enable the filmmaker to take back maximum control over the rights once the agent's appointment has terminated.

48.11   Better still, if the agent is making a deal at a market - or indeed anywhere else - then it should be signed by the agent as 'agent with actual authority on behalf of the principal' so that there is clear privity of contract between the rights owner and rights user. By providing for privity of contract between the rights owner and the distributor the rights owner may enforce its rights directly against the distributor and not need to rely upon the agent to do so. Experience tends to suggest that once a deal has been done and income flowing, some agents may be less concerned in dealing with the policing and monitoring of a distributor or other licensee's performance at a level that meets the overriding commercial and legal needs of a rights owner.   For further discussion regarding privity of contract see paragraphs 25.20-25.22.

48.12   Filmmakers and rights owners need to be consistently vigilant about the extent of authority their agents seek and to ensure that appropriate safeguards are written into the suite of agreements pursuant to which valuable copyrights and profit shares may be handled. Producers whose expertise is in making films or programmes should always be wary of signing agreements that are held out as standard forms that may not apparently be changed - particularly when they are materially and obviously deficient.

49   Distribution agreements

49.1   Introduction

Having made the considerable effort necessary to develop a project, raise finance, attract and engage talent and crew, prepare for production, shoot, edit and post-produce, filmmakers face the further frustration that may be encountered in securing arrangements by which to attract an audience. Festival selection may prove a good starting point. Some filmmakers will be fortunate enough, especially in the early days of their careers, to attract funding that brings with it the promise – and even the reality – of distribution and/or broadcast.

49.2   Entry level distribution

However, even fully-funded features are not guaranteed sales, distribution or even commercial television broadcast. Depending on the size of the budget and the stage the filmmaker has reached in her/his career, there are numerous easily available, low cost online media that may help a filmmaker to establish creative and commercial credibility. Vimeo (https://vimeo.com/) and Vodo (http://vodo.net/) are two sites that work well at entry level and beyond. Films may also be distributed via iTunes which works through a number of aggregators such as:

- Indieflix   https://indieflix.com/filmmakers

- Distribber   https://www.distribber.com/

- New Video Group   http://www.newvideo.com/

49.3   Nevertheless, filmmakers will often believe that they have only arrived if their feature is exhibited on a big screen or their ground-breaking documentary shown on network television. An ambitious filmmaker may find it hard to resist a potentially lucrative deal that includes a guaranteed theatrical release and/or prime time television broadcast. Whether a deal is right and should be accepted will depend on a whole host of factors, some of which may include: the standing of the filmmaker, the nature and budget of the project, pressure from investors, the offer of a further commission. Nevertheless, a filmmaker should carefully evaluate not only the exposure offered by a deal but the terms that are attached to it. A balance needs to be weighed between the overall benefits of the opportunity that are offered such as visibility and an advance on the one hand and, on the other, the detailed terms attaching to the proposal.

49.4   Evaluating a distribution agreement

In negotiating a distribution agreement, the general principles applicable to contracts discussed at section 24 and much of the substance of section 25 will apply. When evaluating the terms of a distribution agreement or other licence for exploitation in any medium - physical, digital and/or otherwise – key terms to consider and questions about them to ask will include those set out in the following paragraphs. Inevitably any evaluation of a contract must look at how all of the component parts fit with each other and their applicability in the context of the overall commercial and creative matrices within which the film has been made.

49.5   Rights and media for distribution including holdbacks

In considering a proposal, a filmmaker should address the following issues:

(a)   Is this distributor a suitable party to exploit the film in all of the media that are sought in the proposal? In particular is a blanket grant of rights for all media, or even for all digital media, appropriate?

(b)   The media defined in any agreement require to be evaluated in the context of the territory/ies in which rights are sought.

(c)   What is the extent of the territory sought by the distributor? Is the distributor a suitable party to control the rights throughout all of that territory? What is the nature of the relationships that a distributor has with its sub-licensees/specialist distributors within a territory?

(d)   Are the holdbacks sought appropriate – or, if none are mentioned, should they be? Holdbacks define the periods during which exclusivity in particular media may be preserved. Even in the digital era, strictly defined holdback periods may still be important, especially if there is a possibility of a significant theatrical release. The type of holdback arrangements that may be proposed are as follows:

   •   the first holdback may define the period during which a film may be exploited exclusively via theatrical release;

   •   this may be followed by a holdback for a window within which the film may be released on DVD then streamed and/or broadcast on pay-per-view television;

- finally the film may be shown on free-to-air network television.

(e)   If the agreement permits sub-licensing there should be control over the terms of sub-licences such as rights granted and the length of term of a sub-licence. There will also be a need for restrictions imported into sub-licences; i.e. a limit on the number of DVDs that may be manufactured in the last period of a term so that the market is not flooded after the term ends. It is accepted that in many territories DVD is now a medium of declining commercial significance.

Example

*In seeking to conclude the financing of its £1.2m budget feature drama based on a true story, Producer secured a relatively modest amount of gap funding from a regionally based UK television broadcaster (**Broadcaster**). Key elements of the film's story took place and were shot in the region where the Broadcaster was located. In addition to free television broadcast rights that were subject to a holdback that enabled Producer to negotiate a theatrical release, the Broadcaster included in the agreement a provision giving it limited rights to include the film on its VOD service that were not subject to the holdback. The Broadcaster also negotiated a share of the back-end profits from the Film which were to be accounted for via a CAMA. In its eagerness to showcase its involvement, the Broadcaster made the film available on its VOD platform, albeit for a limited period, ahead of the projected theatrical release date. The theatrical exhibitors cancelled the theatrical release on the basis that its holdback had been breached. Both the Producer and the Broadcaster lost out, not only on their respective shares of what would have been a profitable theatrical release but also the additional exposure that release would have given the film for its exploitation in other paying media.*

49.6   Term

When evaluating the term – or period – for exploitation, a filmmaker should consider whether the term sought is too long and bear in mind the following:

(a)   If the term is intended to be lengthy, is its continuation made subject to defined performance thresholds in terms of volume of overall sales and/ or income being passed back to the filmmaker or rights owner?

(b)   Is there any mechanism by which, in given circumstances, the filmmaker might terminate a term for non-performance or breach? If so, what are the consequences of termination?

49.7   Options

Distributors may look at acquiring options in respect of which the following considerations apply:

(a)   Is the distributor looking for an exclusive option for further films or programmes? In circumstances where a television network breaks a programme, an exclusive option may be justified, but for how much further content and on what terms?

(b)   Does the option relate to sequels/prequels or is there an attempt to place a blanket over all of the filmmaker's subsequent output and, if so, for how long and on what terms?

Options are discussed in more detail at paragraphs 10.7-10.12.

49.8   Territory

The extent of territory in which the distributor or licensee may seek to exploit the rights poses the following questions:

(a)   Is the territorial coverage sought realistic and reasonable?

(b)   Does the distributor have the capability to deliver throughout the entirety of the territory sought or will it need to bring in sub-distributors for different parts of the territory and, if so, on what terms?

In the light of Brexit, the position with regard to licensing/distribution of UK productions in the rest of the EU was not known at the time of writing. Simply stated, irrespective of contractual exclusivity, under EU competition rules, once rights are lawfully available in any one EU member state, the licensee/distributor may validly exploit them in any other EU member state. The logical corollary of Brexit and a withdrawal of the UK from the free market may mean that UK licensees will no longer be able to benefit from this free movement (unless their grant is specified to include all of the EU) and, likewise, those in other member states will no longer be able to exploit within the UK without a specific grant of rights that will enable them to do so.

49.9   Distributor failure

In the event that the distributor fails:

(a)   Where does this leave the filmmaker in terms of policing and enforcing rights that have been sub-licensed?

(b)   Can the filmmaker collect payment from the distributor or sub-licensee?

(c)   Can the rights granted be readily terminated in the event of breach by the distributor?

(d)   If the rights are terminated what are the consequences? (See paragraph 49.14)

49.10   Censorship and editing

A view requires to be taken as to the extent to which a distributor may be permitted to edit the film, whether for the purposes of censorship or otherwise. Distribution contracts invariably provide for the rating that a film should achieve, failing which the distributor may reject the film. There may also be pre-agreed parameters within which a distributor may be permitted to edit a film whether required by censors or otherwise. Censorship in the UK is discussed at section 50.

49.11   Marketing and other expenses

The following matters require consideration:

(a)   A distributor may be entitled to deduct defined expenses and disbursements from the income it generates.

(b)   The nature of and the terms upon which those expenses may be incurred need to be carefully negotiated: how much, when and to whom and, then, how these payments may be recouped against income or otherwise paid.

49.12   Record keeping, accounting and reporting, payment, inspection and audit rights

Reference should be made to the discussion of these matters at section 47.

49.13   Delivery requirements

In relation to delivery requirements:

(a)   Distributors and licensees generally issue standard lists of delivery materials. These lists are often extensive and should always be carefully checked by the filmmaker or other party responsible for making delivery. If a self-producing writer/director or executive producer does not have the requisite technical knowledge to properly evaluate a delivery schedule, then it is essential that someone with that knowledge undertakes the task.

(b)   Frequently, upon reviewing a 'standard' delivery list, filmmakers may identify that it contains requirements that are neither available nor necessary.

(c)   Not delivering an item that is on a list may constitute a breach of contract which, in turn, may impact on payment of advances and initial release of the film in the distributor's market.

(d)   Lists of delivery materials should properly reflect what is necessary and available; the list needs to be signed off by both parties.

49.14   Termination and its consequences

As with any agreement, the circumstances in which a distribution contract may be terminated should be carefully set out. These may include:

•   an irremediable breach by a distributor;

•   failing to remedy a curable breach after a given period of notice – perhaps 14, perhaps 28 days;

•   upon the distributor becoming insolvent.

Examples of what may constitute an irremediable breach may include:

- licensing a theatrical feature as a cover-mount without the consent of the rights owner where required by the terms of a distribution contract;

- failing to comply with a key holdback;

- a broadcaster editing a documentary in such a way as to fundamentally distort its message.

The consequences of termination should be carefully described. In particular, the filmmaker or rights owner will want to ensure that all and any rights granted to the distributor terminate and revert to the filmmaker and delivery materials are either returned or destroyed. Additionally, if the distributor has granted sub-licences, the filmmaker will want to be able to collect directly any further income arising from exploitation of rights by the sub-licensee. This latter problem may be diminished, if not alleviated altogether, where the profit participants are parties to a CAMA; see paragraph 48.5.

49.15   Governing law and jurisdiction

The discussion at paragraphs 25.29-25.30 applies.

50   Censorship

50.1   Film

In the UK, film classifications are determined by the application of guidelines published by the British Board of Film Classification (**Guidelines**, **BBFC**) which are regularly updated. The Guidelines result from extensive public consultation, research and the continuing experience of the BBFC.

50.2   Classifications by the BBFC also cover the following species of material:

(a)   Films, trailers and advertisements that are to be shown in cinemas. This function is exercised by the BBFC on behalf of local authorities who are responsible for licensing cinemas.

(b)   Commercial video recordings that are offered for sale or hire within the UK as required by the Video Recordings Act 1984.

(c)   Video works which are distributed over the internet under a voluntary, self-regulatory service.

(d)   Commercial and internet content distributed via mobile networks under a voluntary, self-regulatory service.

50.3   In assessing whether content requires censoring, BBFC considers discrimination, drugs, horror, imitable behaviour, language, nudity, sex, sexual violence, theme and violence. The examiners also consider context, tone and the potential impact of a work (e.g. how it makes the audience feel) and even the release format. For example, as DVDs are watched in the home, there is believed to be a higher risk of underage viewing).

50.4   Where a filmmaker is dissatisfied with the BBFC classification accorded to a film, the filmmaker may take advantage of a formal reconsideration procedure.

50.5   The following are the current BBFC classifications:

U   Suitable for all

PG   Parental Guidance

12A   Cinema release suitable for 12 years and over

12   Video release suitable for 12 years and over

15   Suitable only for 15 years and over

18   Suitable only for adults

R18   Adult works for licensed premises only

50.6   More information may be accessed at http://www.bbfc.co.uk/sites/default/files/attachments/BBFC%20Classification%20Guidelines%202014_0.pdf

50.7   Television

Broadcasters are required to take all reasonable steps to protect people under eighteen. There is in place a 'watershed' establishing that material unsuitable for children (aged 15 or younger) should not be shown before 21.00 or after 05.30.

50.8   Appropriate scheduling is judged according to:

•   the nature of the content;

•   the likely number and age range of children in the audience, taking into account school time, weekends and holidays;

•   the start time and finish time of the programme;

•   the nature of the channel or station and the particular programme;

•   the likely expectations of the audience for a particular channel or station at a particular time and on a particular day.

51   IP and Social Media

51.1   The parameters of this Guide do not permit a comprehensive analysis of the use of content in social media. However, by taking two of the most popular platforms and considering their respective terms of use, filmmakers' eyes will be open to the questions they need to ask when either making material available on or using material taken from social media platforms.

51.2   Facebook

Facebook's terms of service (**FB Terms**), which will be found at https://www. facebook.com/terms.php, provide that users *'own the content that they create and share on Facebook ... nothing in these Terms takes away the rights they have to their own content'.*

However, by sharing, posting or uploading content that includes copyright or other intellectual property rights, users grant Facebook a *'non-exclusive, transferable, sub-licensable, royalty-free and worldwide license ... to host, use, distribute, modify, run, copy, publicly perform or display that content".*

51.3   Users may terminate Facebook's licence at any time by deleting content or an account. Notwithstanding such termination, users need to be aware that *'for technical reasons (sic), content (that users) delete may persist for a limited period of time in back-up copies (though it will not be visible to other users). In addition, deleted content may continue to appear if it has been shared with others and they have not deleted it.'*

In other words, by virtue of the extensive rights granted, once a filmmaker uploads content to Facebook it is 'out there' and may be difficult, if not almost impossible, to remove from the internet altogether.

51.4   Facebook's Terms of Service and Community Standards, which will be found at   https://www.facebook.com/communitystandards/,   prohibit   users   from posting content that infringes third party IP rights. Users may submit reports to Facebook identifying content on the platform believed to infringe users' IP rights. Provided it is satisfied that an infringement has occurred, Facebook endeavours to act promptly to remove content that infringes copyright or trade marks. Facebook also reserves the right to disable accounts of users who repeatedly infringe others' IP rights.

51.5   Using others' copyright material on Facebook may be permitted by way of the doctrine of 'fair use'. Unless considered to be a 'consumer' a party seeking to prove fair use must refer to the doctrine as applied by California courts. The elements of this fair use doctrine – criticism, commentary, news reporting, teaching, scholarship and research – are broadly similar to those discussed under English law at section 11. However, there are differences in the way fair use may be assessed under California law.

51.6   An individual user who is to be considered a 'consumer' will be subject to the laws of the country in which s/he resides that will apply to any claim against Facebook that relates to the Terms, which may be resolved in any competent court in that country that has jurisdiction over the claim. Before uploading content, those concerned to establish fair use should seek dedicated advice.

51.7   Facebook Help site is located at https://www.facebook.com/search/str/ facebook+help+site/keywords_search

51.8   Twitter

        In terms, Twitter's services are protected by copyright, trade mark and other laws of not only the US but also those of 'foreign countries'.

51.9   Twitter Terms of Service, which will be found at https://twitter.com/en/tos (**Twitter Terms**) provide that users retain their rights to any content they submit, post or display on or through Twitter. However, similarly to Facebook, by submitting, posting or displaying content on or through Twitter, users grant Twitter a *'worldwide, non-exclusive, royalty free license (with the right to sublicense) to use, copy, reproduce, process, adapt, modify, publish, transmit, display and distribute such content in any and all media or distribution methods'*. Ownership of the copyright in an original photograph taken by a user and posted on Twitter remains vested in that user but subject to an extremely broadly drawn licence which grants Twitter extensive rights. The same principles will apply to other copyright works including audio and audio-visual content.

51.10   The Twitter Terms also require that content submitted will not contain material subject to third party copyright or other intellectual property rights, unless those posting have the necessary permission or are otherwise legally entitled to post the material and grant Twitter the licence described at paragraph 51.9; 'legally entitled' would arguably extend to cover fair use (see section 11 and paragraph 51.5).

51.11   Twitter responds to complaints of copyright infringement submitted in accordance with the provisions of the US statute, the Digital Millennium Copyright Act (**DMCA**). The DMCA contains a procedure for formally reporting copyright infringement and how an affected party can appeal a removal by submitting a compliant counter-notice. Twitter will respond to reports of alleged copyright infringement. If a complaint satisfies the DMCA requirements, Twitter will take action on request which may include removal of infringing material.

51.12   Immediately before going to press, a new EU Copyright Directive was introduced that includes provisions applying to online content sharing services that 'primarily exist' to give the public access to 'protected works or other protected subject matter uploaded by users'. The provisions will cover the likes of YouTube and Soundcloud but could also be applied to social media platforms. Such services will need to licence copyright-protected material from the rights holders. How these provisions will work in practice is presently unknown. Certain of the fair uses of copyright discussed at section 11 may apply. Initial reactions to the Directive were mixed. As the Guide was being published, the necessary discussions between content owners and content-sharing platforms as to how the Directive was to be implemented had barely begun.

MISCELLANEOUS

52 Project vehicle – using a limited company

52.1 In the simplest of analyses, using a limited company (or limited partnership) for a film production provides a degree of immunity and protection against certain personal liabilities of the individuals responsible for developing and producing a film. Limited companies will be used by filmmakers for a number of reasons of which the main ones are as follows:

(a) where a limited company enters into a contract for goods or services with a third party then it is the company's liability to pay for those goods or services and not that of the individual directors or other authorised personnel;

(b) a limited company may be used to acquire, own and subsequently control and protect the use of all of the rights in a film;

(c) a separate company may be incorporated to undertake the physical line-production of a film; see section 43.

52.2 Filmmakers using limited companies need to bear in mind a number of key matters:

(a) a limited company has a separate legal personality to (i) those who own it – the shareholders, and (ii) to those who manage the business of a company – the directors. The same individuals do not necessarily have to be both shareholders and directors of a company. The directors are those who are appointed to manage the company for the benefit of all of the shareholders;

(b) filmmakers should require each individual creating rights and/or performing services for the film to grant or transfer those rights to the company pursuant to the terms of contracts that will then provide for the company's obligations to those individuals; see section 6;

(c) once incorporated, limited companies require to be maintained. Amongst other things, annual statements need to be filed at Companies House and tax returns sent to HMRC;

(d)   changes in a company's directors, constitution and other statutory details require to be promptly notified to Companies House;

(e)   limited liability does not extend to protect an individual who is responsible for the commission by a company of a 'tort'. Torts of most relevance to filmmakers include copyright and trade mark infringement, defamation and negligence. In other words, if defamatory comments are included in a documentary the individual director of that documentary may be personally liable for any damage arising even if s/he has made the film using a limited company;

(f)   limited liability may be lost if individual director(s) permit a company to trade insolvently; more simply stated, individual directors may become personally liable for debts that are incurred when those directors know or ought to know that the company is not in a position to meet the obligation to pay its bills as and when they fall due for payment;

(g)   there are costs involved in incorporating and maintaining a limited company. Failure to provide for and pay the applicable fees may lead to the company being struck off from the register with adverse consequences. Rights and other assets vested in a limited liability company (or partnership) may be lost if a company or limited partnership is dissolved; see discussion at paragraphs 6.13 and 37.9;

Example

In early 2014, Sam and Janet establish Disruption Productions Limited, which is allotted company number 1231231234 by Companies House. They use the company to acquire an outright assignment of the rights to a script by Phineas Smith entitled 'Disruption'. They fail to raise funding and they also fail to keep the company's filings up-to-date and, at the end of 2016, without either Sam or Janet realising it, the company, number 1231231234, is struck off the register. In December 2017, they finally secure funding commitments to make the film. In undertaking its due diligence, the funder points out that Disruption Productions Limited (company number 1231231234) has been struck off. Undeterred, Sam and Janet incorporate a new company under the name Disruption Productions Limited to which Companies House allocates the number 7897897890. However, this new company has no rights in the script. Simply renegotiating with Phineas will, of itself, not be sufficient to cure the problem. As the rights were assigned outright to company number 1231231234, the new company (number 7897897890) will need to acquire those rights from the Crown via the Treasury Solicitor; alternatively, Sam and Janet will need to apply to restore company number 1231231234 to the register. Either way, the process may be time-consuming and complex and, potentially, costly as well.

52.3   Entry level filmmakers may decide that the overall administration burden and cost of establishing and maintaining a limited company is more trouble than it is worth. Nevertheless, a filmmaker may subsequently transfer ownership – and therefore, management – of a film into a limited company. Before doing this, the filmmaker will need to check to see if there are any particular provisions in any of the contracts with any of the providers of goods and services to the film that restrict such a transfer and, if necessary, seek their consent.

52.4   An individual or individuals not operating their activities by using a limited company or limited partnership will assume unlimited personal liability to third parties arising from and out of the making of the film including all and any contractual obligations.

53   Role of the lawyer

53.1   It often falls to the lawyers to endeavour to balance the competing creative and commercial requirements of contracting parties. It's a cliché, but art and business seldom make easy bedfellows.

53.2   Quite apart from the complexities of the words on the page of a contract, the inexperienced filmmaker should also carefully consider what it is that is being offered to him by the other party to a deal. Early stage filmmakers working with modest budgets may be disadvantaged as much by lack of experience as they may be by lack of sufficient knowledge; both are required to evaluate the commercial worth of what is offered by financiers, sales agents, distributors, commissioning broadcasters or potential co-producers. Ultimately, a filmmaker must make her/his own decisions. However, a properly instructed lawyer should provide insight as to the potential for both the upside and the downside of terms offered to a filmmaker and the consequent effects on the filmmaker's creative and commercial objectives.

53.3   The negotiation process starts with the parties themselves agreeing headline points. In order to reach this stage, the parties need to have a clear understanding of what they each seek to achieve from an agreement with the other(s). The parties may then proceed to negotiate and finalise the terms of an agreement – whether it is a formal contract, a summary of key terms or a series of email exchanges. It is seldom too early to bring a lawyer into a deal, even if it is just for an initial sounding. The examples are many and varied of the truly horrible messes that could have been avoided by involving lawyers at an earlier stage in a project.

53.4   On numerous occasions clients will ask their lawyers whether or not they should proceed with a deal or not. Sometimes a client's inclination to accept a less than generous deal may be conditioned by her/his lacking any negotiating muscle; alternatively, the client may be desperate for a pay day and/or in need of a credit on a resumé. Even allowing for these factors – and others – the client may realise that the deal on the table is a poor one. As a lawyer, one needs to retain distance from the emotional aspects of negotiating deals. Lawyers can point out the good and bad aspects of a contract or its specific terms and project what the consequences may be of taking a particular course. In the course of negotiation, lawyers may be able to persuade another party or its lawyer that given provisions in a contract are unacceptable. Nevertheless, the other party may have a self-defined cut-off point beyond which they will negotiate no further and the deal then being offered is on a 'take-it-or-leave-it' basis.

53.5   At this stage, the filmmaker client must ask her/himself whether any deal is better than no deal? The lawyer ought not to be the one answering this question. Having said that, there are inevitably situations that arise where the terms offered to a client are so egregious that a lawyer has no alternative but to dissuade a client from proceeding. Some of these situations are conditioned as much by a lawyer's previous experience of the individuals or companies involved in a proposal as they may be by the particular terms on offer.

53.6   In addition to the legal aspects of a deal, lawyers may be referred to for all-round advice on the why and the wherefore of a deal as much as the how and the when. In a word, the most valuable commodity that a lawyer may contribute to a project is experience. After working in the industry for a while, a lawyer will become acquainted with not only how to collect together the disparate elements that comprise a film, but also the way in which the industry works, with some of those who work in it and, most importantly, strategies for approaching and overcoming some of the innumerable obstacles and road-blocks that may continually obstruct the progress of a filmmaker.

53.7   A major concern for filmmakers in the independent sector is often legal fees. Lawyers working with independent production companies are accustomed to working on fixed or capped fees, the amount of which will be determined by a line item in a film's budget. A good way to proceed is to sound out the lawyer before committing to that budget figure. No filmmaker should be dissuaded from instructing a lawyer by assuming the fees will be prohibitive. Nevertheless, filmmakers are encouraged to understand that lawyers in the UK do not, as a rule, necessarily want to become, in effect, investors in a project by writing off vast swathes of their time for no tangible reward. Thus a realistic discussion of what a lawyer will and will not do within a given budget for legal fees and a clearly drafted engagement letter may provide benefits all round both to the filmmaker and to the lawyer.

53.8   Another area of activity in which lawyers will be involved is in the resolution of disputes. Litigation should be the last resort in a dispute. Quite apart from the fact that even before proceedings are filed at court, legal costs may rapidly escalate, the time and human resource required make it an exercise that should not be embarked upon lightly. With goodwill on both sides, experienced lawyers with commercial sense and detailed instructions ought to be able to negotiate a sensible resolution to a problem. Engaging the services of an independent mediator may also prove to be worthwhile. Nevertheless, there are cases where mediation will not work and entrenched positions make a court case – or an arbitration – unavoidable.

54   Brexit

Following the proposed departure of the UK from the EU, in addition to the specific items mentioned in various sections of the Guide, there are a number of matters for UK filmmakers to consider by which they may be affected. Some of these include the following:

•   The loss of EU grants and subsidies including those available from Creative Europe Programme and Media Programme.

•   The possibility that UK content may become less attractive to European broadcasters by virtue of the fact that in some EU countries minimum quotas are imposed on the amount of European content TV broadcasters must show. In the past, such quotas have led to an increased demand for UK films and television shows which may diminish after Brexit.

•   The introduction of working visas and possibly tariffs/duties that may make it harder for UK filmmakers to film in the EU and work with citizens and companies in the remaining 27 EU member states.

•   Changes in the laws on free movement of goods and services reintroducing territorial integrity for UK-only licensing deals; see paragraph 49.8.

•   With the decline in the value of the pound that has followed in the wake of the Brexit vote, the UK has arguably become a more attractive location for overseas producers to make films. Numerous Hollywood productions take advantage of not only the excellent facilities at Pinewood, Shepperton and other studios but also the extensive experience and high standards of British talent both on and off camera.

•   EU rules on state aid and distortion of competition currently prevent the UK from favouring British productions. After Brexit, the UK government will be in a position to encourage British productions by introducing more favourable tax credits, though whether successive governments will actually do this is presently unknown.

55   **Disclaimer**

This Guide does not purport to contain a definitive statement of the law nor provide definitive legal advice that will be universally applicable to every project. This Guide comprises a compilation of information derived from the writer's practice and experience as a solicitor working, qualified and regulated in England & Wales in the entertainment sector generally and in the film, music, audio-visual and digital industries in particular. The information contained in this Guide and the forms of specimen documentation annexed are not intended to be substitutes for tailored advice that filmmakers should seek from solicitors or others duly qualified to give that advice and who may then negotiate and draft the agreements that will be required by a filmmaker. Neither the author, Tony Morris, nor the firm to which he is a consultant, Swan Turton LLP, take any responsibility or assume any liability to any person, firm or corporate or other body

(a)   for any view, decision or action that may be taken by that person, firm or corporate body or omission made,

and/or

(b)   for use made of any one or more of the specimen agreements included in the Appendices or any part or parts thereof, as a consequence of considering and/or based on and/or suggested by any of the content, information, material, examples, opinions, suggestions, observations, web-links or specimen agreements comprising, contained, mentioned, included or referred to in the Guide. All opinions expressed in the Guide are the personal opinions of the author.

APPENDICES

Introduction

No	Type of agreement	Key mention
1	Non-disclosure Agreement	Paragraph 7.5
2	Life Rights Release	Paragraph 10.6
3	Option to acquire underlying literary work	Paragraph 10.7-10.12
	Exhibit A: Acquisition Agreement	Paragraph 10.9
4	Shopping/Attachment Agreement	Paragraphs 10.13-10.14
5	Music licence (short form)	Paragraph 13.5, 13.7-9
6	Music - Composer	Paragraph 13.11-13.13
	Schedule 2: Performer/Contributor Release	Paragraph 13.11
7	Location Agreement	Section 20
8	Writer's Agreement	Section 27
9	Director's Agreement	Section 28
	Schedule: Inducement Letter	Section 36
10	Producer's Agreement	Section 29
11	Performer's Agreement	Sections 9, 30 and 31
12	Performer's Consent (Short Form)	Sections 9, 30 and 31
13	Interviewee Release (Short Form)	Section 33
14	Crew Agreement (Short Form)	Section 35
15	Assignment of Rights	Section 37; Paragraph. 6.1
16	Investor Agreement	Section 40
17	Commissioning Agreement	Paragraphs 41.1 - 41.4 & 6.2
18	Collaboration Agreement (Short Form)	Paragraph. 44.1

Index

- The documents included in these Appendices (**Precedents**) are provided as guides to the type of forms of agreement that may be of interest to a filmmaker. The Precedents are not holy writ, should not be slavishly followed and, if used in whole or in part, will need to be carefully considered and tailored for each individual project.

- The Precedents are not intended to be substitutes for bespoke agreements drafted to meet the detailed commercial, creative and legal requirements of each individual project.

- Many of the Precedents are not and are not intended to be long forms and will not necessarily cover every detailed aspect of the relationships provided for by each Precedent for every project.

- Certain of the provisions mentioned in the applicable sections of the Guide may not be included in the Precedents.

- Provisions used in various of the Precedents may be appropriate to and adapted for use in others.

- Text in italics, some of which is in square brackets, contains suggestions, some in the alternative that, if not appropriate, may need to be replaced with other information.

- Bracketed and other sections that are blank require to be completed.

- Attention is drawn to the footnotes in which there are comments on the text and drafting of documents.

- The relevant sections of the Guide in which each precedent document is discussed are noted at the beginning of each Appendix.

- Neither the writer, Tony Morris, nor Swan Turton LLP, the firm to which he is a consultant, take any responsibility for the use or consequences thereof of any one or more of the Precedents or any part or parts thereof.

Appendix 1

Non-disclosure Agreement
Paragraphs 7.5-7.8

From:[1]

To:[2]

Date:[3]

Dear Sirs,

I am writing to you in relation to a *[television format][movie project][4]* provisionally entitled "[5]   " ("**Project**").

This letter sets out the terms upon which I am prepared to share with you the information ("**Confidential Information**") contained in the *[format bible][script][graphics] [treatment][outline][summary][storyboard][6]* for the Project ("**Materials**").

1   I am willing to make available the Confidential Information to you in order that you may evaluate the same with a view to assessing the possibility of entering into an arrangement with me pursuant to which you may *[acquire certain rights in and to the Project] [use or exploit the Confidential Information] [participate in the Project][7]* on such terms as we may hereafter agree ("**Evaluation**").

2   For the avoidance of doubt, any data, information, item or other matter disclosed by me to you after the date hereof, whether orally, in writing or by any other means or in any other media, shall be conclusively deemed to be Confidential Information unless otherwise stated in writing by me.

3   *[For the purposes of this letter, "Confidential Information" shall include all and any information in relation to the Project which was disclosed by me to you*

---

1 Insert name and address of author of script, deviser of format or owner of idea for which protection is sought
2 Insert name and address details of recipient of information
3 Insert date of document
4 Amend as appropriate to describe nature of project
5 Insert title of project
6 Amend as appropriate
7 Amend as appropriate

prior to the date of this letter.] [8]

4   In consideration of the disclosure by me to you of the Confidential Information, you hereby undertake that you shall not at any time after the date of disclosure without my prior written consent

    (a)   make any part of the Confidential Information available to any third party; nor

    (b)   use the Confidential Information for any purpose other than the Evaluation; nor

    (c)   make any kind of copy of the whole or any part of the Confidential Information unless strictly necessary in order to carry out the Evaluation; nor

    (d)   develop and/or produce and/or exploit any programme, film or other project using the Confidential Information or any part of it.

5   As long as I am notified in advance in writing, you may disclose all or part of the Confidential Information to any of your employees who need to review the Confidential Information in connection with the Evaluation. However, you shall ensure that all and any such employees are bound by obligations of confidentiality which are no less strict than those set out in this letter *[and, if required by me, you will procure that such persons confirm their obligations of confidentiality to me in writing]*[9].

6   The obligations provided for in this letter of agreement shall not apply to any part of the Confidential Information which you can clearly demonstrate to me:

    (a)   has become public knowledge other than through you (including any of your employees); or

    (b)   was already known to you before I disclosed it to you; or

    (c)   was received from a third party who did not owe me a duty of confidence in respect of it; or

---

8 Delete as necessary
9 Amend as appropriate or omit

(d)   is required to be disclosed by a court or statutory body.

7   You hereby acknowledge and agree that the Materials, together with the Confidential Information, comprise and incorporate original copyright works in respect of which:

(a)   copyright in and to Materials, as well as all and any other content containing and/or reproducing the Confidential Information as the same is recorded and reproduced in the Materials together with all other intellectual property and proprietary rights in and to the Confidential Information and the Project is and shall remain my exclusive property; and

(b)   the Materials belong solely and exclusively to me; and

(c)   taken as a whole the information and materials provided and to be provided by me to you in connection with the Project constitute a disclosure of Confidential Information, notwithstanding that individual component elements thereof may not of themselves be confidential;

(d)   the title of the Project is a *[registered] [unregistered]*[10] trade mark of which I am the owner and in which goodwill vests in me.

8   You shall, at any time if requested by me, cease to use and immediately return to me or, at my option, destroy all files, documents or other media whether in hard copy or digital formats (and all copies) which pertain to or reproduce Confidential Information and produce to me evidence that you have so done.

9   This letter of agreement constitutes the entire understanding and agreement between us and supersedes any prior agreement, whether oral or written, between us.

10   The terms of this letter shall be governed by English law and disputes shall be referred to the courts of England and Wales.

---

10 Delete which does not apply

Please signify your acceptance of the foregoing by signing and returning to me the attached duplicate of this letter.

Yours sincerely [11]

Agreed and Accepted[12]

---

11 Signature of the provider of the information
12 Signature of the recipient of the information

Appendix 2

Life Rights Release
Paragraph 10.6

AGREEMENT dated[13]

PARTIES

(1)   [14]   ("**Grantor**")

(2)   [15]   ("**Producer**")

        each a "**Party**" and collectively the "**Parties**"

RECITALS

(A)   Producer is intending to develop and produce *[a theatrical motion picture]*
        and/or [television series] and/or [programmes] and/or [other entertainment
        production(s)][16] (individually and/or collectively "**Film(s)**") *[including*
        remakes, sequels and prequels] [17] which Producer proposes (but does not
        undertake) to produce and distribute to be based upon and/or that may include
        storylines, incidents, themes or episodes based upon experiences and events in
        the Grantor's life ("**Life Story**").

(B)   The Parties have entered into this agreement ("**Agreement**") to provide for the
        exclusive grant by Grantor to Producer of the right to make the Film(s) on the
        terms and conditions herein provided[18].

---

13 Insert date of agreement
14 Insert name and address details of Grantor
15 Insert name and address details of Producer
16 Delete/amend as appropriate
17 Include/amend as appropriate
18 An agreement to acquire Life Rights could also be subject to the grant of an option; see Appendix 3

OPERATIVE PART

1   Grantor hereby grants to Producer forever and throughout the universe the exclusive[19] right to portray, represent. impersonate and depict Grantor and the Life Story in any manner whatsoever, whether factual, fictional, or both, by any actor or actors which Producer may select, under Grantor's own name or any other name Producer may select and the non-exclusive right to use Grantor's name, actual or simulated likeness, and voice ("**Grantor's Attributes**") in the Film(s) and in or in connection with any exhibition or exploitation of all or any part of the Film(s), in all media whether now existing or hereafter devised and all means of publishing, all forms of merchandising and all manner of advertising and publicity in connection with the Film(s) and/or any such exhibition or exploitation (all of the foregoing rights and entitlements collectively referred to as the "**Rights**").

2   Producer shall have the right to fictionalize, adapt, dramatize, rearrange, add to and subtract from the actual facts of the Life Story in the preparation of any story or screenplay for the Film(s) and/or any other material prepared for or in connection with the exhibition or exploitation thereof.

3   Grantor hereby agrees that Grantor will not at any time claim or assert that any portrayal, representation, impersonation or depiction of Grantor or any exploitation of Grantor's Attributes pursuant to this Agreement constitutes a violation of any of Grantor's rights including, without limitation, any or all of Grantor's right of privacy, publicity, false light and Grantor's right to bring and prosecute an action for defamation, whether such exploitation or use is made by Producer or Producer's successors, licensees or assigns. Grantor hereby releases Producer, Producer's successors, assigns, licensees, and employees from any and all claims by or under Grantor's authority arising out of or in connection with any portrayal, representation, impersonation, or depiction of me or any exploitation of Grantor's Attributes pursuant to this Agreement.

4   In full and final consideration for the Rights hereby granted Producer shall pay Grantor the sum of £   (thousand pounds) to be paid in the following instalments[20].

---

19 This form contemplates the Grantor giving exclusive rights to the Producer. The agreement may require to be amended to reflect a more restricted grant. If Grantor reserves the right to work subsequently with other filmmakers and/or on other projects, Producer should require a period of exclusivity sufficient to prevent a derogation from the rights acquired from the Grantor.
20 Insert instalment or other payment details

5   Grantor hereby represents, warrants and undertakes to Producer that Grantor:

(a)   is the sole owner of all rights granted to Producer herein;

(b)   has not granted or accorded to any person, firm or corporation any of the rights or privileges which Grantor has granted or agreed to grant to Producer pursuant to this Agreement nor will Grantor grant any such rights that will or may derogate from the Rights;

(c)   has not authorized or consented to any person exercising such rights.

6   Grantor hereby grants to Producer all consents necessary (including Grantor's express consent in respect of sensitive personal data) pursuant to the Data Protection Acts 1998 and 2018 ("**DPAs**") to store, handle and/or process my personal data (which may include information given on camera) and, if applicable, sensitive personal data, for the purposes of the making and/or exploitation of Film(s) in any manner or medium worldwide which may include sharing information with broadcasters and/or other distributors which grant shall not derogate from Producer's obligations to Grantor under the DPAs; further in granting Producer the consents provided for by this Clause 6, Grantor acknowledges and understands that Producer has a clear legitimate interest in processing the personal data hereinbefore mentioned and specifically Grantor acknowledges that

•   as a consequence of Producer's investment of finance and resource into the Film(s), Producer is pursuing a genuine business interest in continuing to process the personal data;

•   the processing is absolutely necessary in order for Producer to pursue that interest;

•   the processing is balanced against the impact the processing will have on such fundamental rights and freedoms as Grantor may have.[21]

7   This Agreement shall bind and inure to the benefit or Grantor's and Producer's respective heirs, legal representatives, successors and assigns and all or any of Producer's rights hereunder may be licensed or assigned by Producer.

---

21 See discussion at 16.9-16.20

8   Under no circumstances are Producer or Producer's successors or assigns to be in a less favourable situation than Producer or they might have been had Producer not secured from Grantor the rights, privileges, powers and/or immunities contained herein.

9   Nothing contained in this Agreement shall be construed to be or operate in derogation or limitation of any rights to which Producer may be entitled as a member of the public if this Agreement was not in existence.

10   Grantor shall not be entitled to any equitable relief to restrict or interfere with Producer's right to produce, distribute, market or exploit Films or other productions produced pursuant to this Agreement or contemplated herein (including, but not limited to, derivative works) and the ancillary rights therein or to otherwise exploit or exercise any of the rights granted to Producer hereunder.

11   This Agreement includes the Parties' entire understanding with respect to the subject matter hereof, and all prior and concurrent oral agreements, and all prior written agreements with respect to such subject matter have been merged herein. No representations or warranties have been made to Grantor or by Grantor other than those expressly provided for herein. This Agreement may not be modified. except by a written instrument signed by the Parties.

12   This Agreement shall be construed. interpreted and enforced in accordance with, and governed by, English law and disputes shall be referred to the non-exclusive jurisdiction of the English courts unless another jurisdiction shall constitute a forum conveniens.

....

Grantor   **Producer**

Appendix 3

Option to acquire underlying literary work
Paragraphs 10.7-10.12

Exhibit
Paragraph 10.9

AGREEMENT dated[22]

PARTIES

(1)   [23]   (**"Owner"**)

(2)   [24]   (**"Producer"**)

RECITALS

(A)   Owner is the author[25] of the literary work entitled "   [26]"(**"Work"**)

(B)   Owner has agreed to grant to Producer the sole and exclusive option to purchase certain rights in and to the Work upon the terms and conditions of this Agreement.

OPERATIVE PART

1   Option

1.1   In consideration of the sum of   pounds (£   ) paid by Producer to Owner (receipt and the sufficiency of which Owner hereby acknowledges) Owner hereby grants to Producer an exclusive option ("**Option**") to acquire the rights in the Work specified in Clause 2 of the agreement attached as Exhibit A ("**Acquisition Agreement**") which said sum *[shall be][shall not be]* in advance and on account of the Purchase Price (as defined in the Acquisition Agreement) but shall not be returnable in any event.

---

22 Insert date
23 Insert name of owner of work
24 Insert name of production company; include registered number and registered office as appropriate
25 Unless the author and Owner are different in which case the recital will need amendment
26 Insert name of book between inverted commas

1.2 Producer may at any time before the end of the period of *[12][18][24]*[27] calendar months from the date of this Agreement either:

    (a) extend the Option by notice in writing to Owner for a further period of [   ] months accompanied by payment of a further sum of £ (which sum *[shall/shall not]* be on account of the Purchase Price);

    or

    (b) exercise the Option by notice in writing to Owner accompanied by payment of the Purchase Price.

1.3 All sums payable hereunder shall be exclusive of any Value Added Tax payable thereon which if payable shall be paid by Producer upon delivery to Producer of a valid and appropriate Value Added Tax invoice.

2 Execution of the Acquisition Agreement

2.1 Within fourteen (14) days of the exercise of the Option, Owner will at her/his own expense execute and deliver to Producer an engrossment of the Acquisition Agreement.

2.2 If Owner fails or omits to execute or deliver the Acquisition Agreement to Producer within fourteen (14) days of the exercise of the Option as required, it is agreed that on the due exercise of the Option, all rights in and to the Work agreed to be granted or transferred to Producer under the Acquisition Agreement will be deemed vested in Producer with effect on and from the date of the exercise of the Option.

---

27 Amend as appropriate

3   **Representations and Warranties**

All the covenants, representations, undertakings and warranties to be made or given on the part of Owner set out in the Acquisition Agreement are deemed to be incorporated in this Agreement and will be binding while this Option subsists.

4   **Assignability**

Producer is entitled to assign the benefit of this Agreement to any third party ("**Assignee**") subject to and conditional upon procuring that Assignee shall first enter into a direct written covenant with Owner that Assignee shall perform all of Producer's obligations provided for in this Agreement including but not limited to the obligations provided for by this Clause 4 as if primary obligor thereof.

5   **Notices**

Notices by either party:

(a)   must be in writing addressed to receiving party at the address set out in this Agreement or at such new address as the receiving party may from time to time notify to the other for the purpose of this clause; and

(b)   will be effectively served on the following business day, where hand-delivered; on the following business day, where sent by facsimile message so long as a valid facsimile transmission receipt is received; on the second business day following the day of posting of any letter sent by first class prepaid mail if such notice is sent from and to an address in the same country; or on the fifth business day following the day of posting to an overseas address of any prepaid airmail letter.

6   **Confidentiality**

The terms and the subject matter of this Agreement and all and any information provided hereunder shall be and is deemed to be confidential and may only be used for the purposes of this Agreement.

7   **Governing Law**

This Agreement is governed by and to be construed in all respects in accordance with English law and the parties agree to submit to the exclusive jurisdiction of the English courts in respect of any claim or matter arising in relation to this Agreement.

IN WITNESS whereof the parties have executed this Agreement the day and year first above written

SIGNED by   **SIGNED** by   [28]

Owner   for and on behalf of Producer

---

28 Insert individual signing on behalf of the Producer, if a company

Exhibit A

Acquisition Agreement[29]

AGREEMENT made[30]

(1)　　　[31]　　　　　　　　　　　　　　　　　　　　　　　**("Owner")**

(2)　　　[32]　　　　　　　　　　　　　　　　　　　　　　　**("Producer")**

(together referred to as the "**Parties**" and each where the context admits as a "**Party**")

RECITALS

(A)　　　　　　　　　　　　　　　　　　　　　[33] is the author of the literary work
　　　　entitled "　　　　　　　　　　　　[34] " ("**Work**").

(B)　　　Pursuant to an agreement between the Parties dated
　　　　[35]("**Option Agreement**"), Owner granted to Producer an exclusive option to
　　　　acquire certain rights in the Work. Producer has exercised its option under the
　　　　terms of the Option Agreement.

(C)　　　Owner has agreed to grant to Producer certain rights in and to the Work upon the
　　　　terms and conditions of this Agreement.

OPERATIVE PART

1　　　Definitions

1.1　　　In this Agreement, except where a different interpretation is clear from or
　　　　necessary in the context, the following expressions have the following meanings:

　　　　"Budget"　　　the final estimated above and below the line cost of production
　　　　　　　　　　　　of the Film (it being acknowledged that this may include a

---

29 See paragraph 10.9
30 Insert date
31 Insert name of owner of work
32 Insert name of production company; include registered number and registered office as appropriate
33 Unless the author and Owner are different in which case the recital will need amendment
34 Insert name of book between inverted commas
35 Insert date of Option

production fee and overhead payable to Producer) less any overhead charged by a third party financier, completion guarantee fees, deferred payments, legal fees, finance costs (including but not limited to interest, arrangement fees, commitment fees, finders' fees and the like) and contingency payments;

"Film"   the first film based on the Work[36] and produced pursuant to this Agreement including the soundtrack of such film;

"Net Profit"   shall be computed and determined in accordance with the definition contained in the principal financing and distribution agreement(s) for the Film;

"Producer's Net Profit"

shall mean the Net Profit payable to and actually received and retained by Producer;

"Purchase Price"   shall mean a sum equal to   % of the total Budget of the Film subject to a minimum of £   and a maximum of £ [37] .

1.2   All references to statutory provisions or enactments include references to any amendment, modification, or re-enactment of any such provision or enactment (whether before or after the date of this Agreement) and to any regulation or order made under such provision or enactment.

1.3   Headings are for ease of reference only and not to be taken into account in construing this Agreement.

1.4   References to the Parties, clauses, sub-clauses and paragraphs, are (unless the contrary appears) respectively to the Parties, the Recitals and Schedules to, and the clauses, sub-clauses and paragraphs of this Agreement.

2   **Grant of Rights**

---

36 Or as may be the case; i.e. television programmes
37 Complete all figures

In consideration of the payment by Producer to Owner of the Purchase Price, Owner with full title guarantee hereby assigns to Producer the worldwide *[motion picture][dramatic] [radio][and television]*[38] rights in and to the Work to enable *[one full-length feature theatrical motion picture] [television series]*[39] to be made of the Work for the full period of copyright and any and all renewals, extensions, reinstatements or reversions thereof and thereafter (insofar as may be possible) in perpetuity.

3 Payments

3.1 In consideration of the assignment of rights in Clause 2, Producer shall pay or procure the payment to Owner:

(a) forthwith upon execution of this assignment, the Purchase Price (the receipt and sufficiency of which Owner hereby acknowledges);

and

(b) sums equal to [40] of the Producer's Net Profit from exploitation of the Film which shall be accounted for and paid to Owner within sixty (60) days of each calendar quarter for the initial three years after first exploitation of the Film and thereafter within thirty (60) days of each half year.

3.2 All sums payable hereunder shall be exclusive of any Value Added Tax which, if payable, shall be paid by Producer within twenty-eight (28) days of the receipt by Producer of a valid Value Added Tax invoice.

3.3 In the event that Producer or any party deriving title from Producer or its assigns enters into a collection account management agreement, Producer shall procure that Owner shall be made a direct party to and beneficiary of such agreement.

3.4 Producer shall and shall procure that those deriving rights in or to the Film from Producer shall maintain true and complete books of account containing an accurate record of all data necessary for the proper computation of payments hereunder, and Owner shall have the right by itself or its duly authorised

---

38 Amend as required
39 Amend as required
40 Assuming there is a back-end share agreed, then complete with relevant figure

representative to examine such books at all reasonable times (but not more than once in each calendar year) for the purpose of verifying the accuracy of the computations rendered by Producer. Upon reasonable advance notice, such examination shall be made during normal business hours at the principal place of business of Producer. If such examination reveals that statements furnished by Producer were inaccurate by more than *[5%][10%]* and that amounts in excess of those paid to Owner are due, such sums shall be paid to Owner forthwith following such examination and the cost of such examination shall be borne by Producer and Producer shall pay Owner's reasonable costs of and occasioned by the said audit *[excluding costs of travel, subsistence and accommodation]*[41].

3.5   In the event that Producer fails to make full payment of sums to Owner when due, Owner shall be entitled to charge Producer interest at a rate of two percent (2%) above the base lending rate from time to time of Barclays Bank PLC on all sums which are not paid when due calculated from the date such sums were due until paid.

4   Warranties

4.1   Owner hereby represents, covenants and warrants that:

   (a)   it has the right to enter into this Agreement and to grant the rights herein transferred or granted or agreed to be transferred or granted;

   (b)   it has not entered into and will not during the subsistence of the Option hereby granted and (if the Option is exercised) at any time thereafter enter into any arrangement or agreement granting the same or similar rights as are transferred or granted or agreed to be transferred or granted hereunder or any other rights to exploit the Work.

4.2   Owner agrees to keep Producer indemnified from and against all actions, claims, proceedings, costs, expenses and damages incurred or awarded or paid in respect of or arising out of any breach or non-performance of all or any of Owner's covenants, warranties and representations set out in this Agreement.

---

41 Or as may be the case

5   **Credit**

5.1   In *any Film* [42] made by Producer based on the Work, Owner shall receive a credit on-screen and in major paid advertising (subject to normal industry exclusions) issued under Producer's control as follows:[" [43]"]

5.2   No casual or inadvertent failure to accord credit on the parts of Producer or any third party shall constitute a breach of this Agreement

6   **Proceedings for infringement**

Owner authorises Producer, at Producer's expense, in any countries of the World to institute and prosecute such proceedings and to do such acts as Producer may decide are expedient to protect the rights granted or transferred under this Agreement and for the recovery of damages and penalties for any infringement of such rights and if necessary to use Owner's name for such purposes and in any such proceedings Owner will give Producer all reasonable assistance in proving and defending the rights granted or transferred to Producer under this Agreement. Any net sums recovered by Producer pursuant to any such proceedings shall be treated as net profits and in respect of which Owner will be entitled to receive its percentage share pursuant to Clause 3 of this Agreement.

7   **Assignment**

Producer shall be entitled to assign, transfer, sub-licence, sub-distribute, mortgage, charge or in any way dispose of its rights, interests or obligations under this Agreement in whole or in part without the prior written consent of Owner provided always that as a condition of any such assignment Producer shall first procure that any assignee shall enter into a direct covenant with Owner to be bound by all of the terms and provisions of this assignment including but not limited to the provisions of this Clause 7.

8   **Further Assurance**

Owner hereby undertakes with Producer that it will at the request and expense

42 Amend as appropriate
43 Insert details of credit; additional information may be required in relation to position of the credit and whether or not it is single-frame or otherwise

of Producer do all such further things and execute all such further documents as Producer may from time to time require for the purpose of confirming Producer's title to the rights pursuant to Clause 2 as the Producer may require.

9   Relationship between the Parties

Nothing in this Agreement is intended to or shall be deemed to constitute a partnership, agency or joint venture between the Parties hereto and save as expressly provided herein neither party shall have any authority to bind the other in any way or to pledge the other's credit for any purpose whatsoever.

10   Remedies

Owner's sole and exclusive remedy for any breach of this Agreement by Producer shall be money damages and in no event shall Owner be entitled to terminate or rescind this Agreement or to prevent the exercise of any of the Rights or any other right granted hereunder or to seek to apply for any form of injunctive or equitable relief against Producer and/or the Rights and/or the Film.

11   Notices

Notices by either Party:

(a)   must be in writing addressed to receiving party at the address set out in this Agreement or at such new address as the receiving party may from time to time notify to the other for the purpose of this clause;

and

(b)   will be effectively served on the following business day (being a day (other than a Saturday or Sunday) when banks are open for business in England), where hand-delivered; on the following business day, where sent by facsimile message or by email or other print-out mechanism so long as a valid transmission receipt is received; on the second business day following the day of posting of any letter sent by first class registered or recorded prepaid mail if such notice is sent from and to an address in the same country; or on the fifth business day following the day of posting to an overseas address of any prepaid airmail letter.

12   Third Party Rights

A person who is not a party to this Agreement shall have no right under the Contracts (Rights of Third Parties) Act 1999 to enforce any term of this Agreement, but this shall not affect any right or remedy of a third party which exists or is otherwise available apart from that Act.

13   Confidentiality

The terms and the subject matter of this Agreement and all and any information provided pursuant to it about the Film shall be and is deemed to be 'Confidential Information' no part of which shall be disclosed or made available to any third party. The obligations provided for in this clause shall not apply to any part of the Confidential Information which can clearly be shown as in the public domain or if released by Producer in relation to the announcement and/or promotion of the Film.

14   Governing Law

This Agreement shall be construed and shall take effect in accordance with the laws of England and the Parties hereby irrevocably submit to the exclusive jurisdiction of the English courts to resolve any dispute which may arise.

IN WITNESS whereof the parties have executed this Agreement the day and year first above written

SIGNED by   )

for and on behalf of Owner   )

SIGNED by   )

for and on behalf of Producer   )

Appendix 4

Shopping/Attachment Agreement
Paragraphs 10.13-10.14

AGREEMENT dated[44]

PARTIES

(1)   [45]   ("**Creative**")

(2)   [46]   ("**Producer**")

each a "**Party**" and collectively the "**Parties**"

RECITALS

(A)   Creative has written an original motion picture screenplay presently entitled " " ("**Work**")[47] the rights to which are exclusively owned and controlled by Creative[48]

(B)   Producer is interested in the development and possible production of a theatrical motion picture and/or television series and/or programmes and/or other entertainment production(s)[49] to be based upon the Work (each, a "**Film**")

(C)   For a period commencing on the date of this agreement ("**Agreement**") and continuing through and including the date that is *twelve (12)*[50] months from the date of full execution of this Agreement ("**Shopping Period**") Creative has agreed to enable the Producer to seek finance for the Film on the terms of this Agreement

---

44 Insert date of agreement
45 Insert name and address details
46 Insert name and address details
47 The agreement may be adapted for works other than screenplays; i.e. TV formats or an online audio-visual work
48 Insert details of WGA registration if appropriate
49 Amend as required
50 Alter as appropriate

OPERATIVE PART

1. The terms of this Agreement shall apply with respect to any third party sponsor, buyer, cable or broadcast network, studio, financier and/or other applicable third party and/or, as applicable with respect to the Producer in the event Producer elects to finance and produce the Film (**"Financier"**), to whom the Film and/or Work is submitted.

2. The Parties agree that Producer shall have the *[exclusive][non-exclusive]*[51] right to shop the Film and Work during the Shopping Period in order to obtain financing from a Financer.

3. *Creative shall not engage in any further development, production, distribution and/or other exploitation of the Film during the Shopping Period*[52].

4. In the event that Producer succeeds in raising finance on terms that are acceptable to Creative, then subject to Financier's agreement, Producer may be attached to the Film as a *[non-]* [53] exclusive *producer/executive producer*[54]. Creative shall have absolute discretion whether or not to accept terms proposed by a Financier.

5. If, at the conclusion of the Shopping Period, bona fide negotiations are in progress with a Financier in connection with a Film, then the Shopping Period shall be automatically extended for the duration of such bona fide negotiations *[subject to a final cut-off of   months]*[55].

6. In the event that the Shopping Period expires prior to the Film being "set up" for development (as customarily understood in the entertainment industry) with any Financier, Producer shall have no further rights in and to the Work or any Film and shall transfer to Creative the right, title and interest in or to any materials developed by Producer[56] on behalf of Creative and Producer shall cease to represent the Work to Financiers.

7. If at any time after the period of six (6) months following the expiration of the Shopping Period (as the same may be extended), Creative enters into an

---

51 Alter as appropriate
52 Unless the shopping appointment is non-exclusive in which case this clause needs to be amended
53 Amend as appropriate
54 Delete as appropriate
55 Amend as appropriate
56 If turnaround applies see, for example, Guide paragraph 38.9

agreement with a Financier to whom the Work was submitted by Producer at any time during the Shopping Period then Producer shall remain attached to the Film/Work.

8. Creative shall be entitled to negotiate the terms of the sale, option, license and/or other disposition of the exclusive rights to make a Film. Creative shall negotiate the terms of any additional engagement of Creative's input by any Financier (or by Producer, in the event Producer becomes the producer of the Film) as a non-exclusive executive producer. Creative shall be entitled to retain one hundred percent (100%) of any fees and contingent compensation payable to Creative for such services.

9. Producer shall negotiate the terms of Producer's engagement as *[producer]* *[executive producer]* of the Film by any Financier introduced by Producer. Producer shall be entitled to retain one hundred percent (100%) of any fees and contingent compensation payable to Producer for such services. Failure by Producer to come to terms with Financier shall not entitle Producer to prevent Creative from concluding an agreement with Financier, however, in such circumstance Creative shall account for and pay to Producer a sum equal to *[10% of all sums]*[57] received by Creative from the production and exploitation of the Film.

10. Creative warrants, represents and undertakes that:

    (a) Creative has full power and authority to enter into and perform its obligations under this Agreement;

    (b) Creative is and will remain at all material times a "qualifying person" for the purposes of the Copyright, Designs and Patents Act 1988;

    (c) Creative has not licensed, assigned or encumbered nor will s/he licence, assign or encumber the whole or any part of the copyright, goodwill and/or other rights in the Work;

    (d) the Work is original to Creative and does not and shall not infringe the copyright or any other rights of any third party;

---

57 Or as may be the case

(e)   the Work does not and shall not contain any defamatory or obscene material.

11.   The Parties shall keep the terms and the subject matter of this Agreement confidential save as may be necessary for proper performance of the Agreement.

12.   This Agreement represents the entire agreement between the Parties as at the date hereof with respect to the subject matter hereof.

13.   This Agreement shall be governed by and construed in accordance with the laws of England and Wales whose courts shall be courts of competent jurisdiction.

....

Creative   **Producer**

Appendix 5

Music licence (short form)
Paragraphs 13.5, 13.7-13.9

LICENCE dated

PARTIES

(1)   [58]   (**"Composer"**)

(2)   [59]   (**"Producer"**)

RECITALS

(A)   Composer is the composer and first owner of the copyright in the original musical compositions entitled "[60]   " and "   "   (collectively the "**Compositions**")

(B)   Composer is the producer and first owner of copyright in the original sound recordings of the Compositions ("**Recordings**") and to which Recordings Composer has also contributed musical performances

(C)   Producer is the producer of a *[short]* *[feature film]* entitled "[61]
" ("**Film**") and wishes to use the Compositions and the Recordings on the soundtrack to the Film.

---

58 Insert name and address details of Composer
59 Insert name and address details of Producer including registered office and number if a company
60 Details of the Compositions
61 Title of Film

OPERATIVE PART

1   Grant of Rights

1.1   In consideration of *[the sum of   now paid by Producer to Composer[62]]* and of Producer undertaking to provide credit to Composer as provided for at Clause 3 of this licence ("Licence"), Composer hereby grants to Producer, Producer's successors, assigns and licensees the *[non-][63]*exclusive and irrevocable licence in respect of the Compositions and Recordings to include Composer's musical performances included in the Recordings and to reproduce, mix, remix, synchronise and perform the same in whole or in part and to exploit the same as part of the Film by all means and in all media now known or hereafter invented or devised and in any advertising or publicity of or for the Film for the life of copyright in the Film and all renewals, revivals, reversions and extensions, throughout the world; insofar as the licence extends to the Composer's musical performances the grant hereby made is pursuant to the provisions of s182 of the Copyright, Designs and Patents Act 1988 ("**Rights**").

1.2   Notwithstanding the foregoing Producer may not use the Compositions or the Recordings other than as permitted by the terms of this licence which restriction extends to prohibiting Producer from releasing or exploiting Recordings in any way as sound recordings only.

1.3   For a period of five years commencing upon the first communication of the Film to the public, Composer shall not grant rights to use the Compositions or the Recordings for the soundtrack of any other film or audio-visual production.

2   Warranties

Composer warrants, confirms, undertakes and represents that:

(a)   Composer is the sole author of the Compositions and sole producer of the Recordings;

(b)   *Composer has secured written consents from all and any other persons who have in any way contributed to the Recordings as performer or otherwise enabling Composer to grant the Rights without any restriction or encumbrance;[64]*

---

62 Complete as appropriate; add VAT if applicable, subject to valid VAT invoice
63 Amend as required
64 Use, for example, the form to be found as Schedule 2 to the composer agreement at Appendix 6

(c)   Composer is the absolute and unencumbered legal and beneficial owner of the copyright and all and any other rights in the Compositions and the Recordings;

(d)   Composer has full right, power and authority to enter into this Licence and to grant the Rights and has not and shall not enter into any arrangement which may conflict with it;

(e)   Producer shall be entitled to edit the Recordings for the purposes of synchronising them with the Film;

(f)   upon execution of this Licence Composer shall deliver copies of the Recordings to Producer in *[.wavformat]*[65] suitable for synchronising onto the soundtrack of the Film.

3   Credit

Producer undertakes to include the following credits on every copy of the Film

Opening credits:[66]   *Music by*

End credits: *Music by*

4   Protection of copyright

Producer agrees that it will take all necessary steps to protect the copyright in the Film and hence the Recordings and the Compositions and will not do or authorise to be done or omit to do anything whereby such copyright and the protection of the same will or may be prejudiced.

5   Law and jurisdiction

This Licence sets out the entire agreement and understanding between the parties regarding the Compositions and the Recordings and supersedes any prior agreements or arrangements (whether oral or in writing) relating to the same and shall be governed by and construed in accordance with the laws of England the courts of which shall be courts of competent jurisdiction.

Composer   **Producer**

---

65 Include appropriate format
66 Include details of credits

Appendix 6

Music: Composer
Paragraphs 13.11-13.13

AGREEMENT made the

PARTIES

(1)   [67]("**Company**")

(2)   [68]("**Composer**")

(each a "**Party**" and collectively "**Parties**")

RECITAL

Company is producing a full-length motion picture feature film provisionally entitled [69] ("**Film**") and wishes to engage Composer to compose, arrange, record and perform musical works for inclusion in the Film and Composer has agreed to render his services to Company on the terms and conditions of this Agreement.

OPERATIVE PART

1   Definitions

In this Agreement these terms are defined as follows:

"**Agreement**"   means this agreement together with its Schedules;

"**Compositions**"   means the musical works and accompanying literary works (if any) composed, arranged, performed, recorded and produced by Composer pursuant to this Agreement for inclusion in the Film and the Derivative Film Material as more particularly described at Clause 2.2;

"**Delivery Date**"   [70];

67 Insert name of production company
68 Insert name of composer
69 Insert title
70 Insert date

"Delivery Materials"	means materials set out in Schedule 1 to this Agreement;
"Derivative Film Material"	means all trailers, documentaries, making of films or other productions based on the Film and like material connected with advertising and promoting the Film and all or any so-called music videos whether in long or short form;
"Rights"	the rights granted by Composer to Company as more particularly described at Clause 3;
"Recording(s)"	means the sound recordings of the Compositions;
"Schedules"	means the schedules to this Agreement; and
"Term"	means the term of this Agreement[71] *commencing on the date of this Agreement and continuing until* [72]*the date on which Company notifies Composer in writing of its approval of all Delivery Materials delivered by Composer to Company.*

2 Commitment

2.1   During the Term, Company engages Composer and Composer agrees to render the following services (**"Services"**) to Company on an *[exclusive][first call]*[73] basis:

(a)   to compose, arrange, perform, record and produce the Compositions in accordance with the directions of Company and/or its agents;

(b)   to make such alterations to the Compositions and/or the Recordings as may be reasonably required by Company from time to time;

---

71 Amend as may be appropriate
72 Insert date or details of when the Delivery Materials are required
73 Or as required

(c)   to engage technicians, musicians, performers or other artists and to hire studio and other facilities for recording the Compositions, provided always that the payment for the services of any such third parties shall be made by Composer at his own expense;

(d)   to deliver to Company the Delivery Materials by no later than the Delivery Date with time being of the essence; and

(e)   to advise, assist, consult and collaborate fully with Company and any individual producer and director of the Film and any other person Company may nominate in relation to the Recordings and the Compositions, and for such purposes to attend at such times and in such places as Company may reasonably request *[and subject to reimbursement of Composer's travel expenses]* provided always that Company's decision in relation to all matters connected with the Compositions including those involving artistic taste shall be final.

2.2   When recorded the Compositions shall comprise not less than *[minutes]* of original soundtrack music for which the specifications shall include the following[74]:

2.3   Composer shall render the Services in a competent, conscientious and professional manner.

2.4   Composer hereby acknowledges and agrees that the Compositions and Recordings may not necessarily be used in the Film.

3   Grant of Rights

In consideration of the payment by Company to Composer of the sum of
            [75] (the "**Fee**") payable in accordance with the provisions of Clause 5, together with all and any royalties in accordance with Clause 6 below, Composer hereby:

---

74 Set out any particulars of styles, genres and other requirements for the Film, specific sections of the Film for which soundtrack music is required etc
75 Insert amount; add VAT if applicable, subject to valid VAT invoice

3.1   in relation to the Recordings:

(a)   irrevocably, and with full title guarantee, assigns to Company the entire copyright, and all other rights, title and interests of whatsoever nature, whether vested or contingent, in and to the Recordings, free of all encumbrances throughout the world, including (but not limited to) the right to exploit the Recordings in all media and by all means now known or hereafter invented, for the full period of copyright and all renewals, revivals, reversions or extensions, save that such Recordings may be used by Composer for resume/curriculum vitae purposes;

(b)   accepts and agrees that Company shall be the sole owner of the copyright in the Recordings and, further, that for the purpose of the copyright law of the United States of America, the Recordings are and shall be deemed to be made as "works made for hire"; and

3.2   in relation to the Compositions:

(a)   grants to Company the right to reproduce and exploit the Compositions in all media and by all methods now know or hereafter invented, including (but not limited to)[76] the sole and exclusive right:

(1)   to synchronize the Compositions with the soundtrack of the Film and the Derivative Film Material so that the same may be used as part of the soundtrack of the Film in all media now known or hereafter invented for the life of copyright of the Film and for all and any purposes connected with the Film including but not limited to all and any marketing, advertising or promotional purposes connected with and related to the Film including but not limited to trailers, teasers, and other clips, and

(2)   without further payment to reproduce and exploit the Compositions as part of the Film in all forms of mechanical devices whether capable of reproducing sound with images or sound alone and whether such devices are now known or hereafter to become known or invented to include but not be limited to CDs, DVDs, cassettes, compact video discs and/or via digital downloads, and

---

76 Assumes Composer retains ownership of copyright in the Compositions

(3)   to publicly perform, distribute and exploit for profit or otherwise, and to authorise others to do so, the Compositions as synchronized with the Film and the Derivative Film Material;

(b)   to authorise or licence others to exercise any or all of the above rights.

3.3   Composer irrevocably and unconditionally waives in perpetuity all moral rights that the Composer may have in and to the Compositions, the Recordings and his performances included therein, whether arising under sections 77 to 85 (inclusive) of the Copyright, Designs and Patents Act 1988 or otherwise, save that Composer shall be accorded the following credit on the positive copies of the Film made by or to the order of Company[77].

3.4   The Parties hereby acknowledge that Composer shall be the sole owner of the copyright, together with all rights, title and interests of whatsoever nature, in and to the Compositions[78].

3.5   Composer hereby accepts and agrees that no further payment or licence shall be required to synchronize the Compositions with the soundtrack of the Film or with the Derivative Film Material. In particular, but without limitation, no mechanical licence fees shall be payable or paid where the Film is reproduced in CDs, DVDs, cassettes, compact video discs and/or via digital downloads or any other medium for which a mechanical licence may otherwise be required. Company acknowledges that Composer will retain 100% of the public performance rights in the Compositions which the Composer may register in his name with those performing rights organisations with which Composer is registered and/or affiliated[79].

4   Composer's Warranties and Undertakings

Composer warrants and undertakes to Company that:

4.1   Composer is and shall be the sole composer and writer of the Compositions and performer on the Recordings[80] which are and shall be wholly original to Composer and that nothing contained in the Compositions or Recordings infringes or shall infringe the copyright or any other rights of any third party;

4.2   Composer has full authority to enter into this Agreement and copyright in

---

77 Insert credit details
78 If this intended to be the case
79 This precedent does not address issues relating to soundtrack albums which may need to be considered on a case-by-case basis
80 Amend as appropriate

Compositions and Recordings shall subsist or may be acquired in all countries of the world whose laws provide for copyright protection;

4.3 Composer has not and will not at any time do or omit to do anything relating to Compositions and Recordings as a result of which the copyright or any part of the copyright in the Compositions or Recordings may be destroyed or impaired;

4.4 Neither the Compositions nor the Recordings shall infringe the rights of any other person, nor shall they contain any description of or reference to, any person, thing or incident which, if published in any manner or form, would confer upon any person or entity a right of action or claim for damages against Company;

4.5 Neither the Compositions nor the Recordings shall contain any defamatory, blasphemous or obscene matter;

4.6 Composer shall procure that any technician, musician, performer or other artist engaged by Composer or on Composer's behalf to undertake any role, contribute to the creation of any copyright material including but not limited to Compositions, perform on any one or more of the Recordings in relation to this Agreement signs a written release in favour of Company and in the form set out in Schedule 2 to this Agreement, provided always that the payment for any such release shall be made by Composer at Composer's own expense;

4.7 Composer is a qualifying person for the purposes of the Copyright, Designs and Patents Act 1988; and

4.8 *[For a period of [seven (7) years] following the first [theatrical release] [in the UK/US] of the Film, Composer shall not grant any right to any third party to incorporate any Composition in the soundtrack of any theatrical motion picture other than the Film.]* [81]

5 Consideration

5.1 The Fee shall be paid by Company to Composer as to:

(a) [82]on signature by Composer of this Agreement (receipt of which Composer hereby acknowledges); and

(b) on the date on which Composer delivers the Delivery Materials to Company and Company accepts such Delivery Materials.

---

81 Include/omit/amend as may be required
82 Complete as required

5.2   For the avoidance of doubt, Composer hereby accepts and agrees that all recording costs shall be paid by him out of the Fee.

5.3   All payments hereunder are exclusive of Value Added Tax which shall be paid by Company upon receipt of a VAT invoice from Composer.

5.4   Composer agrees that the payments provided for in this Agreement shall be inclusive of all and any claims Composer may have for equitable remuneration.

6   Royalties

6.1   In relation to the Recordings[83] and notwithstanding termination the Term and delivery of the Delivery Materials, Company hereby agrees to account for and pay to Composer for *[50% (fifty per cent)]*[84] of income actually received by Company which is wholly, directly and identifiably attributable to the exploitation of the Recordings as standalone works (including, but not limited to, income received in respect of the sale of copies of any soundtrack of the Film) less any actual deductions, payments, commissions and expenses incurred by Company to any third party in respect of such income.

6.2   Company shall keep proper books and records of account in respect of exploitation of the Recordings and shall make up statements of account showing the royalties due to Composer in respect of each Recording at half yearly intervals ending on 30 June and 31 December in each year until Company shall cease to derive income from such Recording. Company shall forward such statements and make payment of the amounts shown due to Composer within 90 days of 30 June and 31 December each year; and not more than once in any year subject to reasonable notice, Composer may appoint a chartered accountant to inspect the relevant parts of Company's books and records in order to verify the accounts. Any audit shall be at the usual place of business of Company during normal business hours and shall be at the sole expense of Composer. Composer may not inspect the books or records in respect of royalty accounts rendered more than three years previously.

7   Assignment

Either party may assign its rights under this Agreement in whole or in part to any third party, subject to and conditional upon the party effecting the assignment procuring that the assignee covenants directly with the non-assigning party in writing to perform the assigning party's obligations under this Agreement, which covenant shall also include a provision that any subsequent assignee shall

---

83 If applicable
84 Amend/delete as appropriate

be bound by the terms of this Clause 7.

8   Further Assurance

Each party hereby undertakes that it will at the request and expense of the other party do all such further things and execute all such further documents as the other party may from time to time require for the purpose of confirming the other party's rights pursuant to this Agreement and/or giving effect to the provisions of this Agreement.

9   Indemnity

Composer indemnifies Company, and shall keep Company indemnified, from and against all claims, demands, actions, proceedings, costs, damages, losses and expenses, which shall include legal costs, expenses and VAT whether suffered or incurred directly or indirectly by Company or any compensation paid or agreed to be paid by Company to any third party or arising out of any breach, non-performance or non-observance of any of the covenants, warranties, representations, undertakings and agreements of Composer contained or implied in this Agreement.

10   Termination

If during Term, Composer fails, is unable, or refuses to observe and perform any of Composer's obligations in this agreement and if Composer fails to remedy a breach (to the extent that it is remediable) within seven days after receipt from Company of a notice specifying the nature of such breach, then Company may terminate this agreement without prejudice to any claim it has for damages for such breach. Regardless of any termination, the Rights shall remain vested in Company. Upon a termination prior to the end of the Term, the provisions of Clause 5.1 shall cease to have effect and Company shall not be liable to pay Composer any more than a quantum meruit fee.

11   Notices

11.1   Any notice required to be given under this Agreement shall be in writing and shall be delivered to the other party's last address either by hand or by fax or other print-out mechanism but shall in any event be confirmed by its being sent by prepaid registered or recorded delivery post.

11.2   Any notice to be given or served pursuant to this Agreement shall be treated as having been received no later than two working days after the date upon which such notice has been posted within the United Kingdom and twelve working days if posted outside the United Kingdom.

11.3   The addresses stated at the beginning of this Agreement shall be the appropriate addresses for service unless and/or until a new address is notified, it being the obligation of each party to keep the other informed of any changes of address.

12   Legal Advice

Composer confirms that s/he has been given the opportunity of taking and has taken independent legal advice from a lawyer experienced in music agreements before signing this Agreement.

13   Miscellaneous

13.1   Each Party is an independent contractor and nothing in this Agreement shall be construed as constituting either Party a partner, joint venture, agent or legal representative of the other or as conferring on either Party any right, power or authority to create any obligation, express or implied, on behalf of the other.

13.2   Neither of the Parties has entered into this Agreement in reliance upon any representation, warranty or undertaking by or on behalf of any other party which is not expressly set out in this Agreement.

13.3   No delay or failure by either Party to detect, protect or remedy the failure of the other Party to perform any obligation under this Agreement shall constitute a waiver of the aggrieved Party's rights. No waiver of any provision of this Agreement or any rights or obligations of either Party will be effective unless agreed in writing and signed by the relevant Party waiving compliance. Any such waiver will be effective only in the specific instance and for the specific purpose as put in writing.

13.4   The clause headings in this Agreement are for the convenience of reference only and are not part of the clause and do not form part of this Agreement and shall not be used in construing this Agreement.

13.5   If any one or more of the provisions of this Agreement is found to be unenforceable, it or they shall be deemed to be removed and the rest of this Agreement shall stand as long as it continues to evidence the basis upon which the Parties have entered into this Agreement.

13.6   A person who is not party to this Agreement has no right under the Contracts (Rights of Third Parties) Act 1999 to enforce any terms of this Agreement.

13.7   Company shall be entitled to injunctive or other equitable relief to prevent a breach of this agreement by Composer. Composer acknowledges that any breach could cause irreparable damage to the commercial prospects of the Film.

13.8   The terms and the subject matter of this Agreement and all and any information provided by Company to Composer about the Film shall be and is deemed to be

'Confidential Information' no part of which shall be used by Composer otherwise than for the purposes of this Agreement nor disclosed or made available to any third party. The obligations provided for in this clause shall not apply to any part of the Confidential Information which can clearly be shown as in the public domain unless (a) has become public knowledge other than through Composer or any party to whom Composer provides the same or (b) was received from a third party who did not owe Company a duty of confidence in respect of it or (c) is required to be disclosed by a court or statutory body.

13.9   Composer acknowledges and agrees that Composer's sole and exclusive remedy for any breach of this Agreement by Company shall be money damages and in no event shall Composer be entitled to terminate or rescind this Agreement or to prevent the exercise of any of the rights granted by you to Company nor may you seek to apply for any form of injunctive or equitable relief against Company and/or the Rights and/or the Film.

13.10   This Agreement shall be governed by and construed in accordance with the laws of England, and, failing mediation, disputes shall be referred to the High Court of Justice in London, England.

EXECUTED as a deed for and on behalf of
[85]

by its director [86]

In the presence of:[87]

EXECUTED as a deed by
[88]

In the presence of:[89]

---

85 Insert name of production Company
86 Insert name of individual director signing the Agreement
87 Insert name, address and occupation of witness
88 Insert name of Composer
89 Insert name, address and occupation of witness

Schedule 1

Delivery Materials[90]

Schedule 2

Performer/Contributor Release[91]

From: [92]("**Company**")

To: ("**you**"/"**your**")

Date:

Dear

"   [93]" ("**Film**")

This letter of agreement ("**Agreement**") shall constitute the terms upon which you agree to render your performances *[services]* as *[a musician][a vocalist][engineer][mixer]*[94] (your "**Performance**") in connection with the making of recordings *[whose titles or provisional titles are set out in the Appendix hereto]*[95] (the "**Recordings**") for use in connection with the Film.

1   In consideration of the sum of £[[96]], the receipt of which you hereby acknowledge, you hereby irrevocably:

1.1   agree and consent to participate in the Recordings and to the filming, recording and/or broadcasting of the Performance and to the mixing, remixing, editing, copying, adaptation or translation of the Performance and that such filming, recording mixing, remixing, editing, copying, adaptation, translation or broadcasting may be incorporated in the Recordings and/or the Films in whole or in part at Company's discretion (but you acknowledge that Company is under no obligation to use such film and recording);

1.2   consent to the reproduction, exhibition and exploitation of the Recordings and/ or the Film or any part thereof (including the Performance) by all means and in all media and formats whether now or hereafter invented throughout the world for the full life of copyright in the Film to include all extensions, renewals, revivals and reversions thereof and insofar as possible in perpetuity (including for the purposes of advertising, publicity and promotion of the Recording and/ or the Film) and further you waive the benefit of any moral rights to which you may be entitled;

1.3   consent to the use and reproduction of your name, photograph, likeness and biography in connection with the Performance and the reproduction of the Recordings and/or the Film or any part thereof by all means and in all media throughout the world insofar as possible in perpetuity;

1.4   grant and assign to Company us all rights in the Performance and all consents necessary to enable Company to make the fullest use of the Performance worldwide in perpetuity in any and all media, whether now known or hereafter developed or discovered, without payment, liability or acknowledgement to you;

1.5   waive and release Company from any claim, action or demand arising out of or in connection with the Performance; and

1.6   agree not to disclose to any party any information relating to the subject matter of this Agreement and/or the Film; and

1.7   accept the Fee as inclusive of all and any entitlement to any equitable remuneration;

1.8   in consideration for our agreeing wherever consistent with industry practice to accord you a credit in the end titles to the Film for your performance, you hereby waive all moral rights arising in relation thereto.

2   You warrant and undertake that you are fully entitled to grant all rights in the Performance to Company and that nothing in the Performance shall infringe the rights of any third party or breach any contract or duty of confidence and that you are at least 18 years old.

3   You acknowledge and agree that copyright and all and any other intellectual property rights in the Recordings and the Film shall be owned by Company and that Company may assign or license the whole or any part of the benefit of this

Agreement to any third party.

4   This Agreement shall be governed by and construed in accordance with English law.

Please signify your acceptance of the foregoing by signing and returning to us the attached duplicate of this Agreement.

APPENDIX

(BEING THE LIST OF RECORDINGS)[97]

Yours sincerely   Agreed and Accepted

[98]for and on behalf of   [99]

[100]

---

97 If required
98 Insert name of individual signing on behalf of Company
99 Print name of individual contributor
100 Insert name of Company

Appendix 7

Location Agreement
Section 20

From: [101]   (**"we"**, **"us"**, **"our"**)

To: [102]   (**"you"**, **"your"**)

Date: [103]

Dear [104]

"[105]   "(**"Film"**)
Premises located at   (**"Premises"**[106])

We are writing to confirm that this letter of agreement ("**Agreement**") shall constitute the terms upon which you hereby grant to us permission to use the Premises in connection with the production of the Film, which we propose but do not undertake to produce.

1   In consideration of the sum of £   [107] (**"Fee"**), which Fee shall be paid by us to you as follows:

    (a)   deposit of £   which sum shall be paid on or before ;

    (b)   sum of £   , which shall be paid on the first day of principal photography, *[currently scheduled for   [108]];* and

---

101 Insert details of producer; if a production company include registered office and number details
102 Insert details of location owner; if a company include registered office and number details
103 Insert date of agreement
104 Insert name of producer or, if a company, Dear Sirs
105 Insert name of Film
106 It may be necessary to delineate particular areas of the Premises to which the production is restricted
107 Insert appropriate amounts
108 Complete as appropriate

(c) sum of £ which shall be paid on the final day of principal photography, *currently scheduled for*   ,

you hereby grant to us (including our successors, assigns, licensees, employees, agents, independent contractors and suppliers) permission during the period commencing on   and terminating on   [1] [0] [9]
("**Licence Period**") to enter upon, photograph, record and use the Premises together with all access, facilities and utilities at such Premises until we have completed filming, photographing or other recording, including, without limitation, filming of any retakes or additional scenes for 24 hours a day for such purposes as we may require in connection with the production, exhibition, distribution, advertising, publicity and/or other exploitation of the Film.

2   Access may be gained to the Premises via[110]   . Parking areas will be designated *[as per the plan attached]* [111]   .

3   You agree that during the Licence Period (and any return or continuing period) we shall have the exclusive use of the Premises[112] and no other person shall be permitted to take any photograph or make any film or audio or audio-visual recordings in, upon or around the Premises.

4   You hereby grant to us the option of returning to or continuing to use the Premises during additional day(s) or hours, as needed, for filming beyond the Licence Period, and for which use of the Premises an additional fee £
per day shall be payable in respect of each additional day of use, provided that any delay is not caused by you or within your control and/or is not as a result of a breach of this agreement by you, in which case no further compensation shall be payable. VAT shall be payable if applicable subject to the provision to us of a valid VAT invoice.

5   You hereby accept and agree that all rights, including any and all copyright in the films, photography, recordings and/or any other work(s) made, taken or otherwise created by us at the Premises (collectively the "**Works**") shall vest in us and that we may use the Works in any manner we consider fit by all means and in all media now known or hereinafter invented for the full life of copyright

---

109 Insert dates
110 Describe how and where
111 Explain, perhaps by reference to a plan of the area; provide how parking is to be supervised and by whom
112 Or otherwise as may be the case

together with all renewals, revivals, extensions as well.

6   You hereby warrant and represent that:

    (a)   *[you are the owner of the Premises and/or that you are the owner of all rights in and to the Premises[113]and that]* you are fully authorised to enter into this Agreement, and that you have the right to grant us the use of the Premises;

    (b)   no consent of any other party is necessary to grant the rights and licences granted in this Agreement and the signatory of this Agreement is duly permitted to sign it;

    (c)   no depiction or references to the Premises or its contents will constitute any copyright or trade mark infringement, act of defamation or invasion of privacy or otherwise infringe the right of any third party; and

    (d)   the Premises are safe for their intended use;

    (e)   you have in place public liability insurance for the Premises that will cover the intended use of the Premises by us.

7   We undertake that we will leave the Premises in the condition in which we found them at the commencement of the Licence Period and that we will make good all and any damage caused by or as a consequence of the production.

8   Security at the Premises *[and for the production]* will be provided by on the following basis[114]:

9   At all times we shall have in place all relevant insurances to cover the production and third party liabilities arising as a consequence of any default, neglect or breach of statutory duty by members of the cast and crew.

10   We shall provide you with a credit in the end credits of the Film.

11   We shall be entitled to assign or licence the whole or any part of the benefit of this Agreement to any third party involved in the production of the Film provided that we shall first require such third party to undertake directly to you to be bound by and responsible for all of our obligations arising under this Agreement.

12   You will keep confidential the terms of this Agreement and shall not disclose

---

113 Amend as necessary
114 Provide as appropriate

nor divulge any matter or information about the Film or about our production of it and, in particular, prior to the first public exhibition of the Film, you shall not make any public announcement nor release any press or other statement about your connection with the Film or in relation to our using the Premises without our prior written consent.

13   This Agreement shall be governed by and construed in accordance with English law.

Please signify your acceptance of the foregoing by signing and returning to us the attached duplicate of this Agreement.

Yours sincerely

....

[   ]
for and on behalf of
[   ][115]

Agreed and Accepted

....

[   ]
for and on behalf of
[   ][116]

---

115 Name of location owner's signatory
116 Name of production company signatory

Appendix 8

Writer's Agreement
Section 27

From: [117]   (**"Producer"**, **"we"**, **"our"**, **"us"**)

To: [118]   (**"you"**, **"your"**)

Date: [119]

Dear   [120]

Reference is made to our recent discussions and this letter of agreement (**"Agreement"**) sets out the terms and conditions upon which you are being engaged by Producer to write an original screenplay *[adaptation of the [novel] [original stage play)] [the "**Original Work**"]* [121]entitled "   " (**"Screenplay"**) for a film which Producer proposes but does not undertake to produce (**"Film"**):-

1   Works

In consideration for the payments provided for at paragraph 3.1 below you will write and deliver to us the following works in the *English* [122] language:-

(a)   a treatment (**"Treatment"**);

(b)   a first draft of the Screenplay (**"First Draft"**);

(c)   a second draft of the Screenplay (**"Second Draft"**);

(d)   a polish of the Screenplay (**"Polish"**);

(e)   a final screenplay (**"Final Screenplay"**);

(**"Works"**) [123]

---

117 Insert name and address details
118 Insert name and address details
119 Insert date of agreement
120 Insert first name of writer
121 Amend as appropriate
122 Or as otherwise may be the case
123 Clause 1 may need to be amended to address requirements for additional/alternative drafts, polishes etc

2   Delivery

2.1   You will deliver the Treatment by no later than [124].

2.2   You will deliver the First Draft *[by no later than forty (45)[125]]* days after Producer notifying you in writing that delivery is required.

2.3   By no later than *[seven (7)]* days after delivery of the First Draft Producer will revert to you with any comments it may have on the First Draft.

2.4   By no later than *[fifteen (15)]* days after Producer submits its comments to you on the First Draft, you will deliver to the Producer the Second Draft.

2.5   By no later than *[fifteen (15)]* days after Producer submits its comments on the Second Draft, you will deliver to the Producer the completed Polish.

2.6   By no later than *[seven (7)]* days after delivery of the Polish, Producer will revert to you with any comments it may have and you will then have a further 10 days in which to deliver the Final Screenplay.

2.7   Time shall be of the essence of all of your obligations as contained in this Agreement.

3   Payment

3.1   In full and final consideration of your writing the Works, Producer shall pay you the total sum of [126] as follows:

      (a)   the sum of [127]upon your countersignature of the Agreement and its return to Producer; and

      (b)   the further sum of within seven days of delivery of the First Draft as provided for at paragraph 2.2; and

      (c)   the further sum of upon acceptance by Producer of the Final Draft which acceptance if not notified by Producer to you in writing shall be

---

124 Insert date for delivery
125 Amend italicised provisions of 2.2- 2.5 as appropriat
126 Insert all amounts required in 3.1; milestones may need amending depending on what is agreed between parties
127 Insert instalment amounts in each of these sub-clauses – or as otherwise may be the case

deemed to be given no later than ten days after delivery of the Final Draft.[128]

3.2   Producer shall procure that all income derived from exploitation of the Film is to be collected and accounted for by an independent third party pursuant to the terms of a collection account management agreement ("**CAMA**") which the parties hereto and others connected with the financing, production and exploitation of the Film propose to negotiate and conclude hereafter and of which Producer shall procure Writer to be a direct beneficiary.

3.3   Additionally, Producer shall pay or procure that those responsible for collecting and accounting for the profits of the Film shall pay to you[129]   % (per cent) of the Producer's net profits from exploitation of the Film with "net profits" being defined as per the principal agreements entered into for the finance, post-production and distribution of the Film and which sums shall be paid at such time and in such proportions as shall hereafter be negotiated by the parties in good faith at the same time of negotiation of recoupment schedule for the CAMA;

3.4   VAT shall be payable if applicable subject to the provision to Producer of a valid VAT invoice.

3.5   The payments and other consideration provided for in this Clause 3 shall constitute the full extent of your entitlement to be remunerated for your work and shall be deemed to include all and any right that you may have to any equitable remuneration or other remuneration arising from any rental and lending rights that you may otherwise have.

4.   Warranties

4.1   You hereby warrant, represent and undertake as follows:

(a)   you will provide your services to the best of your ability;

(b)   your services will be provided to Producer on an exclusive basis;

---

128 If Writer is offered a share of producer's net profit additional provisions such as those as Appendix 9 sub-clauses 7.1(c)-(e) may be included
129 Insert payment details

(c)   *[save for those elements of the Original Work that are incorporated into the Work,]*[130] you will be the sole author of all of the Work which will be wholly original and no third party's copyright will be infringed;

(d)   copyright will subsist in the Works;

(e)   the Works will not be defamatory;

(f)   you have not entered into any agreement which might conflict with the terms of this Agreement or with the provision by you of your services under this Agreement;

(g)   you are a qualifying person for the purposes of the Copyright, Designs and Patents Act 1988.

4.2   Producer hereby warrants, represents and undertakes as follows:

(a)   that Producer has the right to enter into this Agreement;

[(b)   that it has obtained the [screen] [television][131] *rights in and to the Original Work*[132]*]*;

and

(c)   that any use made by you of the Original Work will not infringe the rights of any third party[133].

5.   Copyright

5.1   By your countersignature to this Agreement you hereby assign to Producer all of the copyright in and to the Works for the full term of copyright to include all and any reversions, extensions, revivals and renewals thereof throughout the territory of the world and in so doing you hereby waive all and any of your moral rights therein.

5.2   Each of the Works constitutes within the meaning of the copyright laws

---

130 Include words in italics if appropriate
131 Amend as required
132 Include as appropriate
133 Include as appropriate

of the United States of America, a "work made for hire" for Producer and as between Producer and you Producer owns and shall own all right, title and interest in and to the Works including without limitation the copyright therein and the copyright in the Film and all and any rights arising under the copyright laws of all and any jurisdictions including but not limited to the United States of America exclusively in perpetuity, and Producer may exploit the same throughout the Territory by all means and in all media whether now known or hereafter devised, including, without limitation. If for any reason the Works or any of them are not deemed to be a "work made for hire", you irrevocably assign and grant to Producer all rights of any kind in and to the Works as herein contemplated.

6.   Credit

6.1   In the event that the Film is made, Producer undertakes that it will accord you a screen credit in the form "Screenplay by   [134]". If other writers are brought in to work on the Screenplay, and Producer reserves the right to bring in other writers as it may decide, you shall share a credit with those other writers, but those other writers shall be in a position below yours. The credit shall be a single card credit and will appear in the main titles, whether at the beginning or end of the film. The credit will also appear in any paid ads, including DVD and home video box covers, where the director's, producers', and lead actors' credit appears, except congratulatory ads.

6.2   For the avoidance of doubt and notwithstanding the provisions of paragraph 6.1 you accept that any inadvertent failure to accord any credit will not be regarded as a breach of this Agreement so that no right will thereupon arise whereby you might seek an injunction or claim other relief against Producer or its assigns with the only obligation consequently arising being an obligation to use reasonable endeavours to rectify the omission of the credit.

7   Indemnity

You hereby indemnify Producer in the event of any breach by you of any of your several warranties or obligations and undertakings contained in this Agreement. Producer hereby agrees to defend and indemnify you in the event of any breach by Producer of any warranties or obligations and undertakings contained in this Agreement, or any claims that arise from the Screenplay or the exploitation of

---

134 Complete as required

the Screenplay except those claims which relate to a breach of this Agreement by you.

8 Acknowledgement

8.1 Producer is not obliged to make any use of the Works nor to make or release any Film.

8.2 Producer is hereby entitled to use and authorise others to use your name and likeness in connection with its proposed production and subsequent exploitation of the Film.

9 Turnaround

9.1 If a firm start date for commencement of principal photography of the Film shall not have been set within two (2) years of the delivery to the Producer of the Final Screenplay then you shall have an exclusive option to purchase all of Producer's rights in the Work.

9.2 The price payable by you pursuant to paragraph 9.1 for the rights in the Work shall be the sum of Producer's costs[135] incurred in respect of the Work plus interest thereon at two percent 2% per annum compounded annually over Barclay's Bank Base Rate from time to time ("**Purchase Price**"). Unless otherwise hereafter agreed in writing, Producer shall not be obliged to transfer or release to you any rights unless and/or until you have made full payment of the Purchase Price.

10 Further Assurance

You hereby undertake to execute such further or other documents and do such further or other things as may be necessary to give effect to the terms and conditions of this Agreement.

11 Writer's Default

If at any time you fail, or are unable to or neglect or refuse to perform your obligations under this Agreement and within seven (7) days after the receipt

---

135 May include cost of drafting a full blown budget and other costs wholly and necessarily incurred in developing the Film

from Producer of a notice specifying the nature of any of the breaches you failed to remedy the same, then Producer may immediately terminate this Agreement but without prejudice to any other claim or rights it may have against you nor to use any of the Works that you may have completed at the time of termination.

12   Assignment

Producer may assign, license or grant the benefit of this Agreement or its rights or benefits under this Agreement in whole or in part to any third party and all of your representations, warranties and undertakings herein contained shall enure for the benefit of such third party. However, Producer shall remain liable under this Agreement unless it procures that such third party enters into a direct covenant whereby it assumes direct liability to you, and that such third party is financially solvent.

13   Notices

Any notice to be given or served under this Agreement shall be in writing and shall be delivered personally, by facsimile or by first class, prepaid, registered or recorded delivery (if available) post (air mail if posted to another country) to the party to be served at the address set out at the head of this Agreement (or such other address as either party may from time to time notify in writing to the other) and shall be deemed to have been served within five (5) business days of being sent.

14   General

14.1   A waiver by either party of any term or condition of this Agreement shall not be deemed or construed to be a waiver of such term or condition for the future or any subsequent breach thereof. All remedies, rights, undertakings, obligations and agreements in this Agreement shall be cumulative and none of them shall be in limitation of any other remedy, right, undertaking, obligation or agreement of either party.

14.2   You acknowledge and agree that your sole and exclusive remedy for any breach of this Agreement by Producer shall be money damages and in no event shall you be entitled to terminate or rescind this Agreement or to prevent the exercise of any of the rights granted by you to Producer nor may you seek to apply for any form of injunctive or equitable relief against Producer and/or the rights and/or the Film.

14.3   The terms and the subject matter of this Agreement and all and any information provided by us to you about the Film shall be and is deemed to be 'Confidential Information' no part of which shall be used by you otherwise than for the purposes of this Agreement nor disclosed nor made available to any third party. The obligations provided for in this clause shall not apply to any part of the Confidential Information which can clearly be shown as in the public domain unless (a) has become public knowledge other than through you or any party to whom you provided the same, or (b) was received from a third party who did not owe us a duty of confidence in respect of it, or (c) is required to be disclosed by a court or statutory body.

14.4   If any provision of this Agreement is adjudged by a court to be void or unenforceable, such provision shall in no way affect any other provision of this Agreement, the application of such provision in any other circumstance or the validity or enforceability of this Agreement and such provision shall be curtailed and limited only to the extent necessary to bring it within legal requirements.

14.5   This Agreement replaces, supersedes and cancels all previous arrangements, understandings or agreements between the parties either oral or written with respect to the subject matter of this Agreement and expresses and constitutes the entire agreement between Producer and you and no variation of any of the terms or conditions of this Agreement may be made unless such variation is agreed in writing and signed by both parties to this Agreement.

14.6   This Agreement shall be construed and shall take effect in accordance with the laws of England and it is hereby agreed that the Courts of England shall have jurisdiction (and the parties hereby irrevocably submit to the exclusive jurisdiction of the English courts) to resolve any dispute which may arise.

Kindly confirm your agreement to and acceptance of the above terms and conditions by countersigning the duplicate of this letter and returning it to me.

Yours sincerely   Agreed and Accepted

For and on behalf of [136]   [137]

---

136 Signature of the individual signing on behalf of Producer and, if applicable, the name of the production company
137 Signature of the Writer

Appendix 9

Director's Agreement by way of a loan-out agreement
Inducement letter[138]
Sections 28 & 36

PARTIES

(1)   [139]   (**"Producer"**)

(2)   [140]   (**"Company"**)

RECITALS

(1)   Producer is intending (but does not undertake) to produce a motion picture feature Film entitled "[141]   " (**"Film"**).

(2)   Company is solely entitled to (a) the services of the Director as a film director throughout the world for a period exceeding the term of this Agreement and (b) the entire copyright and all other rights in and to the products of such services and the right to make such services available to others.

(3)   Company has agreed to supply the services of the Director to the Company to assist in the development of and subject to the terms of this Agreement, to direct the Film on the terms and conditions of this Agreement

OPERATIVE PART

1.   Definitions

"**Act**"   the Copyright, Designs and Patents Act 1988 as amended from time to time or any other enactment which replaces it;

---

138 The structure of this agreement is where the director provides services via a loan out company; this form may be adapted for others who provide services via their loan-out companies; this is also a longer form agreement than many included in these Appendices and has been adapted from a form used for films with significant budgets. See section 36 for a discussion of loan-out agreements
139 Insert name, registered office and registered number details of Producer
140 Insert name, registered office and registered number details of Director's loan- out company
141 Insert name of film

"Agreement"	this agreement and its Schedule;
"Budget"	the budget for the Film agreed by Producer and the financiers of the Film;
"Business Day"	a day (other than a Saturday or Sunday) when banks are open for business in England;
"Commencement Date"	to be notified in writing by Producer to Company;
"Director"	[142]
"Force Majeure"	any cause outside the control of Producer including but not limited to fire, casualty, accident, riot, war, act of God, strike, lock-out, labour conditions, judicial order, enactment or the incapacity or death of Director, the producer, leading cast member or a senior technician of the Film;
"Inducement Letter"	the inducement letter of even date in the form attached as the Schedule;
"Production Period"	the period commencing with effect from the Commencement Date *[being no later than]*[143] being a date at the commencement of pre-production and prior to commencement of principal photography, or otherwise as Producer may determine and expiring on *[completion of principal photography]*[144];
"Production Schedule"	the schedule for the production of the Film approved by Producer as of the first day of principal photography;

---

142 Insert name of director
143 Insert relevant dates
144 Insert relevant details

"Products"	the products of Director's services provided by Company to Producer pursuant to the terms of this Agreement;

"Recoupment Schedule"	the recoupment waterfall to be agreed between those participating in income to be generated from exploitation of the Film;

"Screenplay"	the screenplay entitled[145] " " written by

"Schedule"	the schedule to this Agreement;

"Term"	the term of this Agreement being a period starting on the Commencement Date and concluding upon delivery to and acceptance by the Producer of the final cut of the Film.

## 2.	Engagement

2.1	Producer hereby engages Company to provide the services of Director to direct the Film and Company hereby agrees to procure that Director render his services as director of the Film upon the terms and conditions of this Agreement from and after the Commencement Date.

2.2	During active pre-production and principal photography, Producer shall use reasonable endeavours to provide a private office or other suitable working space for the Director including adequate environmental controls, lighting, personal computer and telephones etc.

## 3.	Exclusivity

3.1	Company agrees that Producer shall be entitled to the exclusive services of Director *[in any part of the world]*[146] during the Production Period, during the edit, grading, ADR and VFX work on the Film and at all other times both prior to and after the Production Period Company shall procure that Director shall render Director's services to Producer on a non-exclusive first call basis (as

145 Insert details
146 Or as may be agreed

that expression is understood in the Film industry) for all and any purposes connected with the production, editing, promotion and marketing of the Film.

3.2   Company agrees that Producer shall also be entitled to make use of Director's services subject to his then prior professional commitments free of charge to Producer (except only for the payment of expenses in accordance with Clause 8) in connection with publicity interviews, personal appearances and the like.

4.   Director's services

4.1   Company shall provide the services of Director to take primary responsibility for performing all of the Company's obligations set out in this Agreement and shall procure that Director executes the Inducement Letter which Company shall deliver to Producer upon execution of this Agreement.

4.2   During the engagement of Company, Company shall procure that Director shall render his services as, where and when Producer shall reasonably require in a competent, conscientious and professional manner having due regard for the production of the Film within the Budget and as instructed by Producer in all matters, including those involving Director's taste and judgment.

4.3   Without limitation to Clauses 4.1 and 4.2, Company shall procure that Director shall:

(a)   consult with, advise and assist any person who may be engaged in writing or contributing to the Screenplay and carry out all such revisions to the Screenplay as may be discussed and agreed with Producer;

(b)   render services before the Commencement Date free of charge in connection with wardrobe, costumes, tests, auditions, rehearsals, consultations and the like;

(c)   to such extent as Producer may require, assist Producer in the preparation and revision of the Production Schedule and the Budget for the production of the Film;

(d)   assist in the casting and all necessary preparations for the photography of the Film as may be required by Producer;

(e)   direct the photography and recording of the Film in the manner of and carry out all services customarily undertaken by a first-class director and in a professional manner and in accordance with the Screenplay, Production Schedule and the Budget;

(f)   not make any addition to or deletion from the Screenplay or Production Schedule without the prior approval of Producer other than minor changes required by the exigencies of the production;

(g)   not make any commitment for services, rights, facilities or materials nor engage any personnel nor incur any liability on behalf of Producer nor pledge the credit of Producer, nor hold himself out as being entitled to do so, nor use, nor license the use of, nor record any music for or in connection with the Film without the specific written approval of Producer in each and every case;

(h)   not incur any further costs beyond those which are set out in the Budget unless such expenditure has been approved in writing by Producer;

(i)   upon the completion of principal photography of the Film, supervise the titling, editing, scoring, dubbing, cutting and completion of the Film to the extent required by Producer, so that the Film is completed in a first-class condition fit for exhibition to the public as first-class entertainment;

(j)   where requested by Producer, render services for promotional films, trailers and the like and assist Producer in the production of any so-called "making of" films, such services to be rendered either during or after the term of this Agreement, but if after the term subject to Director's then prior professional commitments. For the avoidance of doubt, the Director shall not be primarily responsible for initiating the production of any promotional materials in connection with this sub-Clause 4.3(j);

(k)   make himself available as may reasonably be required for the purposes of supporting Producer in promoting and marketing the Film, attending at festivals, undertaking interviews and the like.

4.4   The answer print of the Film in the form to be delivered by Company to Producer will have a running time of between *[90 and 100 minutes]*[147] including main and end titles (as designated by Producer) and will qualify with the MPAA *[for an 'R' or less restrictive rating]* [148]and shall be accompanied by such other materials as may be required by Producer as notified to Company during Term.

4.5   Until two weeks before the anticipated first day of principal photography of the Film or such earlier date as the exigencies of production may require, Company shall procure that Director shall endeavour to agree with Producer the selection of actors to play the principal roles in the Film, the cameraman, the editor, the art director, the costume designer, the production designer and director of photography, and all other key creative elements. After such period and after consulting with Director (provided that such consultation shall not delay or interfere with the timely production of the Film), Producer shall make the final decision in respect of such of those elements as have not by then been agreed and in respect of any necessary replacement for any previously agreed element.

4.6   Company shall procure that Director shall prepare an assembly of the Film in sequence. After Producer has had an opportunity of examining the assembly, Director shall prepare the so-called 'director's cut' of the Film. After Producer has had an opportunity to view the director's cut, Director shall then prepare the so-called 'final cut' in respect of which the decision shall be taken by the Director in consultation with the Producer and by agreement with the individual producer irrevocably appointed by the Producer for that purpose and in the event of any dispute the decision of the Producer as to 'final cut' which decision shall be final and binding. Producer shall market and distribute the final cut. Editing of the Film shall be carried out under the Director's supervision.

4.7   The Director shall have approval over the shooting script, save that Producer shall have the right to veto any material which it deems to be unsuitable and thereafter the right to make such additional cuts as it may in its complete discretion deem necessary.

4.8   All of Director's rights and entitlements pursuant to Clauses 4.5, 4.6 and 4.7 are subject to Company procuring that Director performs obligations in such a way and with such cognisance of Producer's time strictures as will enable Producer to timely meet all delivery requirements of distributors of the Film provided the

---

147 Amend italicised words as appropriate
148 Amend italicised language as required

same are within customary and reasonable parameters and in compliance with legal considerations.

5. Copyright and rights

5.1 With full title guarantee Company (a) hereby irrevocably assigns to Producer all and any of its and (b) shall procure that Director assigns to Producer all of his right title and interest in and to the Products including the copyright therein and in and to any physical materials of any kind reproducing the Products. Such assignment shall be effective immediately and where the subject matter is not yet in existence such assignment shall be by way of present assignment of future copyright. If the subject matter is copyright the assignment shall be of the entire copyright for the full period thereof (including any extensions, revivals and renewals) notwithstanding termination of this Agreement for any reason and thereafter in so far as is possible in perpetuity.

5.2 Each of the Products constitutes within the meaning of the copyright laws of the United States of America, a 'work made for hire' for Producer and, as between each of (a) Producer and Company and (b) Producer and Director, Producer owns and shall own all right, title and interest in and to the Products including without limitation the copyright therein and the copyright in the Film and all and any rights arising under the copyright laws of all and any jurisdictions including but not limited to the United States of America exclusively in perpetuity, and Producer may exploit the same throughout the Territory by all means and in all media whether now known or hereafter devised. If for any reason the Products or any of them are not deemed to be a 'work made for hire', Company and Director irrevocably assign and grant to Producer all rights of any kind in and to the Products as herein contemplated.

5.3 Producer is and shall be considered the author and, at all stages of completion, the sole and exclusive owner of the Products and all right, title and interest therein (the "**Rights**"). The Rights shall include, without limitation, all copyrights, neighbouring rights, trade marks and any and all other ownership and exploitation rights in the Products and the Film now or hereafter recognised in any and all territories and jurisdictions.

5.4 Company hereby grants exclusively to Producer forever and throughout the universe the right to use, for no additional consideration, Director's name, image, voice, likeness, photograph and biographical data in connection with the Works and the Film and all ancillary, subsidiary and derivative rights therein and thereto.

5.5 Director hereby waives, pursuant to section 87 of the Act, unconditionally, irrevocably and in perpetuity, in favour of Producer, all rights under Sections 77 to 85 inclusive of the Act in respect of the Products and all other moral and author's rights of a similar nature whether now existing or hereafter conferred under the laws of any jurisdiction.

6. Warranties

6.1 Company hereby represents, warrants and undertakes on behalf of itself and on behalf of Director that:

    (a) Director will be the sole author of his contribution to the Products (except insofar as the same directly comprise material submitted to Director by Producer) which will be wholly original to Director and nothing therein will infringe the copyright or to Director's best knowledge any other rights (including any rights of confidentiality and/ or privacy) of any third party;

    (b) the Products will not (except insofar as the same directly comprise material submitted to Director by Producer) to the best of Director's knowledge and belief contain any defamatory, blasphemous or obscene matter;

    (c) the rights hereby granted and assigned are vested in Company absolutely and Company has not previously in any way dealt with or encumbered same;

    (d) Company will not at any time, without the written consent of Producer, make any disclosure or supply any information to the public or to any third party (other than Director's professional advisers) other than non-derogatory, incidental mentions in primary personal publicity, in relation to any matters arising under this Agreement;

    (e) throughout the Term Company will keep Producer informed of Director's whereabouts;

    (f) Company will deliver to Producer on request or on the completion of Director's services or the termination of this Agreement, whichever is the earliest, all documents, manuscripts, drafts, set designs or other material and copies thereof relating to the Film in the power, possession or control of Director;

(g) for a period of *[fourteen (14)]*[149] days before the commencement of principal photography until completion of all services required of Director, under this Agreement in connection with principal photography, Company shall procure that Director will not engage in any unusually hazardous pursuit without Producer's written consent and in particular Director shall not fly other than on regular scheduled flights without Producer's prior consent;

(h) Company has not entered and shall not enter into any arrangement or agreement to render Director's services to a third party during the period of Director's exclusive engagement under this Agreement;

(i) Company shall procure that Director shall, if required by Producer, without any additional remuneration render such services and will work such hours as are necessary to fulfil Company's obligations under this Agreement. Company agrees that the maximum weekly working time shall not apply to this Agreement or to the provision of Director's services pursuant to this Agreement. This clause shall constitute an agreement in writing for the purposes of Regulation 5 of the Working Time Regulations 1998.

6.2 Company will indemnify Producer against any breach or non-performance by Company or Director of any of the warranties, representations, agreements or undertakings by Company Director in this Agreement.

7 Consideration

7.1 Save as otherwise provided in this Agreement, subject to Company and Director fully and completely performing all of their several and respective obligations set out in this Agreement, Producer:

(a) shall procure that Director is accorded the credits provided for at Clause 9 of this Agreement;

(b) shall pay to Company a fee of £ [150] (pounds) to be paid in accordance with a schedule of instalments to be hereafter agreed in good faith between the Parties[151];

---

149 Amend as required
150 Insert payment details
151 Include payment milestones if agreed

(c) shall procure that all income derived from exploitation of the Film is to be collected and accounted for by an independent third party pursuant to the terms of a collection account management agreement ('**CAMA**") which the parties hereto and others connected with the financing, production and exploitation of the Film propose to negotiate and conclude hereafter and of which Producer shall procure Company as a direct beneficiary;

(d) shall pay or procure those responsible for collecting and accounting for the profits of the Film to pay to Company[152] % (per cent) of the Producer's net profits from exploitation of the Film with 'net profits' being defined as per the principal agreements entered into for the finance, post-production and distribution of the Film and which sums shall be paid at such time and in such proportions as shall hereafter be negotiated by the parties in good faith at the same time of negotiation of Recoupment Schedule for the CAMA;

(e) shall procure that any third party to whom Producer assigns Rights shall first enter into a direct covenant with Company to be bound by the terms of this agreement including but not limited to the provisions of this Clause 7.1(e).

7.2 Company and Director each acknowledge that the compensation payable to Company pursuant to this Agreement includes equitable remuneration in respect of any and all rights of whatsoever kind or nature (including any rental and lending rights and satellite broadcasting and cable re-transmission rights in relation to the Film and all rights which Company and/or Director may have as 'author' of the Film) to which either Company or Director may now be or shall hereafter become entitled under the laws of any country of the world in connection with the exploitation of the Film in any and all media.

7.3 VAT shall be added to all payments provided for in this Agreement if applicable and subject to the provision of a valid VAT invoice.

7.4 Company shall be responsible for paying its own income tax due on remuneration hereunder and any tax or insurance contributions due in respect of Company's engagement of the Director for the Film for all of which Company hereby fully indemnifies Producer.

---

152 Insert payment details

7.5   Producer shall maintain books of account concerning the exploitation of the Film. Company or its duly appointed agent, on Company's behalf, may, at Company's sole expense, examine Producer's said books relating to the exploitation of the Film solely for the purpose of verifying the accuracy thereof, only during Producer's normal business hours, upon reasonable written notice and only at the location where Producer maintains said books and records. Producer's such books relating to any particular accounting statement may be examined as aforesaid only within *[three (3)]*[153] years after the date rendered and Producer shall have no obligation to permit Company to so examine Producer's such books relating to any particular royalty statement more than once. Following such an examination and forthwith upon being notified of the amount of any underpayment either by the Company or its representative, Producer shall pay to the Company the amount of such underpayment together with interest thereon at the rate of *8% (eight percent)*[154] per annum calculated from the date upon which the payment should have been made by the Producer to the Company. In the event the amount of the underpayment exceeds 5% of the total accounted to the Company prior to the audit, Producer shall pay the Company's reasonable audit costs to exclude any travel, subsistence and accommodation costs.

8   Expenses

Producer shall reimburse all Company's expenses wholly and necessarily incurred by it or Director in the course of his performance of his duties under this Agreement subject to the same first being agreed in writing and secondly to the production of receipts for the same; standard and class of accommodation and travel to be agreed between the parties.

9   Credit

9.1   Director shall be accorded a 'Directed by' credit on all positive copies of the Film at the front of the Film on separate card, main titles and in the billing block in all paid ads. Such credits shall be no smaller than any other credit accorded to any third party.

9.2   No inadvertent breach by the Producer of the provisions of this Clause 9 and no failure of third parties to accord the said credit shall constitute a breach of this Agreement by the Producer.

---

153 Amend as appropriate
154 Amend as appropriate

10   Consents

Company shall procure that Director shall and Director hereby irrevocably and unconditional grants to Producer all consents which it may require under Part II of the Act and any similar legislation in any part of the world to make the fullest use of Director's services under this Agreement and the widest possible exploitation of the Products and the Film.

11   Health

Company hereby warrants and represents that Director is not now nor has at any time been subject to or suffering from any ill health, injury and/or incapacity which will in any way prevent Director from rendering Director's services under this Agreement.

12   Further documents

12.1   Company undertakes with Producer that Company and, where necessary, that Director will, at the request and expense of Producer, do all such further things and execute all such further documents consistent herewith as Producer may from time to time reasonably require for the purpose of confirming Producer's title to the rights granted and assigned under this Agreement in any part of the world including and not limited to such short form assignments as Producer may require for the purpose of registration in the United States of America or elsewhere.

12.2   Company hereby irrevocably appoints Producer as agent for each of Company and Director with full power of substitution in the name and stead of each of Company and Director but for Producer's benefit to take any and all steps and to execute, acknowledge and deliver any and all documents and assurances necessary or expedient in order to vest such rights more effectively in Producer.

13   Right of assignment

Producer may assign, license or grant the benefit of this Agreement or its rights or benefits under this Agreement in whole or in part to any third party subject to first procuring that any such third party shall enter into a direct covenant with Company to be bound by all of the terms and conditions of this Agreement as if primary obligor thereof including but not limited to the provisions of this Clause 13 and all the representations, warranties and undertakings of Company in this

Agreement and the benefit of the Inducement Letter shall to the extent of such assignment, licence or grant thereupon enure for the benefit of such third party provided that pending the novation of its obligations to a third party, Producer shall remain liable for its obligations under this Agreement.

14 Suspension

14.1 Director's engagement under this Agreement shall be suspended in any of the following events and Producer shall notify Company of the commencement date of any such suspension:

(a) if Company or Director fails, refuses or neglects to perform or is otherwise in breach of any undertaking, warranty or obligation in this Agreement and fails to remedy the breach within twenty-four (24) hours of notice thereof from Producer provided that where such breach is not capable of remedy or Company or Director breaches this Agreement on a second or subsequent occasion no such period of grace shall apply;

(b) if Director is prevented from rendering Director's services by any disability;

(c) if any act or omission or conduct of Company or Director prejudices the production or successful exploitation of the Film;

(d) if the preparation or production of the Film is prevented, interrupted or delayed by any event of Force Majeure provided that if such suspension continues for forty-two (42) consecutive days or more Company shall be entitled during the continuance thereof to give notice to Producer to terminate Director's engagement, provided further that should Company serve such a notice Producer shall be entitled within five (5) Business Days of such notice to serve a counternotice on Director terminating the suspension which gave rise to Company's notice and thereafter Director's engagement under this Agreement shall be deemed to be resumed in all respects as if no notice of termination had been given.

14.2 Suspension of the engagement shall have the following effect:

(a) it will last as long as the event giving rise to it plus such further period as may be reasonably required by Producer to prepare to resume using

Director's services or until this Agreement is terminated;

(b)   while it lasts payments under Clause 7 will cease to fall due;

(c)   if required by Producer, Company shall procure that Director shall immediately leave the set and cease being actively involved with the production of the Film;

(d)   the Term will continue after the suspension ends (unless it ends by termination of this Agreement) for the length of time unexpired when the suspension began;

(e)   Company and Director shall during the suspension continue to comply with all of their obligations under this Agreement not affected by such suspension and shall not without the prior consent of Producer agree to render services to any third party;

(f)   Producer will remain entitled to all rights hereby granted and assigned to it.

15.   Termination

15.1   Producer shall be entitled by written notice to Company to terminate this Agreement (whether or not the engagement has been suspended for the same or another reason) in any of the following events:-

(a)   if Company or Director fails, refuses or neglects to perform or is otherwise in breach of any undertaking, warranty or material obligation in this Agreement and fails to remedy the breach within forty-eight (48) hours of notice thereof from Producer provided that where such breach is not capable of remedy or Company or Director breaches this Agreement on a second or subsequent occasion no such period of grace shall apply;

(b)   if whilst exclusively obligated to Producer, Director is unable to devote the whole of Director's time, attention and normal ability to rendering Director's services under this Agreement for any reason including any disability for the period of three (3) days whether consecutive or in aggregate;

(c)   as provided for at sub-clause 14.1(d) if any event of Force Majeure continues for a period of 42 days or more;

(d)   if any act or omission or conduct of Company or Director prejudices the production or successful exploitation of the Film;

(e)   if Director fails to submit to any medical examination or Company or Director fails to make or makes untrue or inaccurate replies or statements for the purpose of insurance or if Producer is unable to effect insurance on Director on normal terms unless an insurance carrier has offered insurance on payment of an excess premium which Company is willing to pay at Company's own expense.

15.2   If Producer terminates this Agreement pursuant to Clause 15.1 then, except where termination arises by reason of the default of Company or Director, Producer shall pay that part of the remuneration due under Clause 7.1(b) up to the date of the event giving rise to termination (or the beginning of any suspension preceding termination).

15.3   Producer shall also be entitled to terminate Director's engagement at its sole discretion provided that in such event and subject to the duty of Company and Producer to mitigate any losses which may be incurred by either or both of them as a result of such termination, Producer shall make a quantum meruit payment to Company for services delivered up to the date of termination.

15.4   Forthwith upon termination of this Agreement by the Producer, Company shall procure that Director shall forthwith (a) cease any involvement with the production of the Film and (b) where applicable, leave the set and (c) be relieved of her/his obligation to provide any further services and Producer may forthwith replace the Director.

15.5   If Producer terminates this Agreement pursuant to Clause 15.1 or 15.3, Producer shall continue to pay Director's expenses (if any).

15.6   If Producer terminates this Agreement in accordance with the provisions of Clause 15.1 or 15.3 and makes the payments provided for in Clauses 15.2 or 15.3 and 15.5 then Producer will be under no further liability to Company or Director and Company agrees that any payments made to Company pursuant to such Clauses shall be in full and final satisfaction of all claims (if any) that Company or Director may have as against Producer in respect of the termination of the Agreement. Subject to the foregoing Producer and Company will each remain entitled to enforce any claim against the other arising from any breach of this Agreement that has occurred either before termination or in relation to the termination itself. Producer will in any event remain entitled to all rights hereby granted and assigned to it and Company shall continue to comply with all relevant warranties.

15.7   Notwithstanding termination for any reason all Rights will remain vested in Producer.

16   Notices

Any notice to be given or served under this Agreement shall be in writing and shall be delivered personally or sent by facsimile or other print-out communication mechanism or by prepaid registered or recorded delivery (or its equivalent) post (air mail if posted to another country) to the party to be served at the address set out at the head of this Agreement (or such other address as either party may from time to time notify in writing to the other) and shall be deemed to have been served:-

(a)   immediately in the case of personal delivery;

(b)   in the case of facsimile or other print-out mechanism, on the expiration of four (4) hours from the time of transmission if accompanied by a written acknowledgment that the notice has been sent. In the absence of a written acknowledgement, the original notice shall be sent by post or by personal delivery in accordance with this clause not later than the next Business Day after transmission;

(c)   by prepaid registered or recorded delivery on the second Business Day following the date of posting (the fifth Business Day if posted to another country) or an acknowledgement of receipt if earlier.

17   Institution of legal action

17.1   Company hereby grants to Producer the free and unrestricted right at Producer's expense to institute in the name and on behalf of both Company and Director any and all suits and proceedings at law or in equity to enjoin and restrain any infringement of the rights granted and assigned in this Agreement and Company hereby on its own behalf and on behalf of Director assigns and transfers to Producer any and all causes of action arising or resulting by reason of or based upon such infringement and any and all recoveries obtained in any such action.

17.2 Company's and Director's sole and exclusive remedy for any breach of this Agreement by Producer shall be money damages and in no event shall either Company or Director be entitled to terminate or rescind this Agreement or to prevent the exercise of any of the Rights or any other right granted hereunder or to seek to apply for any form of injunctive or equitable relief against Producer and/or the Rights and/or the Film.

18 Confidentiality

The terms and the subject matter of this Agreement and all and any information provided by Producer to Company and Director about the Film shall be and is deemed to be 'Confidential Information' no part of which shall be used by Company or Director otherwise than for the purposes of this Agreement nor disclosed or made available to any third party. The obligations provided for in this clause shall not apply to any part of the Confidential Information which can clearly be shown as in the public domain unless (a) it has become public knowledge other than through Company or any party to whom Company or Director provided the same, or (b) was received from a third party who did not owe Producer a duty of confidence in respect of it or (c) is required to be disclosed by a court or statutory body.

19 Waiver

A waiver by a party of any term or condition of this Agreement shall not be deemed or construed to be a waiver of such term or condition for the future or any subsequent breach thereof.

20 Entire agreement

This Agreement replaces, supersedes and cancels all previous arrangements between the parties and constitutes the entire agreement between Company and Producer and no variation of this Agreement may be made unless in writing and signed by Company and Producer.

21 Insurance

Director shall be added as an additional insured to any errors and omissions insurance policy and/or general liability insurance policy effected by Producer in respect of the Film, but without any obligation on the part of Producer to effect or maintain such policies and such cover shall not in any way limit or restrict Director's representations and warranties under this Agreement.

22   Premieres

Producer shall provide the Company with two invitations to the first UK premiere of the Film (if any) and five DVD copies of the Film.[155]

23   Law of agreement

This Agreement shall be construed and shall take effect in accordance with the laws of England. Any dispute under this Agreement will be resolved by final and binding arbitration under the Independent Film & Television Alliance ("IFTA") Rules for International Arbitration in effect when the arbitration is filed ("IFTA Rules"), and subject to the disclosure provisions of the IBA Rules. The arbitration will be held in London, England.

AS WITNESS the signatures of authorised officers of Producer and Company and of the Director on the date first before written.

SIGNED by[156]
for and on behalf of PRODUCER

SIGNED by[157]for and on behalf of COMPANY

SIGNED by DIRECTOR

---

155 Amend as appropriate
156 Insert name of Producer's signatory
157 Insert name of Loan out Company's signatory

Schedule
Inducement Letter

From: [158]   ("**I**", "**me**", "**my**")

To: [159]   ("**you**", "**your**")

Date

Dear Sirs

[160]   ("**Film**")

I refer to the director agreement of today's date entered into by you with [161]("**Company**") ("**Director Agreement**"). Unless otherwise stated, capitalised terms used in this Inducement Letter shall have the same meaning as in the Director Agreement.

1.   I confirm that I have been provided with a copy of and have read and fully understood the Director Agreement.

2.   All of my services in connection with the Film are being rendered for Company pursuant to an agreement in that behalf.

3.   I shall perform and comply with all of the terms and conditions of the Director Agreement and I confirm that all the rights and consents expressed to be granted and assigned to you by the Company under the Director Agreement have previously been granted to Company by me and to the extent that is not the case I confirm the provisions of paragraph 6 of this Inducement Letter.

4.   I acknowledge receipt of payment in full of all fixed compensation (including any expense) due to me from Company in connection with the Film. I will look solely to Company for compensation for my services.

5.   I specifically acknowledge that the payments to Company for my services pursuant to the Agreement include equitable remuneration in respect of the

---

158 Director's name
159 Name and registered details of producer/production company
160 Insert title of film
161 Insert name registered office and registered number of director's loan-out company

exploitation of any rights in relation to the Film (including my rental and lending rights, if any) to which I am now or may hereafter become entitled.

6. All results and proceeds of my services (hereinafter, the "**Work**") constitute within the meaning of the copyright laws of the United States of America, a 'work made for hire' for Company and, as between Company and me, Company owns all right, title and interest in and to the Work including without limitation the copyright therein and in the Film exclusively in perpetuity, in all media in any manner, whether now known or hereafter devised, and throughout the universe for all purposes, including, without limitation, any rights arising under the copyright laws of the United States of America or any other jurisdiction and so that Company may assign all and any rights in the Work to you as required by Clause 5.1 of the Director Agreement. If for any reason the Work is not deemed to be a 'work made for hire', I irrevocably assign and grant to you all rights of any kind in and to the Work as herein contemplated. I hereby grant exclusively to Company and to you forever and throughout the universe the right to use, for no additional consideration, my name, image, voice, likeness, photograph and biographical data in connection with the Work and the Film and all ancillary, subsidiary and derivative rights therein and thereto. Insofar as I may possess any right, title, and interest in and to the Work, I hereby irrevocably assign any and all such right, title and interest to Company.

7. I hereby unconditionally, irrevocably and in perpetuity waive pursuant to section 87 of the Act in favour of you, your successors in title and licensees, all rights under sections 77 to 85 inclusive of the Act in respect of the Film, the Work and all other moral and author's rights and rights of a similar nature whether now existing or hereafter conferred under the laws of any jurisdiction.

8. Save that it is agreed that I shall be accorded a single-frame credit as Director of the Film in the opening title sequence of the Film and that said credit will also appear in the billing block in any paid ads, including DVD and home video box covers, where the producer, Director and lead actors' credit appears, except congratulatory ads, all other aspects of my credit shall be at your sole discretion.

9. You may freely assign the Work without my further consent.

10. In the event of breach or alleged breach of the Director Agreement by you or of my agreement with Company, I shall be limited to the right to recover damages in an action at law and in no event shall I be entitled by reason of any breach or alleged breach to enjoin or restrain the distribution or other exploitation of the Film.

11.   You shall be entitled to legal and/or injunctive or other equitable relief against me to restrain, enjoin and/or prevent the breach by me of any of Company's obligations or of any term of this Inducement Letter.

12.   The warranties, representations and agreements by Company in the Director Agreement are true and shall be deemed to have been given to you by Company and me jointly and severally.

13.   I will execute or cause to be executed all documents which either you or Company may   consider necessary to confirm your title to the rights expressed to be granted and assigned by Company to you in the Work or otherwise to achieve the objectives of the Director Agreement. If I shall not execute and deliver any such document after reasonable notice, Company, or in its place, you shall have the right to do so in my name, place and stead, and you are hereby irrevocably appointed my attorney-in-fact for such purposes, which power is coupled with an interest.

14.   I shall give you such reasonable assistance as I am able to provide and defend your rights in the Work and the Film provided that you indemnify me for my costs in connection with any such proceedings.

15.   If Company breaches its agreement with me and/or for any reason my engagement by the Company ends, I will continue to provide my services to you as if I had signed the Director Agreement in place of Company and I will enter into such further agreement as you may reasonably require (provided that it does not impose any further or more onerous obligations on me than those already contained in the Director Agreement).

16.   If at any time Company is unable to perform its obligations as provided for by the Director Agreement, I hereby covenant with and undertake to you that I will perform those obligations as if primary obligor thereof.

Yours truly   Accepted and agreed

Director   **for and on behalf of** [162]

---

162 Insert name of production company

Appendix 10

Producer's Agreement
Section 29

AGREEMENT dated

PARTIES

(1)   [163] (**"Company"**)

(2)   [164] (**"Producer"**)

RECITALS

(1)   Company has acquired the right to produce a full-length feature film entitled
         "   " in respect of which prior to the execution of
         this Agreement it has been engaged in pre-production.

(2)   Company has agreed to appoint Producer to produce the film of the Screenplay
         as more particularly defined below on the terms and conditions hereinafter set
         forth.

OPERATIVE PART

1.   **Definitions**

         "Act"   the Copyright, Designs and Patents Act 1988 as
                                       amended from time to time or any other enactment
                                       which replaces it;

         "Agreement"   this agreement and its Schedule;

         "Budget"   the budget for the Film to be agreed between Compa-
                                       ny, Producer and the Film's financiers (**"Financiers"**);

---

163 Insert full name and registered office and number details of production company
164 Insert name and address details of the individual producer being engaged

"Business Day"	a day (other than a Saturday or Sunday) when banks are open for business in England;
"Cash Flow Schedule"	the cash flow schedule for the Film to be agreed between Company, Producer and the Financiers;
"Commencement Date"	to be notified in writing by Producer to Company;
"Complete Delivery"	delivery of all of the Delivery Materials;
"Delivery Date"	on such date to be agreed between the parties, but no later than
"Delivery Materials"	the materials provided for at Schedule 1;
"Film"	a feature length colour film in the English language shot in *HD Cam SR format and fully mixed Dolby 5.1 soundtrack* provisionally entitled " " with a minimum length of 90 minutes and a maximum length of 100 minutes (including main and end titles);
"Production Account"	the bank account opened by Company and in its name and under its sole control for the purposes of the production of the Film;
"Production Schedule"	*[attached hereto][to be agreed hereafter between the Parties]*[165];
"Recoupment Schedule"	the recoupment waterfall agreed between all those participating in income to be generated from exploitation of the Film;

---

165 Complete as required

"**Rights**"	the copyright in the Film and all of its component parts and all rights to exploit and distribute the Film in all media and by all means now known or hereafter devised;
"**Schedules**"	the schedule to this Agreement;
"**Screenplay**"	the screenplay entitled " " *[which screenplay has been registered with WGA of America;]*[166]
"**Term**"	the term of this Agreement deemed to be effective as of [167];
"**Territory**"	the world.

2. Budget and production

2.1 Producer hereby acknowledges that immediately prior to the execution of this Agreement the Company had delivered to Producer the final Budget which the parties hereby further mutually approve together with *[a draft of]*[168] the Production Schedule and the Cash Flow Schedule for the Film.

2.2 Producer agrees to oversee and manage the entire process of the production of the Film and to deliver the same to Company within the Budget and in accordance with the Production Schedule and the Cash Flow Schedule.

2.3 Producer hereby irrevocably waives in favour of Company all moral rights or authors' rights in and to the Film, and irrevocably assigns to Company all Rights including all lending and rental rights that they may now or shall hereafter own.

2.4 Company shall exercise the sole and exclusive right to make and approve all business, creative and other decisions including but not limited to cast, head production personnel and location.

2.5 For the purposes of United States copyright law, the products of the services

---

166 If appropriate
167 Insert date
168 As appropriate

provided by the Producer pursuant to the terms of this Agreement shall be considered "works made for hire" for the Company.

3. Delivery of the Film

3.1 Producer shall, in accordance with the appropriate allowance provided within the Budget (and Producer confirms that there will be sufficient allowance for this purpose), effect Complete Delivery of the Film to Company to a location that Company shall notify to Producer in writing not later than the Delivery Date.

3.2 The Delivery Materials shall be of a first-class technical quality.

3.3 The Film shall substantially conform to the Screenplay except for material changes thereto approved by Company and/or minor changes necessitated by the exigencies of production and other minor changes that do not alter the story or the principal characters of the Film.

4. Producer's agreements, representations and warranties

Producer hereby agrees, warrants, represents and undertakes, (and all such agreements warranties, representations and undertaking will be deemed repeated on Delivery of the Film save to the extent the same have been discharged):-

(a) that Producer will use best endeavours to ensure that the Film will be produced and delivered as diligently, expeditiously and economically as possible in accordance with the Budget, the Production Schedule and the terms of this Agreement and that the Budget will be deployed in accordance with the Cash Flow Schedule;

(b) there are, and will be on Complete Delivery, no liens, claims or encumbrances of any kind against the Film or any of the literary, artistic, dramatic or musical works comprising any part of it which will interfere with or derogate from any of the Rights or any other right granted;

(c) Company shall be entitled to exploit and assign the Rights and the Film in all media without the payment of any so-called "residuals" and "use fees" to any other persons rendering services in connection with the Film including without limitation any composers or recording artists save for any payments due to local performing rights societies which Company acknowledges are not Producer's responsibility;

(d)   neither the Film nor any part of the Film nor the title of the Film nor the exercise of any of the Rights violates or will violate any personal private civil or property rights copyright or trade mark right or rights of privacy or "moral" rights of authors or any other rights whatsoever of any person, firm, corporation or association whatsoever or constitute libel or slander against the same;

(e)   there are and will be no agreements nor any commitments whatsoever with or to any party that may in any manner affect the Rights or any other right granted to Company pursuant to this Agreement;

(f)   Producer has not granted and will not grant to any third party any of the Rights in and to the Film or any rights the exercise of which would derogate from or be inconsistent with the exploitation of the Rights by Company;

(g)   there are no claims or litigation pending or threatened which will or may adversely affect the Rights;

(h)   all contracts for personnel, studio hire, purchase of goods and services, laboratory work and all other licenses, contracts and obligations in connection with the production of the Film shall be made and entered into by Producer as agent for Company which contracts shall be duly executed as Company may direct and delivered to Company. All such contracts or undertakings shall be consistent with the provisions of this Agreement and industry custom and practice. Such contracts and undertakings shall not be terminated, cancelled, modified or rescinded in any manner which would or might prejudice the rights of Company hereunder. All such contracts shall be assignable and upon demand by Company;

(i)   Producer shall, promptly upon request, supply or procure that there shall be supplied to Company originals or copies of all and any relevant contracts, licences or other documents relating to the use in the Film of any literary dramatic artistic and musical works and any other materials or services of any individual and at Company's expense Producer shall render all such assistance and execute all such documents as

Company shall request to enable Company to secure the registration of the copyright in the Film in any country or countries of the Territory PROVIDED ALWAYS that this obligation shall not extend to cover such contracts, licences or other documents that are solely procured and/or initiated by Company;

(j)   in consultation with Company, Producer shall, prior to the commencement of principal photography of the Film, procure or assist Company with procuration of the following insurances: public liability indemnity for the duration of production of the Film, indemnity with abandonment extension against damage or loss of negative stock for negative and other property and equipment to be used in connection with production of the Film, indemnity with abandonment extension against the risks of accident to or illness or death of the director of the Film, the principal cast and such others as may reasonably be required by Company, employers liability and such other insurances as may be prudent in the circumstances of the Film or as may reasonably be required by Company or by law. Producer shall notify the insurers of Company's interest and upon demand shall provide Company with copies of such policies with Producer and Company's interest noted thereon as named insured;

(k)   Producer shall not settle any claim under any insurance policy without the prior written consent of Company and, unless otherwise agreed with Company, Producer shall credit all sums received in respect of any such settlement to the Production Account to defray the cost of production of the Film. Producer shall not do or permit or suffer to be done any act or thing whereby any of the foregoing policies may lapse or become in whole or in part voidable;

(l)   the Budget is a comprehensive informed and bona fide estimate of all expenditure likely to be incurred in the course of production of the Film including all fees payable by reference to any use or exploitation of the Film or the Rights and that Producer will use its best endeavours to prevent the total cost of production exceeding the Budget;

(m)   Producer is an independent contractor and shall be responsible for paying his own income tax due on remuneration hereunder for which Producer fully indemnifies Company.

5.   Producer's obligations

5.1   Producer shall liaise with Company, the director of the Film and all and any other persons involved in the production. Producer shall appoint personnel and technicians and all and any other crew required, deliver all negative material shot in connection with the Film to the agreed processing laboratory and shall procure that all negative development and rush film printing of all film material for the Film during the course of production shall be carried out by such laboratory.

5.2   Producer shall not without the written consent of Company enter into any contracts which contain terms which might result in the Budget being exceeded.

5.3   Producer shall at weekly intervals during principal photography and fortnightly intervals at all other times give to Company a statement of the requirements that it has for payment to it from the Production Account together with details of actual outgoings since the previous statement and expenditure required to be made in accordance with the Budget during the period until the next statement is due.

5.4   Company shall release payments to Producer from the Production Account in accordance with the Cash Flow Schedule.

5.5   Producer shall keep all true and accurate books of account (and retain all vouchers receipts and records) relating to expenditure made in connection with the production of the Film and Company shall be entitled by itself or its duly authorised agents to enter on Producer's premises and to inspect and take copies of such books of account and records on reasonable notice at all reasonable times.

5.6   Producer shall provide to Company as soon as the same can be prepared and delivered detailed progress reports of the production of the Film on a daily basis during principal photography.

5.7   Producer will co-operate fully with all requests and requirements of Company (including, but not limited to, entering into all agreements reasonably required by Company) and all Producer's rights hereunder will be subject to the rights granted to Company in relation to its obligation to complete and deliver the Film.

5.8   Producer will ensure that all individuals providing services to the production will be included on the payroll and PAYE and NIC accounted for to HMRC in accordance with all applicable procedures unless such persons are specifically excluded from PAYE by the HMRC Film and Television Industry guidelines. Immediately following the execution of this agreement Producer will provide to Company a list of all individuals deemed to be self-employed and the reason why Producer will ensure that all payments paid to individuals, including cash, go through the payroll unless it is for approved and receipted expenses.

5.9   Producer will also ensure that VAT records are kept and that information for inclusion on the VAT return is provided to the Company's accountants, in order that they may submit the VAT return in an accurate and timely manner.

5.10   Producer will provide all information requested and give assistance required to ensure that the Company can submit a claim for the UK film tax credit.

6   Consideration

6.1   Save as otherwise provided in this Agreement, subject to Producer fully and completely performing all of Producer's obligations set out in this Agreement, Company:

(a)   shall procure that Producer is accorded the credits provided for at Clause 10 of this Agreement;

(b)   shall pay to Producer a fee of [169]   (*thousand pounds) of which (   ) pounds shall be paid [within seven days of the completion and signature of this Agreement] [with further sums of   ]to be paid on each of first day of principal photography and on the Delivery Date and, in addition, a further sum of   ("**Deferred Fee**") which shall be paid in accordance with the Recoupment Schedule[170]*;

(c)   *the Company shall pay or procure those responsible for collecting and accounting for the profits of the Film shall pay to Producer   % (per cent) [171] of the Company's net profits from exploitation of the Film with*

---

169 Insert details
170 Include as appropriate
171 Include and complete as appropriate

"net profits" being defined as per the principal agreements entered into by the Company for the finance, post-production and distribution of the Film and which sums shall be paid at the same time as other profit participants in the Film;

(d)   shall procure that all income derived from exploitation of the Film is to be collected and accounted for by an independent third party pursuant to the terms of a collection account management agreement (“**CAMA**”) which the parties hereto and others connected with the financing, production and exploitation of the Film propose to negotiate and conclude hereafter it being agreed that Producer shall be a signatory to and direct beneficiary of the CAMA;

(e)   *shall procure payment of the Deferred Fee in accordance with the Recoupment Schedule.*[172]

6.2   VAT shall be added to all payments provided for in this Agreement if applicable and subject to the provision of a valid VAT invoice.

6.3   Company shall maintain books of account concerning the exploitation of the Film. Producer or his duly appointed agent, on Producer's behalf, may, at Producer's sole expense, examine Company's said books relating to the exploitation of the Film solely for the purpose of verifying the accuracy thereof, only during Company's normal business hours, upon reasonable written notice and only at the location where Company maintains said books and records. Company's such books relating to any particular accounting statement may be examined as aforesaid only within four (4) years after the date rendered and Company shall have no obligation to permit Producer to so examine Company's such books relating to any particular royalty statement more than once. Following such an examination and forthwith upon being notified of the amount of any underpayment either by the Producer or its representative, Company shall pay to the Producer the amount of such underpayment together with interest thereon at the rate of *two per cent*[173] per annum calculated from the date upon which the payment should have been made by the Company to the Producer. In the event the amount of the underpayment exceeds *five/ten* [174]per cent of the total accounted to the Producer prior to the audit, Company shall pay the Producer's

---

172 As appropriate
173 Amend as appropriate
174 Amend as appropriate

reasonable audit costs to exclude any travel, subsistence and accommodation costs. Producer shall procure those entering agreements or other arrangements pursuant to which the Film is exploited shall enter into an obligation equivalent to this Clause 6.3.

7 Termination

7.1 Company shall have the right in addition to its rights at law or in equity to terminate this Agreement by notice to Producer in the event of:

(a) Producer failing to remedy a breach of this Agreement within seven (7) days of the date of receipt by it of a notice in writing that has been given to Producer by Company, assuming such breach is capable of remedy;

(b) forthwith by notice in writing in the event that Producer commit an irremediable breach of this Agreement;

(c) forthwith on Producer committing an act of bankruptcy or becoming insolvent.

7.2 Upon termination of this Agreement for any reason

(a) Company shall be released and discharged from all further obligations under this Agreement and Company shall be entitled to appoint another Producer to complete the Film which appointment shall be made entirely without prejudice to all and any of Company's other rights against Producers; and

(b) Producer shall forthwith deliver up all and any materials in any way connected with the Film to Company and shall fully and completely co-operate with Company to enable Company to complete the Film either by itself or such further or other Producer as Company may decide;

(c) Producer shall immediately vacate Company's premises including its offices and shall also vacate the sets and any locations at which production of the Film is being undertaken;

(d) Company shall retain all Rights in respect of which Producer shall have no claim.

8   Expenses

Company shall reimburse all Producer's expenses wholly and necessarily incurred by him in the course of his performance of his duties under this Agreement subject to the same first being agreed in writing and secondly to the production of receipts for the same; standard and class of accommodation and travel to be agreed between the parties.

9   Rights

9.1   Producer with full title guarantee hereby irrevocably assigns to Company all of Producer's right title and interest in and to the Film, if any, the copyright therein, the Rights and the benefit of any assignments, grants, licences and agreements with any third parties entered into by Producer in connection with the Film and in and to any physical materials of any kind produced in connection with the Film. Such assignment shall be effective immediately and where the subject matter is not yet in existence such assignment shall be by way of present assignment of future copyright. If the subject matter is copyright the assignment shall be of the entire copyright for the full period thereof (including any extensions, revivals and renewals) notwithstanding termination of this Agreement for any reason and thereafter in so far as is possible in perpetuity.

9.2   Producer will deliver and hereby transfers to Company unfettered ownership of the Delivery Materials.

10   Credit

10.1   Producer shall be accorded a "Produced by" credit on all positive copies of the Film at the front of the Film on separate card, main titles and in the billing block in all paid ads.   Such credits shall be no smaller than any other credit accorded to any third party.

10.2   No inadvertent breach by Company of the provisions of this Clause 10 and no failure of third parties to accord the said credit shall constitute a breach of this Agreement by the Company.

11   Producer indemnity

Producer agrees to indemnify Company and to hold Company harmless from and against all damages arising from or in connection with:

(a)   any breach by Producer of any agreement representation or warranty made by Producer pursuant to this Agreement and/or from any damages arising out of the distribution and/or exploitation of the Film or any rights therein except to the extent that Company is in breach or default hereunder or has been negligent in connection with the occurrence giving rise to such damages;

(b)   any breach of any of the undertakings on Producer's part herein contained or by reason of any defect of title in and to the Film and/or the sound dialogue and musical compositions recorded in synchronisation therewith.

12   Notices

Any notice to be given or served under this Agreement shall be in writing and shall be delivered personally or sent by facsimile or by other print-out communication mechanism or by first class prepaid registered or recorded delivery (if available) post (airmail if post to another country) to the party to be served at the address set out at the head of this Agreement (or such other address as either party may from time to time notify to the other) and shall be deemed to have been served:

(a)   immediately in the case of personal delivery;

(b)   in the case of facsimile or other print-out mechanism on the expiry of twenty-four (24) hours from the time of transmission

(c)   in the case of postal delivery on the second business day following the date of posting (the fifth business day if posted to another country) or on acknowledgement of receipt if earlier.

13   Confidentiality

The terms and the subject matter of this Agreement and all and any information provided by Company to Producer about the Film shall be and are deemed to be 'Confidential Information' no part of which shall be used by Producer otherwise than for the purposes of this Agreement nor disclosed or made available to any third party. The obligations provided for in this clause shall not apply to any part of the Confidential Information which can clearly be shown as in the public domain unless (a) it has become public knowledge other than through Producer or any party to whom Producer provided the same, or (b) was received from a third party who did not owe Company a duty of confidence in respect of it, or (c) is required to be disclosed by a court or statutory body.

14 General

14.1 Any waiver (whether express or implied) of any breach of any of the provisions hereof shall not be construed as a continuing waiver or consent to any subsequent breach on the part of the parties hereto.

14.2 Producer shall at Company's expense execute and deliver to Company any other instrument or document reasonably considered by Company to be necessary or desirable to evidence, effectuate or confirm this Agreement or any provision hereof or any of the rights granted. If Producer fail to so execute and deliver such instruments or documents within five (5) days of receiving written notice from Company requesting the same then Company shall be entitled to execute such documents and instruments in the name and on behalf of Producer as Producer's duly authorised agent.

14.3 Either party may assign the benefit of this Agreement subject to providing notice of assignment and requiring any assignee to enter into a direct covenant with the other party to be bound by and to perform all of the assignor's obligations provided for in this Agreement as if primary obligor thereof including compliance with the provisions of this clause.

14.4 Nothing in this Agreement shall be construed or deemed to constitute a partnership or joint venture between the parties and save as expressly provided herein neither party shall hold itself out as agent of the other.

14.5 This Agreement replaces, supersedes and cancels all previous arrangements, understandings, representations or agreements between the parties whether oral or written. No variation of any of the terms or conditions hereof may be made unless such variation is agreed in writing and signed by each of the parties hereto

14.6 Producer's sole and exclusive remedy for any breach of this Agreement by Company shall be money damages and in no event shall Producer be entitled to terminate or rescind this Agreement or to prevent the exercise of any of the Rights or any other right granted hereunder or to seek to apply for any form of injunctive or equitable relief against Company and/or the Rights and/or the Film.

14.7   If any provision of this Agreement is judged by a court to be void or unenforceable such provision shall in no way affect any other provision of this Agreement; the application of such provision in any other circumstance or the validity or enforceability of this Agreement and such provision shall be limited only to the extent necessary to bring it within legal requirements.

14.8   Neither party has nor will without the other's prior written consent:

(a)   enter into any agreement, commitment or other arrangement, grant any rights or do any act or thing which could or might prevent or interfere with the production and completion of the Film or prevent or impede the performance of all of the respective party's obligations hereunder;

(b)   do or fail to do any act which might or could interfere with or otherwise prevent such party from fully complying with all of the terms hereof; or

(c)   engage in any conduct inconsistent with this Agreement or the other party's rights hereunder. The foregoing shall not be interpreted as impairing or preventing Company's absolute right to abandon production of the Film at any time and/or to refrain from or cause the termination of the distribution of the Film.

14.9   The date for performance of either party's obligations hereunder shall be postponed to the extent any event of force majeure delays the commencement of production or the performance of the obligations of either party hereunder.

15   Governing Law

This Agreement has been entered into and shall be construed in accordance with the laws of England. Any dispute under this Agreement will be resolved by final and binding arbitration under the Independent Film & Television Alliance ("IFTA") Rules for International Arbitration in effect when the arbitration is filed ("IFTA Rules"), and subject to the disclosure provisions of the IBA Rules which arbitration will be held in London, England.

Schedule

Delivery Materials

AS WITNESS the hands of the parties the date detailed at the heading to this Agreement

SIGNED by   )

for and on behalf of   )

¹⁷⁵   )

SIGNED by

PRODUCER   )

---

175 Insert name of production company

Appendix 11

Performer's Agreement
Sections 9, 30 and 31

From: 176

To: 177

Date: 178

Dear [179   ]

"   180" (**"Film"**)

I am writing to confirm that this letter of *agreement [which, together with the specific terms set out in the Schedule hereto]*181 (**"Agreement"**) shall constitute the terms upon which you agree to play the part of [   ] in the Film (**"Role"**), which we propose but do not undertake to produce.

1   In consideration of the sum of £[182   ] (the **"Fee"**), which Fee shall be paid *[in [   ] [weekly][monthly] instalments of £[ ] each during the* Term (as defined below) you hereby irrevocably:

        (a)   agree and consent to participate in the Film during the period commencing on 183*[date] and continuing until [such date as may be determined by us by written notice to you][delivery of the Film to its principal distributors]* unless terminated earlier by us in accordance with the terms of this Agreement (**"Term"**);

        (b)   agree and consent to the filming, recording and/or broadcasting of you and your voice and performance (**"Performance"**) and to the editing, copying, adaptation or translation of the Performance and that such

---

176 Insert details of producer, if a production company include registered office and number details
177 Insert details of performer
178 Insert date of agreement
179 Insert first name of performer
180 Insert title of Film
181 Details of special terms in terms of perquisites etc
182 Insert relevant payment arrangements
183 Insert relevant details

filming, recording and/or broadcasting may be incorporated in the Film in whole or in part at our discretion (but you acknowledge that we are under no obligation to use said film and recording);

(c)   undertake that you will comply with the reasonable requirements of the producers and director of the Film;

(d)   attend at rehearsals, on set and otherwise as may be required in order to provide your services and to perform the Role to the best of your ability and as directed by the director of the Film;

(e)   waive the benefit of any moral rights to which you may be entitled save that, wherever reasonable and consistent with industry practices, we shall accord you an appropriate credit;

(f)   consent to the use and reproduction of your name, photograph, likeness and biography in connection with the Performance and the reproduction of the Film and recordings of the Performance or any part thereof for the purposes of advertising, publicity and otherwise enabling us to exploit your performance in the Film by all means and in all media now known or hereafter invented for the full term of copyright of the Film to include all extensions, renewals and revivals thereof;

(g)   where reasonably required by us, attend premieres, special screenings and undertake other publicity appearances and interviews to promote the Film in respect of which we shall reimburse your reasonable out-of-pocket expenses subject to our first agreeing them in writing and to the production by you to us of receipts for them;

(h)   grant to us all rights including without limitation copyright in the Performance and all consents necessary to enable us to make the fullest use of the Performance worldwide in perpetuity without payment, liability (save as specifically set out in this Agreement) or acknowledgement to you;

(i)   waive and release us from any claim, action or demand arising out of or in connection with the Performance; and

(j)   agree not to disclose to any party any information relating to the subject matter of this Agreement and/or the Film.

2   You warrant and undertake that:

(a)   you are fully entitled to grant all rights in the Performance to us;

(b)   you are a self-employed person for tax purposes and will keep us fully indemnified against any claims in respect thereof;

(c)   nothing in the Performance shall infringe the copyright or any other right of any third party or breach any contract or duty of confidence, constitute a contempt of court or be defamatory or blasphemous;

(d)   you are and will remain for the period of the engagement a "qualifying person" within the meaning of Part I of the CDPA and for the purposes of US copyright law the Performance shall be considered "works made for hire" for us;

(e)   you are at least 18 years old;

(f)   you shall keep confidential and shall not disclose to any third party any confidential information, photographs or other material relating to us or the Film or anyone taking part in it which came to your knowledge as a result of your participation in the Film;

(g)   that you are not now nor have at any time been subject to or suffering from any ill health, injury and/or incapacity which will in any way prevent you from rendering your services under this Agreement.

3   In consideration for your hereby waiving all and any moral rights that you may have in the Performance, we hereby undertake to provide you with an on screen credit in the *[opening] and/or [closing]* credits in the form [184].

4   The Fee shall include equitable remuneration in respect of any and all rights of whatsoever kind or nature to which you may now be entitled to or shall become entitled to after the date of this agreement under the laws of any country in connection with the exploitation of the Film and the Performance in all media now known or hereafter created or developed.

5   We shall deduct from the Fee Employer's National Insurance contributions at

---

184 Provide credit details

the appropriate rates.

6   Where you are entitled to holiday leave pursuant to the Working Time Regulations 1998 (the "**Regulations**") the "holiday year" for these purposes commences at the date of engagement and leave entitlement is four weeks per annum (pro-rated as appropriate). You shall give to us at least seven (7) days prior written notice of any proposed holiday dates, which dates shall be considered and granted by us in our absolute discretion, save that if the duration of the Term is more than forty-eight (48) weeks, you shall be automatically entitled to take holiday leave at any time from the beginning of the 49th week of the Term. You hereby accept and agree that any day during the Term on which we do not require your services shall be deemed a holiday date for the purposes of calculating your holiday leave entitlement, and that we may require you to take holiday leave on specific dates as may be notified to you.

7   We shall pay to you holiday pay at a rate of £ [[185]] per holiday day, which holiday pay shall be paid to you on completion of the Term, unless otherwise agreed in writing. If we require you to take holiday leave which exceeds your accrued holiday entitlement, you shall not be paid holiday pay in respect of such additional holiday leave.

8   You hereby accept and agree to work such hours as are necessary to fulfil all obligations under this Agreement and you accept that this may involve working an average of more than forty-eight (48) hours per week. You agree that maximum weekly working time specified in Regulation 4 of the Regulations shall not apply to this Agreement.

9   You hereby grant to us all consents necessary (including your express consent in respect of sensitive personal data) pursuant to the Data Protection Acts 1998 and 2018 ("**DPAs**") to store, handle and/or process your personal data and, if applicable, sensitive personal data, for the purposes of the making and/ or exploitation of the Film in any manner or medium worldwide which may include sharing information with broadcasters and/or other distributors which grant shall not derogate from our obligations to you under the DPAs; further in granting us the consents provided for by this Clause 9, you acknowledge and understand that we have a clear legitimate interest in processing the personal data hereinbefore mentioned and specifically you acknowledge that (a) as a consequence of our investment of money and resource into the Film we are

---

185 Insert details

pursuing a real and legitimate business interest in continuing to process the personal data; and (b) the processing is absolutely necessary in order for us to pursue that interest; and (c) the processing is balanced against the impact the processing will have on such fundamental rights and freedoms as you may have.

10   You acknowledge and agree that we shall not be liable for any loss, damage or injury suffered by you in connection with your participation in the Film other than death or personal injury caused by our negligence.

11   You hereby indemnify us irrevocably against all and any costs, claims, expenses and liabilities (including, without limitation, legal fees and any sums paid on the advice of Counsel) resulting from the breach by you of any of your obligations under this agreement.

12   You acknowledge and agree that copyright and all and any other intellectual property rights in the Film ("**Rights**") shall be owned by us for the full term of copyright to include all extensions, renewals and revivals thereof and that we may freely assign, licence and otherwise deal with the Film and/or the whole or any part of the benefit of this Agreement to any third party.in our absolute discretion.

13   You agree that your sole and exclusive remedy for any breach of this Agreement by us shall be money damages and in no event shall you be entitled to terminate or rescind this Agreement or to prevent the exercise of any of the Rights or any other right granted hereunder or to seek to apply for any form of injunctive or equitable relief against us and/or the Rights and/or the Film.

14   You hereby accept and agree that we may at any time in our discretion terminate this Agreement without specifying any reason by one week prior written notice to you.

15   This Agreement shall be governed by and construed in accordance with English law.

Schedule[186]

Please signify your acceptance of the foregoing by signing and returning to us the attached duplicate of this Agreement.

Yours sincerely   Agreed and Accepted

....

For and on behalf of   [187]
[188]

_____

186 Add Specific Terms, where applicable
187 Insert name of performer
188 Insert name of Production Company/Producer

Appendix 12

Performer's Consent (Short Form)
Sections 9, 30 and 31

From:[189]

To:[190]

Date:[191]

Dear [192][

"[193]   " (**"Film"**)

This letter of agreement ("**Agreement**") shall constitute the terms upon which you agree to render your performances as an actor (the "**Performance**") in the role of [194]in connection with the Film, which we propose, but do not undertake, to produce in the role of   .

1   In consideration of *[the sum of £[   ], receipt of which you hereby acknowledge] [and/or] [our undertaking to give you a credit as provided at Clause 7] [and/or] [our giving you the opportunity to film and record the Performance* [195]*]* you hereby:

           (a)   agree and consent to participate in the Film and to the filming, recording and/or broadcasting of the Performance and to the editing, copying, adaptation or translation of the Performance and that such filming, recording and/or broadcasting may be incorporated in the Film in whole or in part at our discretion (but you acknowledge that we are under no obligation to use such film and recording);

---

189 Insert details of producer, if a production company include registered office and number details
190 Insert details of performer
191 Insert date of agreement
192 Insert name of performer
193 Insert name of Film
194 Insert name of role
195 Amend as required

(b)   consent to the reproduction, exhibition and exploitation of the Film or any part(s) of the Film (including the Performance) by all means and in all media and formats whether now known or hereafter invented throughout the world in perpetuity (including for the purposes of advertising, publicity and promotion of the Film) and further you waive the benefit of any moral rights to which you may be entitled;

(c)   consent to the use and reproduction of your name, photograph, likeness and biography in connection with the Performance and the reproduction of the Film and recordings of your performance or any part thereof by all means and in all media throughout the world in perpetuity;

(d)   grant and assign to us all rights including without limitation copyright in the Performance and all consents necessary to enable us to make the fullest use of the Performance worldwide in perpetuity in any and all media, whether now known or hereafter developed or discovered, without payment, liability or acknowledgement to you;

(e)   waive and release us from any claim, action or demand arising out of or in connection with the Performance;

(f)   agree to keep confidential any information relating to the subject matter of this Agreement and/or the Film and shall not disclose to any third party any confidential information, photographs or other material relating to us or the Film or anyone taking part in it which came to your knowledge as a result of your participation in the Film.

2   You warrant and undertake that:

(a)   you are fully entitled to grant all rights in the Performance to us;

(b)   nothing in the Performance shall infringe the copyright or any other right of any third party or breach any contract or duty of confidence, constitute a contempt of court or be defamatory or blasphemous;

(c)   you are at least 18 years old.

3   You acknowledge and agree that we shall not be liable for any loss, damage or injury suffered by you in connection with your participation in the Film other than death or personal injury caused by our negligence.

4   You hereby indemnify us irrevocably against all and any costs, claims, expenses and liabilities (including, without limitation, legal fees and any sums paid on the advice of Counsel) resulting from the breach by you of any of your obligations under this Agreement.

5   You acknowledge and agree that copyright and all and any other intellectual property rights in the Film shall be owned by us for the full term of copyright to include all extensions, renewals and revivals thereof and that we may freely assign and otherwise deal with the Film in our absolute discretion.

6   We are not under any obligation to use the Performance in the Film nor to broadcast, exhibit or otherwise exploit the Film.

7   We shall give you a credit on all copies of the film that indicates that the role of[196]   is played by you. Position and size of the credit shall be in our absolute discretion.

8   You hereby grant to us all consents necessary (including your express consent in respect of sensitive personal data) pursuant to the Data Protection Acts 1998 and 2018 ("**DPAs**") to store, handle and/or process your personal data and, if applicable, sensitive personal data, for the purposes of the making and/ or exploitation of the Film in any manner or medium worldwide which may include sharing information with broadcasters and/or other distributors which grant shall not derogate from our obligations to you under the DPAs.[197]

9   We shall be entitled to assign or licence the whole or any part of the benefit of this Agreement to any third party.

---

196 Insert name of role
197 This is a scaled down version of the provision to be found at Appendix 12 clause 9

10   This Agreement shall be governed by and construed in accordance with English law.

Please signify your acceptance of the foregoing by signing and returning to us the attached duplicate of this Agreement.

Yours sincerely   Agreed and Accepted

....[198]
for and on behalf of[199]

---

198 Insert name of performer
199 Insert name of production company

Appendix 13

Interviewee Release (Short Form)
Sections 33

From: 200 ("**I**", "**me**", "**my**")

To: 201 ("**you**", "**your**")

Date: 202

Dear Sirs

1.   *[In consideration of the sum of £   now paid to me by you (receipt of which
      is hereby acknowledged),] [OR IF NO FEE: In consideration of your arranging
      to film and record the interview to be given by me to you,]* I agree to the filming
      and recording *and/or broadcasting and/or live relay* of the interview with me on
      [203] ("**Interview**") and to the taking of still photographs of me.
      I further confirm that you may film, record or photograph in premises owned or
      controlled by me *[including those situated at   ]*. 204

2.   You acknowledge that I have made available to you *photographs, images, audio-
      visual content, notes, memorabilia and other items in my possession* for use by
      you ("**Archive Material**") and which Archive Material may be used by you for
      all of the purposes provided for in this letter of agreement ("**Agreement**") but
      without any personal liability provided that any further clearances required to
      use the Archive Material shall be a matter for you and for the absence of which I
      shall not be held liable. The Interview and the Archive Material are collectively
      and severally referred to in this Agreement as the "**Contribution**".

3.   You shall be entitled to cut and edit the Contribution as you deem fit and, as you
      may decide, to include all or any of the Contribution in any film, programme
      or other audio-visual production or medium ("**Production**") and, in respect of
      the Contribution, I irrevocably waive the benefits of and agree not to assert any
      provision of law known as "moral rights" or any similar laws of any jurisdiction.

---

200 Insert details of Contributor/Interviewees
201 Insert details of producer, if a production company include registered office and number details
202 Insert date of agreement
203 Insert applicable date
204 Insert address details if considered appropriate

I also acknowledge that you may decide not to use any of my Contribution.

4.   I hereby give all consents necessary for the reproduction, exhibition, transmission, broadcast and exploitation of the Contribution without time limit throughout the universe by all means and media (whether now known or hereafter discovered or developed) without liability or acknowledgement to me.

5.   I warrant (a) that I am fully entitled to give the Interview, (b) that nothing in the Interview will infringe the copyright or any other right of any person, breach any contract or duty of confidence, constitute a contempt of court, be defamatory or be calculated to bring any broadcaster into disrepute and (c) that all facts expressed by me in the Interview are and/or will be, to the best of my knowledge and belief, true and any opinions I express are genuinely and truly held by me.

6.   I hereby grant you the right to issue publicity concerning the Interview and any Production in which it may be included and for such purpose to use and reproduce my name and image and recordings and/or copies of any description of the Interview.

7.   I acknowledge that it is important for you to control the promotion and marketing of all and any Production(s) and that I will not at any time nor by any means without your prior written consent give any further or other interview or release or make any statement or supply any information or make any disclosure which will or could prejudice or damage you or any Production. I will further maintain and keep the substance of this Agreement confidential (save for my right to discuss the same with my professional advisers) unless required to disclose the same to a court of law or statutory body.

8.   I hereby grant to you all consents necessary (including my express consent in respect of sensitive personal data) pursuant to the Data Protection Acts 1998 and 2018 ("**DPAs**") to store, handle and/or process my personal data (which may include information given on camera) and, if applicable, sensitive personal data, for the purposes of the making and/or exploitation of Production(s) in any manner or medium worldwide which may include sharing information with your broadcasters and/or other distributors which grant shall not derogate from your obligations to me under the DPAs; further in granting you the consents provided for by this Clause 8, I acknowledge and understand that you have a legitimate interest in processing the personal data hereinbefore mentioned and specifically

I acknowledge that (a) as a consequence of your investment of money and resource into the Production you are pursuing a genuine business interest in continuing to process the personal data and (b) the processing is absolutely necessary in order for you to pursue that interest and (c) the processing is balanced against the impact the processing will have on such fundamental rights and freedoms as I may have.[205]

9.   I agree to keep confidential any information relating to the subject matter of this Agreement and/or the Film and shall not disclose to any third party any confidential information relating to the Film which came to my knowledge as a result of my participation in the Film.

10.   This Agreement, the Contribution and all and any rights granted by me to you may be freely assigned or licensed by you. This Agreement shall be governed by and construed in accordance with English law.

Yours faithfully   Agreed and Accepted

                [206]   for and on behalf of[207]

205 See discussion at 16.9-16.20
206 Insert name of production company
207 Insert name of interviewee/contributor

Appendix 14

Crew Agreement (Short Form)
Section 35

From: [208]   (**"we"**, **"us"**, **"our"**)

To: [209]   (**"you"**, **"your"**)

Date: [210]

Dear [211]

"[212]   " (**"Film"**)

I am writing to confirm that this letter of agreement *[which, together with the terms set out in the Schedule hereto]*[213] (**"Agreement"**) shall constitute the terms upon which we hereby engage you to render services as [[214]] for the Film (your **"Services"**), which we propose but do not undertake to produce.

1   In consideration of the sum of [[215]] (the **"Fee"**), which Fee shall be paid [in [   ] *[weekly][monthly]* instalments of £[   ]   each during the Term (as defined below)] *[or on* [[216]]], you hereby irrevocably:

1.1   agree to render your Services on a(n) *[(non-)exclusive]* basis during the period commencing on [   ] and continuing until *[such date as may be determined by us by written notice to you][delivery of the Film to its principal distributors]* unless terminated earlier by us in accordance with the terms of this Agreement (**"Term"**);

1.2   agree to render your Services conscientiously and in a competent manner and to the full limit of your skill, knowledge and ability;

---

208 Insert details of producer, if a production company include registered office and number details
209 Insert details of crew member
210 Insert date of agreement
211 Insert name of crew member
212 Insert name of Film
213 Delete if not applicable
214 Insert job title
215 Insert relevant payments
216 Add details as appropriate

1.3 grant and assign to us to us all rights including without limitation copyright in the products of your Services ("**Products**") and all consents necessary to enable us to make the fullest use of the Products worldwide for life of copyright and insofar as possible in perpetuity by all means and in all media now known and hereafter invented without payment, liability (save as specifically set out in this Agreement) or acknowledgement to you;

1.4 waive the benefit of any and all moral rights to which you may be entitled save that, wherever reasonable and consistent with industry practices, we shall accord you an appropriate credit;

1.5 grant to us any consents in order to enable us to make the fullest use of the Products under this Agreement; and

1.6 grant to us (without further compensation) throughout the world the right to use your name, likeness/photograph and biography in connection with the advertising, publicising, promotion and exploitation of the Film; and

1.7 agree to keep confidential and shall not disclose to any third party any confidential information, photographs or other material relating to us or the Film or anyone taking part in it which came to your knowledge as a result of your participation in the Film;

1.8 acknowledge that we are the owner of the copyright in the Film.

2   You hereby warrant, represent and undertake that:

2.1 you are free to enter into and perform this Agreement and have not entered and will not enter into any professional or other commitment which would or might conflict with the full and due rendering of your Services;

2.2 you are a self-employed person for National Insurance and tax purposes and will keep us indemnified against any claims in respect thereof;

2.3 the Products will be wholly original to you and shall not infringe the copyright or any other rights of any third party;

2.4 the Products will not contain any defamatory matter or breach any contract or duty of confidence;

2.5   you are and will remain for the period of the engagement a "qualifying person" within the meaning of Part I of the CDPA and for the purposes of US copyright law the Products shall be considered "works made for hire" for us;

2.6   the rights granted and assigned by this Agreement are vested in you absolutely and you have not previously assigned, licensed or in any way encumbered those rights so as to derogate from the grant and assignment made by this Agreement, nor will you so assign, license or encumber any such rights; and

2.7   you will indemnify and keep us fully and effectively indemnified against all actions, costs, losses, claims and expenses of whatsoever kind or nature arising from any breach or non-performance or threatened breach or non-performance of any of the warranties, representations, undertakings or obligations on your part contained in this Agreement.

3   The Fee shall include equitable remuneration in respect of any and all rights of whatsoever kind or nature to which you may now be entitled or shall become entitled to after the date of this Agreement under the laws of any country in connection with the exploitation of the Film and the Products in all media now known or hereafter created or developed.

4   Where you are entitled to holiday leave pursuant to the Working Time Regulations 1998 ("**Regulations**") the "**holiday year**" for these purposes commences at the date of engagement and leave entitlement is four weeks per annum (pro-rated as appropriate). You shall give to us at least 7 days' prior written notice of any proposed holiday dates, which dates shall be considered and granted by us in our absolute discretion, save that if the duration of the Term is more than 48 weeks, you shall be automatically entitled to take holiday leave at any time from the beginning of the 49th week of the Term. You hereby accept and agree that any day during the Term on which we do not require your Services shall be deemed a holiday date for the purposes of calculating your holiday leave entitlement, and that we may require you to take holiday leave on specific dates as may be notified to you.

5   We shall pay to you holiday pay of a sum equal to 11% of the Fee, which holiday pay shall be paid to you on completion of the Term, unless otherwise agreed in writing. If we require you to take holiday leave which exceeds your accrued holiday entitlement, you shall not be paid holiday pay in respect of such additional holiday leave.

6   You hereby accept and agree to work such hours as are necessary to fulfil all obligations under this Agreement and you accept that this may involve working an average of more than forty-eight (48) hours per week. You agree that maximum weekly working time specified in Regulation 4 of the Regulations shall not apply to this Agreement.

7   Unless specifically authorised to do so by us in writing, you shall not have any authority to incur any expenditure in our name or for our account or have authority to bind us notwithstanding which expenses first agreed by us in writing shall be shall paid or reimbursed by us subject to production of receipts and/or other applicable paperwork.

8   You hereby grant to us all consents necessary (including your express consent in respect of sensitive personal data) pursuant to the Data Protection Acts 1998 and 2018 ("**DPAs**") to store, handle and/or process your personal data and, if applicable, sensitive personal data, for the purposes of the making and/or exploitation of the Film in any manner or medium worldwide which may include sharing information with broadcasters and/or other distributors which grant shall not derogate from our obligations to you under the DPAs.[217]

9   You hereby accept and agree that we may at any time in our discretion terminate the Term without specifying any reason by one week's prior written notice to you notwithstanding which termination the following provisions of this agreement shall remain in full force and effect: Clauses 1.3-1.8 inclusive, 2.3-2.8 inclusive, 3, 7, 8 and 10

10   We shall be entitled to assign or license the whole or any part of the benefit of this Agreement to any third party.

11   This Agreement shall be governed by and construed in accordance with English law.

---

217 This is a scaled down version of the provision to be found at Appendix 12 Clause 9

Schedule

[Add Specific Terms, where applicable]

Please signify your acceptance of the foregoing by signing and returning to us the attached duplicate of this Agreement.

Yours sincerely

for and on behalf of[218]

Agreed and Accepted
[219]

---

218 Insert name of company
219 Insert name of crew member

Appendix 15

**Assignment of Rights
Paragraph 6.1; Section 37**

DEED OF ASSIGNMENT[220] dated[221]

PARTIES

(1)   [222]   (**"Assignor"**)

(2)   [223]   (**"Assignee"**)

(each a "**Party**", collectively and severally the "**Parties**").

RECITALS

(A)   Pursuant to a number of agreements comprising the Chain-of-Title, brief particulars of which are set out in Schedule 3 to this Assignment, Assignor is the owner of the copyright and all other rights as more particularly defined at Clause 1 of this Assignment ("**Rights**") in and to the motion picture feature film presently entitled "   [224]"   (**"Film"**)   brief particulars of which are set out at Schedule 1 to this Assignment

(B)   Assignor has agreed to assign the Film and the Rights and transfer the Materials to the Assignee upon the terms set out in this Assignment.

---

220 This document is designed for a situation where a single producer has made a film in his/her own name and wishes to assign the rights into a limited company; the document may be adapted for assignments of rights in other copyright works
221 Insert date
222 Insert name and address details
223 Insert name and address details; include registered office and registered number for a limited company
224 Insert title

OPERATIVE PROVISIONS

1   In this Assignment the following terms shall be defined as set out in this Clause 1:

"Chain-of-Title"   all of the documents and agreements that establish Assignor's ownership of the Film and the Rights;

"Materials"   the materials set out at Schedule 2 which consist of and include all of the materials pertaining to the Film;

"Rights"   (1) copyright in and to (a) the Film, and (b) each of the Underlying Works which shall include all rights to exploit the Film and the Underlying Works throughout the world by all means and in all media now known or hereafter devised or invented for the life of copyright of the Film to include all revivals, renewals, reversions and extensions thereto and insofar as possible in perpetuity

(2) unless otherwise disclosed in writing by Assignor to Assignee prior to the execution of this Assignment the right to exploit the Underlying Works as part of and for all of the purposes of the Film and otherwise as Assignee may in its absolute discretion determine;

"Schedules"   the schedules to this Assignment;

"Third Party(ies)"   parties to Chain-of-Title documents other than Assignor;

"Underlying Works[225]**"**   all and any copyright and/or other works comprising and/or included in the Film which Assignor and/or any of its predecessors in title have originated and/or of which rights have been acquired for the purposes of developing, producing and exploiting the Film.

---

225 If there is/are any

2 In consideration of the sum of £1 now paid by Assignee to Assignor (receipt of which Assignor hereby acknowledges) Assignor hereby assigns, transfers and sells to Assignee absolutely with full title guarantee:

 (a) all of Assignor's right, title and interest in and to the Film to include all of the Rights and

 (b) the Materials.

3 Assignor hereby warrants and represents to Assignee[226]:

 (a) that Assignor is the sole legal and beneficial owner of the Film, the Rights and the Materials;

 (b) that the Chain-of-Title is complete;

 (c) that there are no disputes affecting the Film, the Chain-of-Title, the Rights, the Underlying Works or the Materials;

 (d) that all documents and agreements comprising Chain-of-Title are complete and have been executed by each of the parties to each said document and agreement;

 (e) that the Film, the Underlying Works, the Rights and the Materials are free of charges or other encumbrances;

 (f) the Assignor has not assigned the Film, the Underlying Works or any of the Rights;

 (g) immediately prior to the execution of this Assignment all of the Materials were in Assignor's custody, power or possession and Assignor is not aware of any other material comprising or in any way pertaining to the Film or the Rights in the custody, possession or power of any other party.

4 Assignor shall at its own expense execute any documents and do any things that Assignee reasonably requests to give effect to the terms of this Assignment. Assignor hereby appoints Assignee to be its attorney to execute and do any such instrument or thing, and generally to use its name, for the purpose of giving Assignee the benefit of this Assignment.

5 Assignee undertakes that it shall at its own expense enter into such further or other agreements and execute such further or other deeds and documents as may be required to enable it to effectively assume and perform Assignor's obligations

---

226 Not all of the warranties may be required as between an individual creative and his/her own company; however, a third party reviewing chain-of-title at a later stage may want to see a full set of warranties

to Third Parties and in respect of which obligations Assignee hereby undertakes to indemnify Assignor.[227]

6   Any notice to be given or served under this Assignment shall be in writing and shall be delivered personally or sent by facsimile or by other print-out communication mechanism or by first class prepaid registered or recorded delivery (if available) post (airmail if post to another country) to the party to be served at the address set out at the head of this agreement (or such other address as either party may from time to time notify to the other) and shall be deemed to have been served

(a)   immediately in the case of personal delivery;

(b)   in the case of facsimile or other print-out mechanism on the expiry of twenty-four (24) hours from the time of transmission;

(a)   in the case of postal delivery on the second business day following the date of posting (the fifth business day if posted to another country) or on acknowledgement of receipt if earlier.

7   No term of this Assignment is enforceable under the Contracts (Rights of Third Parties) Act 1999 by a person who is not a party to this Assignment.

8   This Assignment constitutes the whole agreement between the Parties and supersedes all previous agreements between the Parties relating to its subject matter.

9   This Assignment may be executed in any number of counterparts, each of which when executed and delivered shall constitute an original of this Assignment, but all the counterparts shall together constitute the same Assignment. No counterpart shall be effective until each Party has executed at least one counterpart.

10   This Assignment shall be governed by and construed in accordance with the laws of England and the Parties hereto submit to the exclusive jurisdiction of the English courts.

---

227 Assignee will need to notify each of those who are to receive benefits from the Film that Assignee has taken over and will be dealing with distribution etc. The formal notices to the participating contributors will constitute additions to the chain-of-title

Schedule 1

(being brief particulars of the Film)

Title:
Screenwriter(s):
Director:
Producers:
Principal cast:

Schedule 2

(being the Materials)

Schedule 3

(being short particulars of the Chain-of-Title)[228]

IN WITNESS whereof the Parties have executed this Assignment as a deed of the day and year first above written.

EXECUTED as a deed by   )

[229]   )

In the presence of[230]

EXECUTED as a deed by   )

[231]   )

for and on behalf of   )

[232]   )

In the presence of[233]

---

228 Insert brief particulars - names and dates of parties - of all chain-of-title documents
229 Insert name of Assignor
230 As this is a Deed, the signatures must be witnessed by an independent person who should state his/her name, address and occupation as well as signing the document
231 Insert individual signing on behalf of the limited company Assignee
232 Insert name of limited company Assignee
233 Details of the individual witness

Appendix 16

Investor Agreement[234]
Section 40

AGREEMENT dated

PARTIES

(1)   [235]   ("**Producer**")

(2)   [236]   ("**Investor**")

(each a "**Party**", collectively "**Parties**")

RECITALS

(1)   Producer is developing and producing a full-length feature film entitled "[237]
" to be based on a screenplay by   [238]*[as the same is registered
at WGA under reference   ]*[239] ("**Film**") into which Investor wishes to
invest.

(2)   The Parties have entered into this agreement ("**Agreement**") that sets out the
principal terms upon which Investor will invest in the Film.

---

234 This is a short form of agreement designed for not much more than a simple investment for a return from receipts
and a back-end share; it may not be suitable for use where, for example, there are significant funds being invested
and the Investor will likely want a host of conditions precedents prior to releasing funds that may, for example,
address issues of title, other investors, FTR and so on
235 Insert details of Producer, if a production company include registered office and number details
236 Insert details of Investor, if a company include registered office and number details
237 Insert title of Film
238 Insert details
239 Insert details of screenplay or any other applicable identifying features of the Film

OPERATIVE PART

1   Principal obligations

1.1   Producer shall be the producer of the Film and shall take responsibility for raising the total of the production budget for the Film ("**Budget**") and for overall supervision, management, completion and delivery of the finished Film.

1.2   Investor agrees to make available the sum of £   [240] (pounds) ("**Investment**") to Producer which sum shall be used as part of the Budget which sum shall within 7 days of the full execution of this Agreement be transferred to Producer's production bank account of which the details are:[241]

("Production Account")

1.3   Release of the Investment shall be made in the following tranches and subject to the following conditions:[242]

2   Finance and Budget Contributions

2.1   Producer shall be responsible for raising the balance of the Budget in respect of which the following is the current breakdown of the Budget ("**Budget Contribution(s)**")[243]

(a)	*Producer*	£
(b)	*Third party UK financiers ("**3PFs**") to be sourced by Producer*	£
(c)	*Investor*	£
(d)	*UK Tax credit ([19%][244] of £)*	£
(e)	*Deferred fees*	£
	Total	£

---

240 Insert amount of Investor's investment
241 Insert details of Production Account
242 Provide details of any instalments and any conditions to which the Investment is subject
243 Complete the following as appropriate
244 Precise percentage will depend on amount of qualifying expenditure

2.2 Producer shall be responsible for procuring that all those contributing to the Budget pay their respective contributions into the Production Account or make such further or other arrangements as may be required to make their respective contributions available for the production and Producer shall advise Investor in writing as and when each Budget Contribution is made.

2.3 *Producer shall be responsible for funding or procuring the funding of any shortfall or increase in the Budget of which the maximum amount shall be no more than a sum equal to [[245]   %] of the Budget.*

3 Rights

Investor acknowledges that the copyright in and to the Film and all and any other works comprising or in any way pertaining to the Film and all rights to exploit and distribute the Film in all media and by all means now known or hereafter devised are and will be exclusively vested in and owned and controlled by Producer and those to whom Producer shall grant or assign rights. Investor acknowledges that, save as may otherwise be expressly provided for by this Agreement or as may subsequently be agreed between the Parties in writing, Investor shall not acquire any right of copyright or other intellectual property or other right or entitlement with regard to the Film, or any other aspect or work in any way connected with, suggested by the Film or any derivative work or project.

4 Investor credits and benefits

Producer agrees to procure that Investor be accorded a credit as executive producer in the opening credits. Producer will arrange two invitations to all main events at which the Film is screened or promoted though the cost of attending the same shall be for Investor to pay.

5 Return of investment and waterfall

5.1 Investor's sole entitlement to recoup his investment in the Film shall be determined in accordance with the provisions of this Clause 5.

5.2 After reimbursement of all sales, marketing and other expenses of and occasioned by the sale and distribution of the Film and all collection expenses

---

245 As required

("**Expenses**") recoupment of the Budget Contributions is proposed to be made in accordance with the following waterfall:

1st position: *the investments of Investor and 3PFs* [246] *pari passu*

2nd position: *deferred fees*

3rd position: *Producer*

5.3   The remaining sums collected from exploitation of the Film after return of the Budget Contributions and after deduction of Expenses, ("**Net Profits**") shall be divided into *two tranches each of 50% (fifty per cent) and shall be paid pari passu, the first of which shall be the "**Financiers' Net Profit**" and the second of which shall be the "**Producers' Net Profit**" Investor shall be entitled to be accounted for and paid [ ] per cent of the Financiers' Net Profit* [247] *pari passu with others entitled to participate therein][on the following basis]*[248]:

5.4   Producer shall procure that an independent collection agent is appointed to collect all of the income derived from exploitation of the Film and that Investor will be a signatory to and beneficiary of the collection account management agreement to be put in place and pursuant to which, following recoupment, the Parties' respective shares in Net Profits will be accounted for and distributed for the life of copyright in the Film.

5.5   Save as provided by this Clause 5, Investor shall have no other entitlement to claim repayment or recoupment of its investment in the Film.

6   Relationship of the Parties

Investor is an independent contractor and shall not act as an employee, agent or broker of Producer and shall be responsible for paying its own income or other tax due on all and any payments that may be made to Investor pursuant to this Agreement and in respect of which Investor fully indemnifies Producer.

7   Notices

Any notice to be given or served under this Agreement shall be in writing

---

246 Waterfall will depend on what has been negotiated
247 Will depend on what has been negotiated
248 Insert as appropriate

and shall be delivered personally or sent by facsimile or by other print-out communication mechanism (including email) or by first class prepaid registered or recorded delivery (if available) post (airmail if post to another country) to the party to be served at the address set out at the head of this agreement (or such other address as either party may from time to time notify to the other) and shall be deemed to have been served:

(c)   immediately in the case of personal delivery;

(d)   in the case of facsimile or other print-out mechanism on the expiry of twenty-four (24) hours from the time of transmission;

(b)   in the case of postal delivery on the second business day following the date of posting (the fifth business day if posted to another country) or on acknowledgement of receipt if earlier.

8   Governing law and jurisdiction

This Agreement is legally binding on the Parties hereto and shall be construed and enforced in accordance with the laws of England and Wales and disputes referred to the High Court in London.

9   General

9.1   Any waiver (whether express or implied) of any breach of any of the provisions hereof shall not be construed as a continuing waiver or consent to any subsequent breach on the part of the Parties hereto.

9.2   Investor shall execute and deliver to Producer any other instrument or document reasonably considered by Producer to be necessary or desirable to evidence effectuate or confirm this Agreement or any provision hereof or any of the rights granted. If Investor fails to so execute and deliver such instruments or documents within five (5) days of receiving written notice from Producer requesting the same then Producer shall be entitled to execute such documents and instruments in the name and on behalf of Investor as Investor's duly authorised agent.

9.3   Nothing in this Agreement shall be construed or deemed to constitute a partnership or joint venture between the Parties and save as expressly provided herein neither party shall hold itself out as agent of the other.

9.4   This Agreement replaces, supersedes and cancels all previous arrangements, understandings, representations or agreements between the Parties whether oral or written. No variation of any of the terms or conditions hereof may be made unless such variation is agreed in writing and signed by each of the Parties hereto.

9.5   Investor's sole and exclusive remedy for any breach of this Agreement by Producer shall be money damages and in no event shall Investor be entitled to terminate or rescind this Agreement or to prevent the exercise of any of the Rights or any other right granted hereunder or to seek to apply for any form of injunctive or equitable relief against Producer and/or the Rights and/or the Film.

9.6   If any provision of this Agreement is judged by a court or arbitral tribunal to be void or unenforceable such provision shall in no way affect any other provision of this Agreement, the application of such provision in any other circumstance or the validity or enforceability of this Agreement and such provision shall be limited only to the extent necessary to bring it within legal requirements.

9.7   Unless obligated by statutory authorities or a court of law Investor shall keep the terms of this Agreement and all information confidential.

AS WITNESS the hands of the Parties the date detailed at the heading to this Agreement

[249   ]

for and on behalf of

[   ]

250

Agreed and Accepted

[251   ]

for and on behalf of

]252

---

249 Name of Producer's signatory
250 Name of production company
251 Investor's name
252 If Investor a company add in company name

Appendix 17

Commissioning Agreement
Paragraphs 41.1-41.4 and 6.2

AGREEMENT dated[253]

PARTIES

(1)   [254]   (**"Producer"**)

(2)   [255]   (**"Creative"**)

RECITALS

(A)   Producer is engaged in the production of a *[short]* film entitled "
[256] " (**"Film"**)

(B)   Producer wishes to engage Creative and Creative has agreed to provide the Services on the terms and conditions of this Agreement.

OPERATIVE PART

1   Definitions

In this Agreement, unless the context otherwise requires, the following words and expressions have the following meanings:

"**Act**"   the Copyright, Designs and Patents Act 1988;

"**Agreement**"   this agreement and its Schedule;

"**Materials**"   digital, physical and other media by and in which the Works are reproduced *as more particularly described in the Schedule*;

---

253 Insert date of agreement
254 Insert name and address details
255 Insert name and address details
256 Insert title

    "Rights"   the rights in the Film vested in Producer as more particularly provided for at Clause 4.1;

    "Schedule"   the schedule to this Agreement;

    "Services"   the services to be provided in accordance with the instructions of Producer and that are more particularly described in the Schedule;

    "Works"   all copyright and other works and products of the services including but not limited to all *artwork, designs, digital works, articles, features, written copy, photographs, illustrations, plans, lettering*[257] and all and any other materials created, particulars of which are set out in the Schedule.

2   Engagement

2.1   Producer hereby engages Creative and Creative agrees to create and deliver the Works and Materials and to perform the Services for and to Producer.

2.2   Creative shall comply with all lawful instructions as may from time to time be given or made by Producer. In particular, Creative shall provide the Services in accordance with Producer's specifications, which shall include specifications relating to the Works required, delivery date and method. Such specifications are more particularly provided for at the Schedule.

2.3   Creative shall deliver the Works and the Materials to Producer in accordance with the requirements of the Schedule.

3   Fee

3.1   In consideration of the rights assigned *and/or granted* in the Works and for Creative's performance of the Services and delivery of the Materials, Producer agrees to pay Creative the sum of £   [258]*which shall be paid in the following instalments:*

---

257 Specify what is being commissioned; this could be used for music though also see Appendix 6
258 Insert details of payment

3.2 All sums payable under this Agreement shall be paid within [259]days of receipt of an appropriate invoice by way of transfer to the following account:[260]

3.3 All sums payable under this Agreement are exclusive of any Value Added Tax or other applicable sales tax, which shall be added to the sum in question, subject to the provision by Creative to Producer of a valid VAT invoice.

3.4 Nothing contained in this Agreement shall be construed as or having the effect of constituting any relationship of employer and employee between Producer and Creative or as constituting a partnership between Producer and Creative.

3.5 Creative shall be responsible for the payment of National Insurance, Income Tax and any other payments required by law to be paid in relation to Creative's engagement.

3.6 Creative hereby indemnifies Producer in respect of any National Insurance contributions or similar contributions, costs, penalties, interest or income tax payable by Creative, or payable by Producer as a result of Creative being deemed to be an employee of Producer for tax purposes.

3.7 The Fee shall constitute a "buyout" of all Creative's rights in and to the Works which shall be deemed to be inclusive of all and any claims that Creative may have for equitable remuneration and thus shall constitute full consideration for the assignment by Creative of the rights in and to the Works.

4 Rights

4.1 Creative hereby assigns to Producer (where relevant by way of present assignment of future copyright) with full title guarantee throughout the world the entire copyright and all other rights of whatsoever kind or nature (including without limitation the rental and lending rights) in and to the Works to which Creative is now or may in the future be entitled under the laws in force in any part of the world to hold the same absolutely unto Producer for the full period of copyright and all renewals, reversions, revivals and extensions thereof and after that (insofar as may be or becomes possible) in perpetuity.

4.2 Creative hereby unconditionally, irrevocably and in perpetuity, waives all rights

---

259 Insert number of days
260 Insert details of Creative's bank account

under Sections 77 to 85 inclusive of the Act in respect of the products of the Services and all other moral and Creative's rights and rights of a similar nature whether now existing or hereafter conferred under the laws of any jurisdiction.

4.3   Creative hereby agrees, accepts and understands that as copyright owner of the Works Producer may use and exploit the Works by all means and in all media now known or hereafter invented throughout the world for the life of copyright of the Works to include all extensions, renewals and revivals thereof which rights may be exercised by Producer or by any party to whom Producer may grant any right or entitlement so to do, save that Creative may use individual Works in connection with his curriculum vitae and/or pitches, provided always that he does not engage in the commercial exploitation of the Works.

4.4   For the purpose of US federal law, all and any Works are deemed to be "works made for hire".

4.5   Rights in and to all and any Materials delivered by Producer to Creative, including copyright, remain vested in Producer but may be used by Creative solely for the purpose of creating the Works and all such materials shall be returned by Creative to Producer on demand.

4.6   Creative acknowledges that the copyright in the Film is and will be vested in Producer and its heirs and assigns and that the Works may be included in the Film which Producer may exploit by all means and in all media now known and hereafter invented for the life of copyright in the Film.

5   Warranties

Creative hereby warrants, undertakes, represents and covenants to and with Producer:-

5.1   the Works are and shall be wholly original and Producer's use thereof will not in any way infringe upon or violate any copyright, right of privacy, publicity or any other third party rights, nor will it constitute a libel or slander against any person, firm or Producer;

5.2   Creative is and will remain a qualifying person as defined in Section 154 of the Act;

5.3   Creative shall not enter into any agreement which might conflict with the rights granted to Producer under this Agreement or which might otherwise interfere with the performance by Creative of Creative's obligations under this Agreement;

5.4   Creative will perform the services to the best of Creative's skill and ability and in accordance with directions given by Producer;

5.5   Creative has secured and/or shall secure all necessary permissions and releases and has made and/or shall make all payments due to any such third parties to enable Producer to exercise the rights granted to it under this Agreement; and

5.6   Creative shall procure that any third party who has made a contribution to the authorship, origination or making of the Works shall execute and deliver to Producer such instruments of transfer and/or other documents required for the purpose of giving full effect to this Agreement.

6   Termination

6.1   Producer shall be entitled to terminate this Agreement on fourteen (14) days written notice to Creative.

6.2   The termination of this Agreement shall not affect the assignment and grant of the rights provided for in this Agreement.

6.3   On termination of this Agreement Creative shall deliver up all Materials and Works including any and all related drafts, copies and unfinished Works.

7   Confidentiality

The terms and the subject matter of this Agreement and all and any information provided by Producer to Creative about the Film shall be and are deemed to be 'Confidential Information' no part of which shall be used by Creative otherwise than for the purposes of this Agreement nor disclosed or made available to any third party. The obligations provided for in this clause shall not apply to any part of the Confidential Information which can clearly be shown as in the public domain unless (a) has become public knowledge other than through Creative or any party to whom Creative provided the same, or (b) was received from a third party who did not owe Producer a duty of confidence in respect of it, or (c) is required to be disclosed by a court or statutory body.

8 General

8.1 This Agreement constitutes the entire agreement and understanding between the parties hereto, and supersedes all prior understandings and/or agreements, whether oral or written, and may not be varied or modified, except by a written document executed by the parties hereto.

8.2 Notices shall be in writing and shall either be delivered in person or by recorded delivery to the address at the head of this Agreement. Notices will become effective on delivery.

8.3 This Agreement shall be governed by and construed in accordance with English law and the parties hereto hereby submit to the exclusive jurisdiction of the English Courts.

Schedule 1

1 Services

The Creative shall provide the following Services: [261]

2 Works and Materials required

Creative will produce and deliver to Producer the following Works and Materials:[262]

3 Delivery

Creative shall deliver the Works and the Materials to Producer on the following date(s):[263]

---

261 Insert description of the Services to be provided
262 Set out in as much detail as required, details of Works and Materials
263 Insert required delivery dates

IN WITNESS whereof the Parties have executed this Agreement the day and year first above written

……………………………………….   ……………………………………………..

Producer   **Creative**

Appendix 18

Collaboration Agreement (Short Form)
Paragraph 44.1

AGREEMENT dated   [264] **("Commencement Date")**

PARTIES

(1)   **("Screenwriter")**

(2)   **("Producer")**

(3)   **("Director")**[265]

(together referred to as the "**Parties**" and each where the context admits as a "**Party**")

RECITAL

Parties have entered into this agreement ("**Agreement**") the terms and conditions of which each Party recognises as having binding legal force and effect and pursuant to which the Parties intend to *[continue to]*[266] collaborate on the development, production and exploitation of a *[motion picture/short film/animation/other]*[267] project currently entitled ["   "] ("**Film**"). The Film, its budget, schedules, screenplay and exploitation are collectively referred to AS THE "**PROJECT**".

OPERATIVE PART

1   Each of the Parties shall use all reasonable endeavours to perform their respective obligations under this Agreement, which shall include but not be limited to the following:

2   Screenwriter shall write and deliver the screenplay for the Film ("**Screenplay**") to the other Parties[268] in respect OF WHICH:

     (a)   the Screenplay shall be an original copyright work of which the Screenwriter shall, unless otherwise agreed, be the sole author and first owner of copyright;

---

264 Insert date
265 Insert name and address details of individual collaborators
266 Amend as appropriate
267 Amend as appropriate
268 Consider whether time periods required and provide for them accordingly

(b)   the Screenwriter shall discuss and review the Screenplay with the other Parties and shall make such revisions and changes and produce such further or other drafts and polishes as the Parties shall discuss and agree between them.

3   Director shall discuss production of Film with Producer and consult with Producer in relation to casting, budgeting and scheduling issues. Director shall organise the crew on set and on location and direct them and the cast; Director shall also be responsible for rehearsing the cast and Director shall adhere to timelines agreed with Producer as well as the Film's budget.

4   Producer shall prepare the budget, shooting schedule and production and post-production schedules for the Film but subject to discussion and review with the other Parties; Producer shall be the principal producer of the Film and assume responsibility for hiring crew and liaising with Director on issues of casting, shooting, post-production and finalising the Film for exhibition and other exploitation. Producer shall be responsible for deciding the final cut of the Film but in making the decision shall give good faith consideration to Director's suggestions in relation thereto[269].

5   Unless otherwise agreed and evidenced in writing, all and any funding required for the Project shall be contributed by the Parties in equal shares.

6   Rights and interests in the Project shall be owned by the Parties as tenants-in-common in the following proportions:

(a)   copyright in the Screenplay is hereby assigned by the Screenwriter to the Parties and shall vest in and by virtue of the operation of this Agreement be owned by the Parties in the following proportions: Screenwriter [•]%; Producer [•]%; Director [•]%;[270]

(b)   copyright in the Film shall vest in and by virtue of the operation of this Agreement be owned by the Parties in the following proportions: Screenwriter [•]%; Producer [•]%; Director[•]%;

(c)   subject to repayment to each of the Parties of all of their respective financial contributions to the Project in the proportions determined in accordance with Clause 2, after payment of all other costs and expenses agreed by the Parties, income derived from the Project shall be divided in the following proportions: Screenwriter [•]%; Producer [•]%; Director [•]%.

---

269 There may be circumstances in which final cut may be subject to other arrangements in respect of which this clause will need amendment
270 Insert percentages in each sub-paragraph

7   Decisions as to whether rights in and or derived from the Project may be exploited by any one or more of the Parties or by any third party shall be decided by *[unanimous][majority]*[271] decision of the Parties and which decisions shall become binding as and when the terms thereof have been negotiated in good faith and thereafter confirmed in writing and signed by all of the Parties.

8   Decisions as to exploitation of the rights in and to the Film whether in relation to its submission to festivals, to exhibitors or other distributors in any medium now known or hereafter invented shall be made by *[the Producer][by unanimous/ majority decision of the Parties]*[272] and which decisions shall be subject to binding written agreements to be negotiated by the Parties, where applicable with third parties, in good faith; without prejudice to the foregoing, the Producer shall have primary responsibility for such negotiations.

9   The Parties agree that each of them will have the following credits in the *[opening][end]* credits for the Film and, where applicable, in relation to publicity and promotional materials for the Film.[273]

11   This Agreement shall be deemed to be effective from and after the Commencement Date and shall continue in full force and effect for the life of copyright of the Screenplay and the Film unless otherwise terminated in accordance with the terms of this Agreement ("**Term**").

12   A Party wishing to withdraw from the Project at any time during the Term shall give written notice to the other Parties whereupon all and any rights in and to the Screenplay, the Film and the Project shall vest in the remaining Parties so that the terminating Party's shares shall be divided amongst the remaining Parties proportionately as provided for in accordance with Clause 6 of this Agreement[274].

13   If the Parties collectively agree to cease development of the Film or the Project, the provisions of Clause 6 shall apply to ownership and control of all rights and any benefits, including financial, to be derived therefrom.

14   If a Party is in breach of this Agreement and, if remediable, the breach is not cured within 14 days of that Party receiving a written notice to that effect from any other Party, then the two Parties not in breach, acting collectively, may dismiss the Party in breach from the Project whereupon the Party in breach shall cease to have any interest in the Film or the Project save for (a) reimbursement of any funding made available for the Project which reimbursement shall only

---

271 State which or what alternative applies
272 State which or what alternative applies
273 Insert details of credits
274 Or state as otherwise maybe the case

be made from net income derived from the Project and (b) such credit on the Film as the remaining Parties shall reasonably determine that the breaching Party's contribution merits.

15   Unless authorised to do so in writing by the other Parties, nothing in this Agreement shall permit any Party to disclose confidential information in any form directly or indirectly associated with, belonging or relating to the Film, the Project or Parties nor will any Party disclose the existence and terms of this Agreement to third parties. Unless demonstrated to be otherwise, all and any information pertaining to the Film and to the Project is deemed to be confidential unless in the public domain at the time of its disclosure.

16   The Parties shall each owe the others a duty of utmost good faith in all of their dealings in connection with the Film and the Project.

17   Any notice given to a Party under or in connection with this Agreement shall be in writing and shall be delivered by email or by hand or by prepaid first class post or other next working day delivery service to the address of each Party.

18   This Agreement is governed by the laws of England and each Party submits to the exclusive jurisdiction of the English courts.

SIGNED by   )

[Full name of Screenwriter]   )

SIGNED by   )

[Full name of Producer]   )

SIGNED by   )

[Full name of Director]   )

ABOUT THE AUTHOR

Graduate in Law from the University of Manchester, Tony Morris was admitted as a solicitor in 1977 and currently practices as a consultant to Swan Turton LLP. Tony has wide experience of working across the broadest spectrum of the media, entertainment and technology industries. He is retained by film and television producers, film sales agents, record companies and music publishers, musicians and bands, talent agents and managers, software creators as well as many individual creatives.

In addition to his work as a practising lawyer, Tony is active as both an arbitrator and a mediator with a special interest in the Media, Entertainment, Creative and Technology Industries. In 2002 he was appointed a Member of the Chartered Institute of Arbitrators, and in 2005 was accredited as a mediator. He is also a member of the Arbitration Boards of the Independent Film and Television Alliance and the WIPO Arbitration and Mediation Center's Film and Media Panel.

Tony has been lecturing regularly since 1997, most recently and currently as the provider of the legal module for the Raindance course for Independent Film Producers, as a guest lecturer at the National Film and Television School and at the University of Portsmouth. Previously he has lectured at the EU Media Business School in Spain on its MEGA Masters course for film producers; for the ECAFIC and AFIC courses promoted by Institut National de l'Audiovisuel and held at the Sorbonne, Paris and on courses for producers at Ravensbourne, London. He has also been a guest lecturer at the Danish Film Institute, Copenhagen, at the Filmakademie, Bad Wurtemburg, Germany, for Screen Training Ireland and at the University of Bournemouth. He has presented at numerous conferences and other events including the Raindance Film Festival, the International Association of Entertainment Lawyers' conference at MIDEM in Cannes, the Edinburgh Television Festival, the New Music Seminar in New York and for the New York Bar Association Entertainment, Arts and Sports Law Section. Tony has published dozens of articles and commentaries on a wide range of media and entertainment legal topics in the industry and national press and online and has appeared as a commentator on both radio and television.

Webpages

https://swanturton.com/people/1900/

https://www.facebook.com/filmmakerslegal/?modal=admin_todo_tour

https://www.linkedin.com/in/tony-morris-a1b818/

Photo by Jessica Morris © 2019 @jmophotoworld